CW00556841

MAKING MUSIC

American Made
Music Series

ADVISORY BOARD

David Evans, General Editor
Barry Jean Ancelet
Edward A. Berlin
Joyce J. Bolden
Rob Bowman
Curtis Ellison
William Ferris
John Edward Hasse
Kip Lornell
Bill Malone
Eddie S. Meadows
Manuel H. Peña
Wayne D. Shirley
Robert Walser

MAKING MUSIC

THE BANJO IN A SOUTHERN APPALACHIAN COUNTY

WILLIAM C. ALLSBROOK JR., MD

University Press of Mississippi / Jackson

The University Press of Mississippi is the scholarly publishing agency of the Mississippi Institutions of Higher Learning: Alcorn State University, Delta State University, Jackson State University, Mississippi State University, Mississippi University for Women, Mississippi Valley State University, University of Mississippi, and University of Southern Mississippi.

www.upress.state.ms.us

The University Press of Mississippi is a member of the Association of University Presses.

Copyright © 2023 by University Press of Mississippi
All rights reserved
Manufactured in the United States of America

Photographs are by William C. Allbrook Jr. except where otherwise noted.

First printing 2023

∞

Library of Congress Cataloging-in-Publication Data

Names: Allsbrook, William C., Jr., author.
Title: Making music : the banjo in a southern Appalachian county /
William C. Allsbrook, Jr..
Other titles: American made music series.
Description: Jackson : University Press of Mississippi, 2023. | Series:
American made music series | Includes bibliographical references and index.
Identifiers: LCCN 2023006345 (print) | LCCN 2023006346 (ebook) |
ISBN 9781496845801 (hardback) | ISBN 9781496845818 (trade paperback) |
ISBN 9781496845825 (epub) | ISBN 9781496845856 (epub) | ISBN 9781496845832
(pdf) | ISBN 9781496845849 (pdf)
Subjects: LCSH: Banjo music—Appalachian Region, Southern—History and
criticism. | Banjoists—Appalachian Region, Southern—Interviews. |
Banjo—History. | Oral history—Appalachian Region, Southern.
Classification: LCC ML1015.B3 A45 2023 (print) | LCC ML1015.B3 (ebook) |
DDC 787.8/80975694—dc23/eng/20230308
LC record available at https://lccn.loc.gov/2023006345
LC ebook record available at https://lccn.loc.gov/2023006346

British Library Cataloging-in-Publication Data available

This book is dedicated to my wife, Jerry. And also, to our children, Nink (Sharon, wife), Luke (Renee, wife), and Jennie (Bryan, husband); and to our grandchildren, Kelley and Michael; Boyd (Samantha, wife), Charlotte, Calvin, and Margaret; Joseph and Nolan; and to our great-grandson Rhys (Boyd and Samantha).

To my parents, William (1909–2001) and Margaret Allsbrook (1911–1989); to my father and mother-in-law, G. H. "Jerry" (1909–1967) and Priscilla Boyd (1915–1978).

And to Bud (1924–2013) and Edith Whisenhunt, who introduced me to Haywood County, and whose lives exemplify the great strengths of its people.

"Making Music." The Bolden Family and Friends. (Photo courtesy of Jeremy Bolden)

ON MAKIN' MUSIC

It was widespread. There were just some great musicians we hung around with when I was growing up. They were all over this county. It was just country folks getting together and singing, visiting, and playing music. Even before we had telephones, it was by postcards. We would get lined up—somebody would write somebody and say, "You goin' over to Poppy's Saturday night (my family called my daddy Poppy)?" We would go to other people's homes. It was just a circle of friends is what done it. We'd be somewhere every Saturday night playing music—for years. It was just entertainment. It was something to do. It was who we were. It really was a remarkable legacy. And I can still remember some of the old songs that we'd sing.
—FRENCH KIRKPATRICK

It was how they entertained theirselves.—PHIL HUNTER

I learned to play the banjo by listening to 45 and 78 records. My Aunt Nellie, who lived just down the road, had a whole stack of them things—the old thick 78 records—had Ralph and Carter Stanley on it, Earl Scruggs, Lester Flatt, and Bill Monroe. I got to listening and I'd play a little bit—I want to learn that. And I would try it—couldn't do it. One of the 78s was a recording of "Cripple Creek." I played it over and over and over. Until, I come to a part that I wanted to really learn—I'd back it up, go through it—back it up, go through it—until I learned that one part. After I played the records over and over, I would go home and practice. That was the first one. It was hard, but I kept driving—until I learned it.—MIKE PRESSLEY

Music was essential for our family.—JEREMY BOLDEN

I guess it's joy. I just—I like playing and getting it right. You know, it's the striving to get it as perfect as I can get it; not to say that that's anywhere near perfect—but to my ability, the best I can. My mind is totally on that, nothing else. And if I was to sum it up in one word—just joy. And a lot of people probably go through life and never know what joy is, you know.
—TRACY BEST

CONTENTS

PREFACE

It was several years ago, a lovely pre-Christmas dinner at our neighbor's home. I did not know it at the time, but the evening proved to be a major moment in my life. Prior to dinner, our host casually asked another guest, "How are your lessons going?" Thinking that he was probably taking a pottery course or a woodworking course at the local community college, I asked, "What kind of lessons are you taking?" He replied, "banjo lessons." A few days later, I was sitting in the studio of his banjo teacher, Larry Watson, who told me, "If you practice, I promise that I can teach you to play a banjo." He was right. Since then, playing the banjo as a "profoundly mediocre" amateur has been a source of great pleasure for me.

I realized, over the ensuing years, that there was a surprisingly large number of good to excellent banjo players in Haywood County and repeatedly heard the words "makin' music," which I assumed, like most, meant "playing music." However, I have come to realize that in Haywood County and other areas of the Southern Appalachians, it is much more than that. "Makin' music" in these areas comes primarily from unique musical roots that were apparently first recognized and described to me by banjo historian George Gibson, who coined the term "in-home folkway." It arose, beginning with the frontier settlement, in homes, though not all homes, along the frontier, and ultimately included "isolated" (topographically and infrastructurally) rural areas of the Southern Appalachians. It was certainly not limited to the banjo but also included other instruments, particularly the Scotch-Irish fiddle, as well as singing and dancing. As the twentieth century progressed, "isolation" decreased and ultimately largely disappeared. Scattered remnants of the in-home folkway remain to this day. This unique story will be discussed at length in chapter 2.

This book is an oral history of thirty-two banjo players who, with two exceptions, were born in the latter two-thirds of the twentieth century in Haywood County. They are talented and intelligent men and women. Twentieth-century changes have continued over their lifetimes, and some of these changes have continued to pose challenges to the remnants of the in-home folkway. However, the surviving remnants of this unique folkway are, to this day, significant and give special meaning to "makin' music" in Haywood County. The book is divided into two parts. Part I, "Historical Perspectives," includes two chapters: chapter 1, "Overview of Banjo History," and chapter 2, "The Banjo in Haywood County." Part II, "Makin' Music," is drawn extensively from the oral histories of the banjo players, and one is able to follow "Makin' Music" in Haywood County from roughly the mid-twentieth century to the present.

Haywood County is located in Western North Carolina, adjacent to the eastern border of Tennessee, and is part of the Southern Appalachian Mountains. Western North Carolina is contiguous with mountainous areas of East Tennessee, western Virginia, and northern Georgia. It is also near eastern Kentucky and West Virginia. These areas of the Southern Appalachians are where the old-time (later "folk") music arose and where it thrived.[1] A portion of the Qualla Boundary (Eastern Band, Cherokee Reservation) in Swain County borders Haywood County. Waynesville, the county Seat of Haywood County, is about twenty-five miles west of Asheville, the largest city in the North Carolina mountains.

The estimated population of Haywood County in July 2018 was 62,839,[2] including 93.1% "white alone, not Spanish, Hispanic, or Latino," 3.74% Hispanic or Latino, and 1.03% African American.[3] There are four incorporated towns in the county with roughly estimated populations: Waynesville (county seat), 10,000; Maggie Valley, 1,200; Canton, 4,200; and Clyde, 1,400.[4] The United States 2010 Census data show a 55.4% rural and 44.6% urban population.[5] Additional Haywood County data are presented in chapter 3 and also in the Appendix: Additional Demographics.

The Great Smoky Mountain National Park and the Pisgah National Forest occupy slightly more than half of the county. The scenic Blue Ridge Parkway runs along most of the county's western boundary. The county is a remarkably beautiful place.

I am neither a historian nor an ethnomusicologist. I have been particularly struck, however, by the general lack of knowledge of banjo history by the great majority of people, musicians and non-musicians alike, whom I have encountered. The history of the banjo is often complex. It begins in this country in the 1600s with the advent of slavery. I have attempted to distill the history into a brief, accurate, and readable account.

I am aware that "banjoist" is currently the preferred and recommended appellation for persons who play the banjo. However, in all the many hours that I have spent with the banjo players in this book, I have yet to hear the term used, and therefore I identify the participants in this book as "banjo players."

Mountain people are generally private people. I have been privileged and deeply honored by the willingness of these men and women to talk with me and by their cooperation, their support, their encouragement, and, yes, their patience. This is their story, not mine.

ACKNOWLEDGMENTS

Many people have helped me bring this book to fruition.

Early on in this project, I met and became friends with Marc Pruett, D.Arts, a native of Haywood County and an exceptional Grammy Award-winning banjo player. Marc agreed with my observations about the large number of banjo players in Haywood County and, further, agreed to collaborate with me. His collaboration gave instant credibility to the project. He also gave wise counsel and support. This book would not have been possible without him.

Four years ago, I met Dr. William Ferris, the eminent professor of history and, at that time, senior associate director of the Center for Study of the American South, University of North Carolina at Chapel Hill. Early on in our conversations, he said, "You've got to write a book." He has supported and encouraged me in my efforts.

George Gibson, a noted banjo scholar, had important input in the late development of this book. He read portions of the manuscript and has offered invaluable guidance, suggestions, and support. His greatest contribution was unselfishly introducing me to his concept of a mountain "in-home" folkway and pointing out its musical significance, including for the banjo. It has proved to be significant for this book as well, and I am truly grateful.

Dr. David Evans, professor of music and ethnomusicology, Rudi E. Scheidt School of Music, University of Memphis, initially reviewed a portion of the manuscript and offered important suggestions and encouragement.

The expert computer assistance from my son-in-law, Dr. Bryan Bibb, was absolutely invaluable. Conversations with him were also very helpful in refocusing the thrust of the book.

The help of Kellen Carpenter, Special and Digital Collections, Hunter Library, Western Carolina University, Cullowhee, North Carolina, in gathering and transferring requested archival information to me was also invaluable.

French Kirkpatrick, one of the banjo players in this project, has also been a strong, unwavering supporter, offering sound advice and insight. He also read portions of the manuscript.

Doug Trantham, another of the banjo players in this project, was very helpful in his descriptions of clawhammer-playing techniques.

Dr. Charles Crumley, Bill Fisher, Larry Clark, Carroll Jones, and my wife, Jerry, read portions of the manuscript, and Mike McKinney, Bill Bell, and my daughter, Jennifer Bibb, read the entire manuscript. All, especially my daughter, offered suggestions and corrections and continually supported and encouraged my efforts.

Dr. John Rodgers and his wife, Gaynell, introduced me to Appalachia (eastern Kentucky) and over the years, I have learned much from them.

Craig Gill, director, University Press of Mississippi, and Jackson Watson, assistant to the director, have been supportive of and patient in my efforts to bring this book to fruition.

Bob Coats, governor's census liaison, North Carolina Office of State Budget and Management, and John Cromartie, Rural Economy Branch/USDA/Economic Research Service, provided much-needed assistance in the demographic analysis.

Randall Pressley, mathematics teacher, Tuscola High School, provided expert statistical assistance.

Dr. Larry Leatherwood, associate superintendent for curriculum, Haywood County Schools (retired), helped me understand the complexities of the Haywood County Schools' consolidation.

Angie Messer and Alisha Messer, Strains of Music, Waynesville, North Carolina, were consistently supportive, upbeat, and encouraging. Alisha also provided expert assistance with audiovisual aspects of the project.

Chris Kuhlman, owner, The Print Haus in Waynesville, and his staff, including Rebekah Russell, Jason Mehaffey, and Bethany Cullen, provided excellent assistance in photography and CD preparation.

Debra Covelli, transcriptionist, expertly prepared transcriptions of the great majority of the interviews.

Austin Bryant, Haywood County Land Records/GIS, prepared the Haywood County maps included in this book. Joey Webb, director, Haywood County Technology and Communications, made improvements to the maps after the book was accepted for publication.

Revs. Robert Prince and Sandy Giles provided valuable information about church attendance in Haywood County.

Lyme Kedic, North Carolina Room, Pack Memorial Library, Asheville, North Carolina, was interested and provided, early on, expert assistance in gathering archival information.

Evelyn Coltman, chair, Historic Preservation Committee, Bethel Rural Community Organization, provided valuable information about her local community, including its logging history.

Lewis Oats, Virginia Oats (his mother), and Dewanda Coleman (his sister) provided insight into the Sunburst Logging Camp history as well as the Haywood County African American Community.

Joyce Cope, archivist, Haywood County Library, Waynesville, North Carolina, and Zachary Jones, circulation supervisor, Haywood County Library, have helped me find archival information about Haywood County.

Ann Melton, local historian, and Alex McKay, local historian and curator, Waynesville Archives, were helpful and encouraging in the historical aspects of the book, including providing historical photographs.

A discussion about banjo history, including Cherokee history, with Dr. Brett Riggs, Department of History, Western Carolina University, was informative and helpful.

A conversation with Joshua Grant, banjo builder, was very helpful in clarifying my thoughts about the gourd banjo.

Daniel Huger provided me with information about the Buncombe Turnpike.

Billy Case and Kyle Edwards enlightened me with their knowledge of Maggie Valley history, including the banjo in Maggie Valley.

Dr. Roland Persson, professor of Educational Psychology, Jonkoping University, Jonkoping, Sweden, helped me learn about giftedness and "flow states."

Conversations with and data from Mark Clasby, executive director (retired), Haywood County Economic Development Council, were important in understanding changes in the Haywood County economy over the years.

Conversations with David Noland and Larry Clark, and especially Bill Teague (retired superintendent, Mountain Agricultural Research Station, Waynesville, North Carolina), were helpful in understanding the agricultural history in Haywood County.

Correspondence with Lee Knight was very helpful in the earliest stage of the project.

The late Larry Watson had input and offered encouragement when I first began considering this project. He also taught me to play the banjo, and for that, I will be forever grateful.

My wife, Jerry, has been, from the inception of this book, an unwavering, steady, and quietly enthusiastic supporter. She has put up with scattered books, piles of notes, vast numbers of reprints, photographs, and at times, a stressed husband. She also suggested "Makin' Music" for the title of the book.

I have appreciated the consistent interest and encouraging support of all the banjo players who participated in this project.

Jared Best
June Smathers-Jolley
Scott Mehaffey
Harold Hannah
Tim Bradley
Travis Stuart
Marc Pruett
Phil Hunter
Smiley Burnette
Larry Watson
Thomas Smathers

Scott Evans
Tracy Best
Pam Sutton
Stan Nichols
Brandon Henson
David Burnette
Thomas Tatham
Charles Rathbone
French Kirkpatrick
Lewin Burrell
Gary Wiley

Patrick Massey
Roger Frady
Jeremy Bolden
Steve Sutton
Mike Pressley
Helena Hunt
Jimmy Burnette
Doug Trantham
Mitchell Rathbone
Joey Massie

Part I

HISTORICAL PERSPECTIVES

Chapter 1

OVERVIEW OF BANJO HISTORY

The slave trade originated primarily in West Africa. From 1501 to 1870, an estimated 12.5 million African men, women, and children were shipped, under appalling conditions, across the Atlantic, first to the Caribbean and Brazil, and later to the United States.[1] The Middle Passage mortality rate in the eighteenth century was 15 percent and for the late eighteenth and early nineteenth century, 10 percent or less.[2] Roughly 300,000 slaves, 2.5 percent of the Middle Passage total, entered the United States, most between 1691 and 1810. The importation of slaves into the United States was proscribed by law in 1808.[3] Most of the slaves prior to 1808 were in Tidewater (in Virginia) and Maryland and the Lowcountry of the Carolinas and Georgia. The Gulf Coast had a lesser number. The sale of slaves continued until the end of the Civil War. Small numbers of slaves were present in the United States "almost everywhere that European Settlement was found."[4]

The slaves, initially in the Caribbean and Brazil, were from displaced nationalities, ethnic groups, cultures, and languages, predominantly from West Africa.[5] Some brought cultural variations of plucked spike lutes with them, and others built instruments of their culture when they arrived.[6] The diverse African music cultures were exposed to European influences, and the instruments, through creolization, evolved over time into the unique gourd banjo.[7]

The gourd banjo, an African American instrument, has existed in the West Indies and North American mainland since the late seventeenth century. It was reasonably well-known, particularly in the American South, by 1810.[8] Early on, the banjo consisted of a carved-out gourd covered by animal skin, the gourd being attached to an elongated, flattened, fretless wooden "neck." There were four strings with tuning pegs. A fifth string was subsequently added. The flattened neck and tuning pegs were European influences.[9] The gourd was largely replaced by wooden "frames" in the 1840s.

3

It is now accepted that, contrary to earlier views, whites had learned to play the banjo at different places and different times, directly (or indirectly) from African Americans (African and European cultural exchanges) before the advent of minstrelsy and, therefore, before the Civil War.[10] Downstroking of the strings, reflecting African roots, was, in the early 1800s, the playing technique taught to European Americans by African Americans. It remained the predominant technique until after the Civil War.[11] It is true that minstrelsy and the Civil War, at least in some instances, may have facilitated the spread of the banjo, but I have found no record of this in Haywood County.

Blackface entertainment had been present in America prior to the Revolutionary War. The bigoted portrayal of African Americans seen at entr'acte music or comedy in theatrical productions, but also at circuses and racetrack busking, was a myth.[12] "Minstrelsy," the first full-length, freestanding (white men in blackface) show, began in early 1843. It became, in spite of and also probably because of its bigotry, wildly popular, first in the Northeast and subsequently in the American South. It also spread internationally. The banjo defined and authenticated it.[13] Minstrelsy's popularity waned in the late 1800s, but fragments of it lasted into the mid-twentieth century.[14] Minstrelsy in Haywood County will be discussed further in the following chapter.

The decades following the Civil War into the early twentieth century were eventful times in the history of the banjo. Frank Converse published, in 1865, a "guitar style" (up-picking and three-finger) banjo instruction book. This book, in addition to bringing guitar tunes to the banjo, opened more musical possibilities for the instrument. George Dobson, in 1874, published a technique that clearly designated right- and left-hand positions and made the banjo easier to play. Frets were also added to the banjo neck to facilitate left-hand finger placements in the "guitar style" techniques. In addition to the playing advances, highly competitive technical as well as ornamental banjo production ensued. Large and many small banjo manufacturing companies were created. Variable-sized and hybrid banjos were also produced, as were affordable instruments. Banjo teachers abounded. There was a major banjo journal. The four-string plectrum (pick) banjo with steel strings and standard banjo tuning was loud and predominated in jazz. It was also used in the rhythm sections of orchestras. The five-string banjo became obsolete and largely disappeared. Ultimately, the loud sound of the rhythm guitar replaced the banjo. This complex topic has been extensively reviewed by Philip F. Gura and James F. Bollman in their excellent book *America's Instrument: The Banjo in the Nineteenth Century*.[15]

In the late nineteenth and into the early twentieth century, an effort was made, especially in the Northeast and mid-Atlantic regions, to "socially elevate" the banjo. The banjo, along with the mandolin and guitar, became popular among the upper classes, including women, as well as in university clubs. A banjo and guitar club was also present in Waynesville and will be discussed in the following chapter. This fad largely disappeared after World War I.[16]

African American banjo influence continued in the late nineteenth and twentieth centuries.[17] The five-string banjo, as will be shown, did survive in the rural South, which includes Appalachia.[18] Downstroking did not completely disappear and is still played, including in the Southern Appalachian Mountains and Haywood County.

During this period, intensive study of Appalachian music identified its largely Anglo/Celtic roots (see chapter 2). This music had also been influenced by other music traditions, including, of course, African American, and became known as old-time (and later, also folk or mountain) music. Hillbilly, subsequently country, music emerged from the Southern Appalachians in the early 1900s. Recordings and early radio were critically important in all of this music's spread.[19] The banjo was usually not a featured instrument in this music.

The African American minstrel image became less and less tenable, and by the second half of the twentieth century, African Americans were no longer associated with the banjo. Most people began to identify the banjo as a mountain instrument, which fit, albeit inaccurately, the "mountain folk" stereotype.[20]

In 1936, Pete Seeger attended the Mountain Folk and Dance Festival in Asheville, North Carolina, and was taken by the music. It was the first time that he had ever heard a five-string banjo. He played one for the rest of his life in his efforts to collect and play old-time/"folk" music as well as in his life of social activism.[21] He was largely responsible for the "folk" music renaissance of the 1950s and early 1960s.[22]

Bluegrass arose out of old time, mountain, hillbilly, and country music traditions in the late 1930s and took its name from Bill Monroe's band, The Bluegrass Boys. It was initially popular among the working, farming, and middle classes, but its popularity subsequently spread. It is now enjoyed nationally and internationally.[23] Earl Scruggs, with his three-finger "Scruggs style," played a major role in the remarkable development of bluegrass banjo music. Thanks to him and the contributions of others, the five-string banjo is now the featured instrument in bluegrass. Scruggs will be discussed further in the next chapter.

The 1960s also saw a bluegrass/country/rock crossover, particularly on the West Coast. A "melodic style" of banjo playing—playing the same or similar notes to fiddle tunes—was also developed.[24] Other contemporary banjo innovators include, among others, Béla Fleck and Noam Pikelny.

Finally, the banjo's history came full circle in 2005, when the Carolina Chocolate Drops, a highly successful band originally composed of four African Americans, was formed. Its purpose was to explore and play African American music and African American-influenced music using instruments, including the banjo, with African American origins.[25] In 2017, one of the founding members, Rhiannon Giddens, was named a MacArthur Fellow.[26]

Chapter 2

THE BANJO IN HAYWOOD COUNTY

INTRODUCTION

This chapter will explore the development of the prominence of the banjo in Haywood County.

In his 1914 history of Western North Carolina, John Preston Arthur wrote that "the banjo and the fiddle have been as constant companions of the pioneers of the mountains of North Carolina as the Bible and the Hymn Book."[1] It is important to recognize that his information came largely from reading old letters and journals, as well as interviews with early pioneers, recalling their youth or stories of their ancestors' youth.[2] John C. Campbell, who traveled extensively in the Southern Appalachians in the late 1800s and early 1900s, acquired a deep knowledge of its social and economic conditions and its people. In his book, published posthumously in 1921, he had written that "strangely enough, the banjo touches at times a deeper note than the violin, perhaps from association. It is more generally played throughout the Highlands, and breathes the life of many a lonely hearth far in the hills."[3] These two observations, as will be seen, are very important because, aside from them, very little had been written about the banjo by mountaineer contemporaries. They all knew about the banjo and fiddle, and there was no need to write about it.[4]

Enslaved African Americans, as shown in the previous chapter, were responsible for the introduction and initial spread of the banjo. By the early 1800s at the latest, European Americans in different locations were beginning to learn to play the banjo from African Americans. There was an active musical interchange, which included the banjo, between enslaved as well as free African Americans, mixed-race people, and European Americans. African Americans, European Americans, and mixed-race people could, in turn, subsequently teach others to play the banjo as well. As the banjo spread from location to location, this led to variations in banjo playing styles, as well as variations in the music, stories, and lyrics of the songs and ballads.

This chapter will begin with an overview of slavery in North Carolina, along with the significance of the development of the state's antebellum society. Subsequently, slavery in Western North Carolina, including Haywood County, will be contrasted with slavery in the remainder of the state. The early settlement of Haywood County will also be reviewed.

The significance of the intensive study of mountain ballads and songs by nineteenth- and early twentieth-century musicologists ("songcatchers"), along with its implications for the banjo, will be discussed. George Gibson recognized that many of the songcatchers' observations were also applicable to the instruments, including the banjo, that were being played for individual and group enjoyment, which included dances. He coined the simple term "in-home folkway" to describe them. Isolation and its importance in the development of the folkway will also be discussed.

The in-home folkway was not the sole source of the banjo in Haywood County. Early reports of the banjo in North Carolina, southwestern North Carolina, and Haywood County will be described. Major developments in this period, as well as subsequent developments which were important in the exposure to and spread of the banjo in Haywood County, will also be noted. Finally, the significance for Haywood County, of Earl Scruggs, of the emergence of the banjo as a "mountain instrument," and of the dilution of the in-home folkway will be reviewed.

SLAVERY IN NORTH CAROLINA

In 1663, King Charles II granted eight Lords Proprietors a vast amount of land (later to become North and South Carolina) south of Virginia. While the Lords Proprietors realized the importance of slave labor, most of the coast of North Carolina was a geographic barrier to the direct importation of slaves. The first permanent settlement in Carolina (later North Carolina) with enslaved African Americans occurred in the early 1700s. Slaves entered the Albemarle area of eastern North Carolina from Virginia to the northeast and entered southeastern North Carolina primarily from South Carolina to the south.[5]

North Carolina was originally a society with slaves which ultimately evolved, with the advent of the plantation system, into a slave society. Members of the society with slaves had interracial (European Americans, European American indentured servants, African American slaves, free African

Americans, and indigenous Americans), social, and musical interchanges (including friendships, cohabitation, sexual relations, mixed-race offspring, and intermarriage) which were fluid and commonplace.[6] At that time, the Chesapeake area of Maryland, Delaware, and Virginia had the greatest concentrations of African American banjo players, and the slaves entering northeastern North Carolina from Virginia were clearly the major initial source of the introduction of the banjo in the state.[7]

As the 1700s evolved into a slave society, the freedom of the free African Americans at the time became tenuous, and, indeed, many of them became enslaved once again. There was a large migration of free African Americans and mixed-race people who left the slave society for the relative freedom of the primitive frontiers of the South. There, the populations were dependent upon one another regardless of color.[8] These free African Americans and mixed-race people were clearly, in addition to African American slaves, another source for the introduction of the African American banjo to European Americans.

Slaves were concentrated where manual agricultural labor was critical, particularly between Albemarle and the lower Cape Fear areas and also a tier of counties along the northeastern border with Virginia. Just prior to the American Revolution, roughly 50 percent of households in those areas owned slaves, most of whom were concentrated on plantations. In 1790, the population of North Carolina included 100,572 slaves (including by natural birth and by importation) and 288,204 whites.[9] There were 5,041 free African Americans.[10] By 1808, the legal importation of slaves into the United States had ceased, and subsequent increases in the African American population were by natural births among the slaves who were already present. The plantation society slowly moved deeper into North Carolina.

The antebellum society in North Carolina was three-tiered. The top tier included the wealthy plantation slave owners, along with prominent politicians, lawyers, newspaper editors, merchants, etc. Slaves were in the bottom tier. The middle tier was, by far, the largest. It was a heterogeneous, poorly defined group of people that included white servants, white indentured servants, yeomen farmers, subsistence farmers, slaveholders with small numbers of slaves, and common laborers. Free African Americans were also in this group.

In 1860, just prior to the onset of the Civil War, there were 361,522 African Americans, which included 30,463 free African Americans in North Carolina, with only a very small percentage living on large plantations. Most slave owners owned five slaves or fewer, and most of those slave owners typically owned only one slave.[11]

SLAVERY IN WESTERN NORTH CAROLINA

While different in some respects, it should be remembered that "slavery, while proportionally smaller than in most areas of the South, was fully entrenched and quite healthy in the North Carolina mountains."[12] The major difference is that even though the mountain slave populations varied, at times widely, from county to county, there were, compared to the rest of the state, fewer, but not negligible, numbers of slaves. There were no large plantations. Of additional importance, slaves in the mountains often worked side-by-side with their owners and, in some instances, lived in the same houses as their owners.

There were 300 slaves in nearby Asheville by 1800.[13] The slave population for the fifteen westernmost North Carolina counties in 1860 was 12,183, representing 3.7% of all slaves in North Carolina. The free African American population of the fifteen counties was 1.3% of the total population.[14]

The second difference between mountain slavery and slavery in the remainder of the state was the diversity of economic interests of mountain slave owners. Historian John Inscoe, reviewing 1860 economic activity of larger slave owners in five "sample" counties, noted: "professional, 32%; mercantile or commercial, 68%; real estate and/or mining, 24%; hotel management, or other aspects of tourist trade, 12%; and agriculture alone, only 8%."[15] Agriculture, the most important aspect of the mountain economy, consisted of "mixed farming," which predominantly included livestock production (meat for South Carolina and Georgia) along with the production of crops, primarily corn, to feed the livestock. The diverse economic interests of mountain slave owners made it possible for slaves to also participate in non-agricultural pursuits and often with increased independence and responsibility. Both the close side-by-side working relationships between slaves and owners as well as the "independence and responsibility" of some of the slaves likely enhanced the spread of music, including the banjo, in the mountains, at times, interacting with the in-home folkway.

There were 160 slaves in Haywood County in 1810.[16] The 1860 population of Haywood County was 5,801, including 303 slaves (5.2% of the population) distributed among fifty-nine owners.[17] Slave percentages of the population in four counties adjacent to Haywood County in 1860 were as follows: Buncombe and Henderson counties had roughly three times the number of slaves in Haywood County; Jackson and Madison County slave populations were similar to Haywood County. Buncombe and Henderson counties had longer histories of sojourners and tourists, including their slaves. There were only fourteen free African Americans in Haywood County.

The Buncombe and Henderson County slave populations increased markedly during the summer months. Wealthy planters and their families, primarily from South Carolina and Georgia, accompanied by some of their slaves, traveled to the area to escape the summer heat, some staying the entire summer. Some purchased land and built homes. Others lodged at hotels, including a number of Grand Hotels, boarding houses, and private homes.[18] This practice, with African American servants (erstwhile slaves), continued after the Civil War and extended inexorably deeper into the mountains, ultimately into areas including Haywood County.

In summary, there were fewer slaves in Western North Carolina, and there were no large plantations. Slaves might work side-by-side with their owners. A greater percentage of the slaves, compared to the rest of North Carolina, had significant and diverse responsibilities. The nascent antebellum tourist industry was also important. All of these factors potentially facilitated the entry and spread of the banjo in Western North Carolina, which included Haywood County.

EARLY SETTLERS

The earliest settlers in present-day Haywood County began arriving in the late 1780s and 1790s, either staking claims or purchasing from major land speculators who owned most of the land.[19] Most of the early Haywood County settlers, like most of the early settlers of the southwestern North Carolina mountains, would come from the North Carolina Piedmont and, to a lesser extent, from the Watauga Settlement environs of East Tennessee.[20] They were largely aware of the area through two experiences. First, some of them were hunters or explorers who had earlier penetrated the mountains. Others had, in September 1776, been exposed to southwestern and Western North Carolina as soldiers in the strategically important and controversial Rutherford Trace Expedition against the Cherokee, some of whom supported the British. The Expedition secured a part of the western flank of the colonists during the Revolutionary War. Many of these soldiers ultimately returned to Western North Carolina, including Haywood County, where they purchased land and settled.[21]

The 1790 census noted two small southwestern mountain communities, the largest with just over 500 people, near present-day Asheville. The settlers continued to come and the "frontier" continued to move rapidly into the mountains. In some areas, including Haywood County, the frontier was ultimately stopped by austere mountain topography. But generally, the frontier did not stop. Over time, many early mountain settlers continued to move farther into Tennessee and Kentucky to the west and northwest and into Georgia and Alabama to the south.[22]

Haywood County was formed in 1808, and its county seat of Waynesville was approved by the North Carolina Legislature in 1810.[23] By the mid-1800s, there were no longer large migrations into or through the Haywood County mountains, most of the subsequent population increase being due to births that increased the size of the family. Also, some former residents had moved back to the mountains.[24]

Scotch-Irish migrations were of major importance in the settlement of the Southern Appalachian Mountains, which included Haywood County. The Scotch-Irish saw, in America, cheap land and a new future. In the 1680s, they slowly began moving, primarily as families, to the United States, with major increases in the early 1700s. Many would pay for their immigration as indentured servants, and between 1717 and 1800, 250,000 persons immigrated, including roughly 210,000 Scotch-Irish, along with lesser numbers of Anglo-Irish and Gaelic-Irish.[25] The major portion of the immigration began around the mid-1700s and occurred over two to three generations. Large numbers of Germans also immigrated along with the Scotch Irish.[26] Most moved from Pennsylvania southwestward down the Great Wagon Road through the Shenandoah Valley, some stopping along the way. They continued into the Piedmont, North Carolina, backcountry between the Catawba and Yadkin rivers, where many of them settled. Indeed, this was the area of most rapid growth in North Carolina in the mid-1700s.[27] A smaller number of this Piedmont population, largely English, had migrated from eastern and Piedmont Virginia and eastern North Carolina. A still smaller group, largely Highland Scots and French Huguenots, came from coastal Wilmington, North Carolina, and Charleston, South Carolina.[28] Many in these Piedmont groups moved into the North Carolina mountains. They were, in general, an independent and self-sufficient people.

It is important to recognize that despite relatively large numbers of Scotch-Irish, the mountaineers were not a racially, economically, ethnically, or culturally "homogeneous" population.[29] In 1810, Scotch-Irish families made up about a third of the Haywood County population. The settlers of the southwestern mountains also included other ethnic groups, particularly English and German, as well as (among others) French, Welsh, and free African Americans.[30] However, at the time of the early settlers in Haywood County, there were essentially no Cherokee east of the Balsam Mountain range, and, therefore, the initial contact between the Haywood County settlers and the Cherokee was limited.[31] A large settlement of Germans

("Deutsch") near Canton became known as "Dutch" Cove. With continued ethnic migration, the relative percentage of Scotch-Irish in Haywood County decreased, but their "social prominence exceeded its size."[32]

Although the Scotch-Irish, English, and Germans were the largest groups of immigrants into the mountain frontier, there were, among all the immigrant groups, back-and-forth cultural (including musical) interchanges of instruments as well as songs. This interchange also included African American slaves as well as free African Americans and mixed-race persons. There was also an eventual interchange with the Cherokee. The African American banjo and the Celtic American fiddle were the major instruments, often played together. "Although the banjo-fiddle pairing did emerge among Blacks in the Upland South before the Civil War, how much earlier blacks attempted combining Celtic-American fiddling with their African banjo tradition is not clear."[33]

The mountain dulcimer evolved from the German scheitholt, which had, in turn, evolved from the zither.[34] The guitar came to the mountains in the early twentieth century.[35] Anglo-Saxon and Anglo-Celtic songs and ballads will be discussed subsequently.

The intercultural musical exchange between European Americans, African Americans, and the Cherokee also led to the evolution of Appalachian dance, with the banjo and fiddle largely providing the music. The dance is beyond the scope of this book, but the reader is referred to the excellent work of Phil Jamison.[36]

ISOLATION, THE SONGCATCHERS, THE IN-HOME FOLKWAY

The isolation of populations is not a rare occurrence and can be cultural, geographical, or physical and can be by choice or by outside imposition. It can also be seen in densely populated areas where it can be either voluntary or forced.[37]

Mountaineer isolation in Haywood County is a remarkable story. It began as a topographic, as well as rural, isolation that subsequently developed into a cultural isolation. It was, by the latter part of the nineteenth century, a well-recognized phenomenon. Songcatchers of the late nineteenth and early twentieth centuries who studied mountain songs and ballads realized that isolation had been present for generations. They were also aware of the banjo and fiddle as well as dancing to the music but paid little attention to them. The songs, instruments, and dances of the isolated areas arose in-home. This section will demonstrate how this developed.

Isolation

The first Haywood County settlers began to clear the forests. Looking for land with agricultural potential, they initially followed and cleared rich river and creek "bottomlands." The Pigeon River, fed by major and secondary creeks, rises in the southern portion of the county and flows north into Tennessee. Tertiary and smaller creeks, generally running from coves and hollows, feed the major and secondary creeks. There are countless springs. As time passed and more settlers arrived, some proceeded farther up the valleys where the adjacent terrain became increasingly mountainous and less suitable for agriculture. Some of the land was still pasturable.

Ultimately, a pioneer settler might, in some instances, be a short distance directly across an impenetrable mountain ridge from his nearest neighbors but much farther away by foot, at times via old animal trails, Indian trails, or dry creek beds. In these areas, there was, in effect, a "topographical" isolation. Ultimately, as noted earlier, the frontier in Haywood County reached its topographical limits, and there it persisted.

Many of the pioneer settlers who moved into the remote areas chose, and were satisfied with, a simple "subsistence" lifestyle in a beautiful setting. Small, close-knit communities, including families and extended families, were often developed in the remote coves and hollows but also, as noted, in less mountainous rural areas as well. While subsistence meant minimal contact with anyone other than neighbors, it did not necessarily mean ignorance or poverty, and many lived comfortable frontier lives. Some could read and write.[38]

Isolation (predominantly from Waynesville, the county's business and cultural center) was not confined to the austere mountainous topography. It was also present in less mountainous rural areas and communities, in this instance largely due to poor county roads, and was widespread.[39] There is no sharp demarcation between the "isolated" and "not isolated" areas. Poor roads continued to be a problem for Haywood County into the mid-twentieth century.[40]

The effects of isolation were changing around the time of the Civil War. The farmer/merchant mountain economy that developed in the antebellum years mitigated at least some of the negative aspects of isolation. The towns, especially county seats and the villages, were the hubs of the mountain economy, and nearby Asheville was the hub of the southwestern North Carolina mountains. The marketing of agricultural goods, particularly beef and swine but also turkey and duck, as well as produce, was active in the mountains. It extended largely through merchants, who at times were

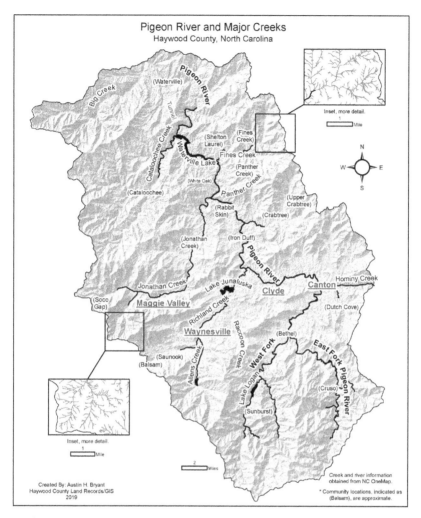

Relief Map. Pigeon River and Major Creeks. Haywood County, North Carolina. Larger rural communities in parentheses, towns in bold print and underlined. (Created by Austin H. Bryant, Haywood County Land Records/ GIS, used by permission.)

"middlemen," into major markets, primarily in South Carolina and Georgia. Goods were sold or bartered, and consequently, capital, dry goods, hardware, and other necessities came back to the county (see Drover's Road, below).[41] Therefore, there were cultural interchanges between the mountain people and "outsiders." However, isolated settler participation in this economy and, therefore, cultural interchanges, were limited. By the end of the antebellum period, most of those who lived in isolation were at or outside the periphery of the evolving, day-to-day Haywood County cultural life.

Wilhelm, in a study of isolation in the northern Blue Ridge Mountains of Virginia following the Civil War, stated that topographical isolation "changed to social, economic, and psychological isolation, causing people to remain in disadvantaged areas and to resist the changes that would bring them in contact with the outside world. The effect of socioeconomic conditions thus became a new cause of isolation, but the new cause was an attitude and not mountain range."

As the people in isolated communities were exposed to new ideas outside their own culture, they evaluated them and either accepted or rejected them, usually the latter. However, if they rejected them, at times to their detriment, they were still capable of living independently within their culture.[42]

Reconstruction was a difficult period in the South, including Haywood County. Following the Civil War, many of the freed African American slaves remained in rural Haywood County, some working on the farms where they had been enslaved. Some moved into Waynesville and Canton and, using skills that they had developed in the mountain slavery system, a few ultimately opened businesses.[43] It is quite possible, although I am not aware of a specific instance, that some who remained in the rural areas, or their descendants, interacted with the in-home folkway. Indeed, as will be seen, some of the ballads and songs identified by the songcatchers were shown to have African American roots.

Cultural Isolation

As noted, John C. Campbell, in the late 1800s and early 1900s, extensively visited and studied economic and social conditions in southern Appalachia, including Haywood County. He wrote in the early 1900s that "a standard of time is needed to indicate the interval between two places [isolated and non-isolated], for they are separated not so much by miles as by years, decades, or generations."

He described three groups of mountaineers: Group 1, Urban and near-urban, and Groups 2 and 3, Rural. Almost all of Group 2 were "prosperous" farmers, along with a few professional people. Many were living in isolated areas. There was considerable overlap between Groups 2 and 3, and Group 3 was more varied than the other two groups. At the bottom of Group 3, generally living in inaccessible areas, were those with "small and usually poor holdings, in distant coves, at the head of streams, and on the mountain and hillsides, tenants, and all who have found it impossible to adapt themselves to the changes taking place." Occasionally, Group 3 persons might be scattered among Group 2 areas.[44] The in-home folkway's major home was in the "inaccessible" and the isolated rural areas.

Cecil Sharp, an English songcatcher, stated in 1917 that the isolated groups were economically independent, hospitable, and interested in, and friendly toward, strangers. Most were illiterate. He further stated that "they possess the elemental wisdom, abundant knowledge and intuitive understanding which those who live in constant touch and face to face with reality seem to be able to acquire."[45] Some were confined to the most remote parts of the mountains, but most were widely scattered about through isolated rural areas.

And what was their culture? Harry Caudill has described the culture of his Appalachian ancestors in early twentieth-century Letcher County, eastern Kentucky. It is applicable to other areas of Appalachia, including areas of Haywood County. I quote it at length because it is seldom mentioned or understood.

> The Bible was the source of nearly all wisdom. . . . Patriotism was the second religion of the hill people. The society was largely patriarchal . . . the grandparents were a living cement that held the generations together and provided for the transmission of folk information. . . .
>
> In the hills a young man grew up as a passable rough carpenter who could "frame out" a house or barn. He could take off a worn sole and repair his shoes . . . He could plow, plant, and harvest a dozen varieties of garden vegetables and knew the seasons when each task should be done. He knew the trees and the low ground-plants of his native hills and could brew tonics and teas that lessened pain and supplied needed vitamins and minerals. He was an adequate smith, and might be able to "draw iron" and fashion it into tools, hinges, and even guns. He could slaughter hogs and cattle, preserve the meat, and tan the hides. He was a skilled hunter . . . His fingers produced dulcimers and banjos, and brought forth tunes to accompany the ancient songs which his imagination embellished and enlarged . . .
>
> In many of these tasks, his wife worked alongside him. She could also clip wool from the back of a sheep, clean it, comb it, card it, and dye it. The ability to spin it into thread and weave it into patterned

cloth had not been wholly lost. She knew how to trim the fat from the guts of hogs and transform it into soap. She could preserve foods by drying, canning, and pickling, and brew remedies from a score of plants. Her "granny woman" often did a creditable job of delivering her babies. . . .

Or consider the grandmother who spun, dyed, wove, sewed, made soap, preserved and cooked food she had grown, milked her cow, and saw to a thousand details without visiting a store. . . .

Frugality was a perpetual and instinctive part of living. All in all, they were a profoundly knowledgeable people. . . . Most of them could read little or nothing. . . . To their sorrow they knew nothing about cover-cropping and crop rotation. Superstitions were rampant. The notion that germs caused sickness was only slowly gaining acceptance, and sanitary standards were shockingly low by today's norms. But when all this is conceded they still knew a tremendous lot.[46]

Larger rural communities were also spread around the county, and several, for example, Dutch Cove, located south of Canton, White Oak, north of Waynesville, and Jonathan Creek, north-northwest of Waynesville, are noted in the map on page 15. Some of these areas would be the homes of some of the banjo players in this book.

One realizes, upon talking with friends and acquaintances whose family roots were in Haywood County and adjacent counties, that the "'isolated' poor people" in Appalachia did not think of themselves as "poor." They were, in general, as noted earlier, a content, proud, and independent people.

It is important to understand that persistent isolation from the time of early frontier settlement allowed the pioneers' in-home folkway, including banjo, fiddle, guitar (later), ballads and songs, and dances, to continue to flourish with little cultural dilution/challenge from outside. The banjo and fiddle provided music in-home, including for dances. This will be discussed further in the next section.

"Corn shuckings" were a time of hard work but also celebration. The early-1900s photo below is from a corn shucking in the White Oak community of Haywood County. Note the fiddle player and banjo player. The fiddle player is James Kirkpatrick, the grandfather of French Kirkpatrick, a banjo player in this book.

But change was inevitable. "The transition was not marked by a radical reorientation of values but rather by a gradual shifting of beliefs and sentiments."[47] That transition continues to this day and is discussed further in chapter 14.

Corn Shucking, Fines Creek Community, Haywood County, early 1900s. French Kirkpatrick's grandfather, fiddle player. (Photo courtesy of Roy French Kirkpatrick)

The Songcatchers, the Banjo, and the In-Home Folkway

Katherine Pettit and May Stone were, in 1902, the first directors of the Hindman Settlement School in Hindman, located in eastern Kentucky. Pettit recognized that some of the ballads and songs that she was hearing had been present in the mountains for generations. They were the product of the in-home musical folkway. Since the ballads and songs were in-home, there were no descriptions of them by the mountain people's contemporaries. Everyone knew them. Consequently, they had been, in effect, "hidden" from outsiders.[48]

A scholarly review of some of these ballads and lyrics, published in 1907, demonstrated their primarily Anglo-Saxon/Anglo-Celtic origins.[49] The songs had been "carried by oral transmission from the cabin on the frontier to the hearth of the mountain home today,"[50] where, for many, the "frontier" had persisted, and the ballads and songs had been preserved.

Olive Dame Campbell, from the fall of 1908 into early 1909, traveled with her husband, John C. Campbell, through the Southern Appalachians, including Haywood County. Their goal was to survey economic and social conditions in this often-isolated area. In early December 1908, Mr. and Mrs.

Campbell visited the Hindman Settlement School. After supper, Katherine Pettit asked Mrs. Campbell if she would like to hear an old ballad, and one of the schoolgirls, Ada B. Smith, sang "'Barbry' Allen." Mrs. Campbell stated:

> Shall I ever forget it? The blazing fire, the young girl on her low stool before it, the soft strange strumming of the banjo—different from anything I had heard before—and then the song. I had been used to sing "Barbara Allen" as a child, but how far from that gentle tune was this—so strange, so remote, so thrilling. I was lost almost from the first note . . . and I seemed to be borne along into a still more dim and distant past, of which I myself was a part.
>
> Of course, I would not rest until I had learned this new fascinating "Barbara Allen"—quite an undertaking . . . I was attracted by both words and songs, but it was the melodies that especially intrigued me, and I began at once to pursue them whenever I had an opportunity.[51]

In 1916, Mrs. Campbell met another songcatcher, Cecil Sharp, and shared her findings with him. The two of them subsequently spent two months in the Southern Appalachians, again including Haywood County, ultimately collecting over one hundred additional songs and ballads which they published in 1917.[52] There were, in addition to Campbell and Sharp, other songcatchers who, in the late 1800s and early 1900s, had begun to come to the mountains in search of ballads and songs.[53]

Cecil Sharp's 1917 comments are instructive. He noted that the people whose music they studied spoke "English" and not "American." They also used outmoded expressions as well as "old-fashioned" pronunciations of words. He believed that they were descendants of England and lowland Scotland emigrants. As noted, the songs had been handed down in-home for generations in the isolated families and communities, and both young and old knew them. Some singers had large repertoires, and there were often variants of the originals, as would be expected in such oral transmission. The ballads were narrative songs, romantic in character, and impersonal—the singer being a "narrator." The songs were more emotional and passionate utterances, usually of personal experiences, very frequently romantic.[54] Josiah Combs, Hindman Settlement School's first graduate, noted that some of the highland songs had African American origins.[55]

The songcatchers were focused on these mountain songs and ballads and, consequently, seldom mentioned mountain instruments. Olive Dame Campbell did mention "the soft strange strumming of the banjo [accompaniment]" by Ada Smith.[56] In John C. Campbell's book, which Mrs. Campbell completed upon his death, there is a very brief overview of the fiddle and the banjo. The dulcimer is mentioned as more of a "curiosity." However, the Campbells, who had become familiar with the mountain people, recognized the banjo and realized that its presence, like the ballads and songs, had been widespread for generations.[57] As noted at the beginning of this chapter, historian John Preston Arthur was also aware of this. The in-home banjo, fiddle, dances, and songs had not been hidden from them.

Cecil Sharp was also aware of the banjo, but the instrument was not his emphasis, either. While visiting the Waynesville area in the summer of 1917, he mentioned two boys who "play the banjo and fiddle rather characteristically." This implies that he had enough knowledge of the banjo and fiddle to recognize that they were often played together. Sharp also mentioned that ballads are more commonly present in remote areas away from population centers (in this instance, tiny Waynesville was a cultural "population center").[58] The same would be true for the banjo and fiddle as well.

So, while the songcatchers were aware of the banjo, it was not their focus, and consequently, it was largely ignored by them. Another reason the banjo story was not pursued is that the banjo, along with the fiddle, provided music for dancing in-home and at community "frolics," which did not meet the approval of many local churches. The banjo was also viewed by the upper classes as an instrument of the lower classes. Local criticism of the banjo, despite Ada B. Smith's mesmerizing banjo accompaniment, led the ladies at Hindman to promote the dulcimer. But dulcimer playing was declining in the early 1900s, and the instrument did not pose a threat to the banjo. Finally, the banjo was also negatively associated with slavery and minstrelsy.[59]

Just as the ballads and songs had been passed down in-home for generations, so had the banjo. However, with the exception of dance references, the banjo was and continued to be largely ignored. Indeed, there was a continued paucity of outside references to the banjo in the mountains until subsequent national folk revivals.[60]

In summary, some of the mountain frontier had "persisted" due to mountaineer isolation. This largely prevented "cultural dilution" from areas of commercial and cultural development, including new songs and dances. Naturally, the songcatchers were active and successful in the rural mountain areas where isolation had taken place. The ballads and songs (and the instruments, including the banjo) had been present there for generations. However, they had been hidden because of a lack of contemporary citations. Folkways being common, the mountain folk rarely mentioned them.[61]

Finally, Cecil Sharp made, in 1917, a prescient comment urging the timely completion of the songcatchers' work. "Already the forests are attracting the attention of the commercial world; lumber companies are being formed to cut down and carry off the timber, and it is not difficult to foresee the inevitable effect which this will have upon the simple Arcadian life of the mountains."[62]

The railroad had been present in Haywood County since the early 1880s. Its presence, as will be seen, had facilitated not only massive logging and lumber production but also a major stockyard, industrialization, and the development of tourism. These changes in Haywood County were well underway when Sharp made his comment and would, indeed, affect the life of the mountains, including its in-home folkway.

THE BANJO, EARLY REPORTS

The Banjo in North Carolina

The banjo, to my knowledge, was first noted in North Carolina on Christmas Day, 1787, in Tarborough (now Tarboro).[63] "After Breakfasting I returned to Tarborough. I dined with Andrew Grier. After dinner saw a dance of Negroes to the Banjo in his Yard."[64] This was likely a slave Jonkonnu ("John Canoe") celebration.[65]

An 1807 article regarding an "after corn husking" slave "frolic" stated that "after the corn had been shucked and the food cleared, dancing would begin to the music of the fiddle and banjo. In almost any gathering of slaves, at least one could be found with a musical instrument."[66]

An 1840s reference from a history of Durham County, North Carolina, stated that "'on moonshiny nights he [Dr. Bartlett L. Durham, 1824–1859, after whom the city of Durham is named] would get a group of boys together and serenade the town.' Thaddeus Richmond remembered on one occasion . . . 'We had some horns, a fiddle and a banjo. We went by a barroom and got some liquor' before waking up the town."[67]

An 1858 Raleigh newspaper published a "For the Register" piece by one "Simon," who described early memories of Piedmont Springs in Stokes County, North Carolina (north of present-day Winston-Salem) in light of its 1858 "luxury."

It seems but yesterday, I used to come to these Springs when in their original native simplicity. The worst kind of "old corn whiskey" was retailed by "Finchem" in a gourd, from a brown jug with a corn-cob stopper. Now champagne, &c, is the order of the day—We then scraped away the "trash," leveled the dirt, and sprinkling down the bran, had the real bran dances of primeval times to the music of the Banjo . . . Then, log cabins, ox wagons, and tents, sheltered our beavers from the mountain showers.[68]

A 1915 retrospective article, "A Visit to His Old Home," described two boyhood friends in northeastern North Carolina playing, prior to 1870, the banjo and fiddle: "Many years ago, we remember, as boys, how we played together, he playing the old banjo and me on the fiddle—not violin—as it was the "banjo" and "fiddle" in our good old boyhood days."[69]

The Banjo in Western North Carolina

The major study of the banjo in Western North Carolina occurred in a mountainous area of northwestern North Carolina adjacent to Tennessee and Virginia. A section of eastern/central Piedmont, North Carolina, was also studied extensively.[70] African American/European American inter-changes occurred in both areas by the early 1800s, prior to the advent of minstrelsy. European Americans, at least initially, learned to play the banjo from African Americans and could, in turn, teach other European Americans to play. It is not surprising, as noted previously, that there were different "styles" as well as songs with varying lyrics and lyrics with varying tunes. African Americans, as well as European Americans, who learned primarily or secondarily from African Americans, took the banjo into the mountains from western Virginia, northwestern North Carolina/northeast-ern Tennessee, and western Piedmont, North Carolina. Others learned to play the banjo from similar sources in the mountains.

The Buncombe Turnpike (Drover's Road)

The Buncombe Turnpike (Drover's Road), which opened in 1827, was probably a significant source of antebellum African American/European American interchanges of the banjo in Western North Carolina, includ-ing Haywood County. In the early 1800s, agriculture, particularly meat production, became increasingly important for the mountain economy. Livestock was driven to markets to both the north and south along "turn-pikes," the Buncombe Turnpike being the most important. It extended over a hundred miles from northeastern Tennessee, southward (upstream) along the French Broad River, through downtown Asheville, and toward South Carolina. In the fall of the year, in addition to routine turnpike traffic, which was considerable, massive numbers of livestock, particularly swine, were driven to markets in the foothills and beyond. In time, roads were extended to Greenville and Charleston, South Carolina, Augusta, Georgia, and also into Piedmont, North Carolina. Another turnpike ran from Canton, near Waynesville (roughly I-40, Exit 37), to Asheville, where it connected with the Buncombe Turnpike.[71] Two of the banjo players in this book, a father and son, grew up on Turnpike Road, originally the Canton-Asheville Turnpike.

Animals, at times over a thousand in a "drove," were herded down the turnpike. The "drove" was sub-divided into groups of roughly twenty to fifty or up to one hundred animals, each driven by one or two "drovers." The drives averaged eight to ten miles per day. At intervals along the roads, there were "stands" or "inns," including large pens where the animals could be sheltered and fed for the night and where the drovers could rest, eat, visit, and sleep before continuing the next day's journey.

The drives were a lucrative undertaking for all participants. In addition to food and shelter for the drovers, thousands of bushels of corn had to be produced for the animals. Farms, primarily devoted to this purpose, sprang up along the route of the turnpike. Upon selling their livestock, the drovers would return home along the turnpike with goods that they had purchased with the money from the sale of their stock and would also pay the stands along the turnpike where they had stayed earlier. The price of the livestock was regulated by the price of cotton.[72]

The drovers, including African Americans, were entrusted with major responsibilities. African Americans also worked in the businesses that catered to these drovers.[73] One of the inns was operated by an African American man named Farnsworth.[74]

These drives offered a significant avenue for cultural interchange among the drovers, the farmers, the people who maintained the inns, and other travelers on the road.[75] They continued, to a lesser extent, after the Civil War until rendered obsolete by the railroads. Banjo exposure must have been present on these drives, at the very least at the stands.

THE BANJO IN WESTERN NORTH CAROLINA,
FURTHER REPORTS

A brief report of voter registration in the south, "Registration Scenes," appeared in 1867 in *Harper's Weekly Magazine* and contained a sketch from Asheville, North Carolina, about twenty miles east of Waynesville. In one part of the sketch, there is an African American man playing the banjo for another African American who is dancing.[76] It is the earliest report of the banjo in the Haywood County region that I have been able to find.

A reference to an impromptu "hoe-down" in Nantahala, Western North Carolina, was reported in 1883. The hoe-down was held in an isolated one-room log cabin several miles into the wilderness. Two young men sat in chairs "before the blazing hearth. One of the twain had a home-made banjo on his knee; the other a violin. . . . Then the music struck up, and such music! The tune was one of the liveliest jigs imaginable, and the musicians sang as they played . . . social ties between the young folks are kept warm principally by the old-fashioned 'Hoe-downs.'"[77] This is a good example of the in-home folkway.

An article from a local historic newsletter about the early 1880s describes the boyhood of Judge Felix Eugene Alley in Jackson County, adjacent to Haywood County. In it, Judge Alley recalls:

From "Registration at the South. Scene at Asheville, North Carolina." *Harper's Weekly Magazine*, September 28, 1867.

When I was eight or nine years old, one of my brothers made for me a banjo, using for material a cheese hoop, a tanned ground-hog skin, and wood that he worked into shape with knife and drawing knife, for the banjo's neck. We made the strings of "J. and P. Coat's Spool Cotton" by twisting strands of the thread into the properly varying sizes, and then waxing them with homemade beeswax. When the banjo was finished, I soon learned to play on it, not only hymns, but all the old mountain melodies that I had ever heard; and for years being the only person in that area who could play a banjo, I made the music for the mountain dances in my own section and in the adjoining counties.[78]

John Campbell, writing about mountain men in the early 1900s, says that "even during periods of hardest labor, they rarely appear hurried or pressed by the necessity of making a living, and there is always time in the long winter season to pick up the banjo."[79]

The earliest banjos in the mountains were gourd banjos. They had no manufactured hardware. The mountaineers, as has been noted, initially learned, directly or indirectly, how to play them and how to make them from African Americans.[80] They were not difficult to make and could be made with simple tools.[81]

Well-known North Carolina banjo players Samantha Bumgarner (1878–1960)[82] and Charlie Poole (1892–1931)[83] both initially learned to play the banjo on gourd banjos.

Homemade gourd banjos were largely replaced by more durable materials, predominantly wood, and early on, these too were homemade.[84] The early homemade "mountain banjo" was a wooden copy of the gourd banjo, and it too contained no manufactured hardware.[85] It was gradually replaced by cheaply manufactured banjos with hardware. Gourd banjos continue to be made and played, albeit uncommonly, in the Southern Appalachians.

As mentioned in the previous chapter, following the Civil War, efforts were made to "elevate" the banjo. They included up-picking, "playing by notes," technical innovations, and manufacturing advances. In the late nineteenth and early twentieth centuries, efforts centered in the Northeast and mid-Atlantic states were also made to "socially elevate" the banjo. The movement progressively expanded into neighboring regions, including North Carolina, and reached Waynesville, the county seat of Haywood County, but largely disappeared after World War I. The focus was on "performance." On the other hand, the cultural focus of the banjo in the mountains, including rural Haywood County, was not performance. It was centered in-home, which provided individual and group enjoyment as well as providing music for in-home and local community dances. There was no need to "elevate," no need for professional teachers, and usually, with the exception of county fairs, no need for "performance." Playing was done by downstroking and was learned by ear. As noted earlier, given the scattered advent of the banjo along the frontier, multiple downstroking techniques developed and evolved. With the advent of bluegrass in the 1940s, up-picking, particularly three-finger Scruggs-style playing, named after Earl Scruggs, a legendary banjo player who is discussed below, would begin to largely, but not entirely, replace downstroking.

THE BANJO IN HAYWOOD COUNTY, EARLY REPORTS

Although early African Americans and mixed-race people also had an in-home musical tradition,[86] I am not aware of any contemporary reports of this in Haywood County. There are, however, three early reports of an African American banjo player in Haywood County.

The earliest (1874), in *Scribner's Monthly*, describing Waynesville in the evening, states, "By nine o'clock at night there is hardly a light in the village: a few belated horsemen steal noiselessly through the street, or the faint tinkle of a banjo and the patter of a negro's feet testify to an innocent merry-making."[87]

There is, in *Harper's Weekly Magazine* of August 1880, a "travelogue" of a visit to Waynesville. A drawing, "On the Porch at Mrs. Bright's," shows an African American banjo player sitting on the porch steps of a building identified as Mrs. Bright's Inn which was located directly across a side street from the current Haywood County Court House. Four or five people are watching and listening. The banjo player is identified in the narrative as "Black Sam," and a young boy is dancing Juba.[88]

The third report is in a letter to the editor published in the May 5, 1920, edition of the *Carolina Mountaineer and Waynesville Courier*. It is a retrospective piece, probably referring to the early 1880s,

> On the street front of the old court house was a large dry goods box, a negro with a banjo drumming up a crowd for an "itinerary" medicine man peddling worm candy guaranteed to rid the county of worms. . . . The negro sang only the one song as he picked the banjo all the time I was in town which, I believe, was more than a week. I remember the words of it yet.[89]

On the porch at Mrs. Bright's. *Harper's Magazine*, August 1880.

This reference also underscores the possibility of the role of traveling medicine show banjo players in the spread of the banjo.

An African American "frolic" occurred on January 2, 1913, in Waynesville (*Waynesville Courier*, January 10, 1913). There were roughly forty African American participants. "They had fiddling and dancing and banjo picking— a general hilarious affair."

It has not been possible for me to identify the first white banjo player in Haywood County. There were, in this book, at least eight great-grandparents (including two great-grandmothers) who played the banjo (see Appendix, Additional Demographics, The Banjo Players, The Great-Grandparents).

The first verified white banjo player in Haywood County that I am aware of was Martha Jane Rathbone (1864-1947). She was the great-grandmother of Charles Rathbone (in this book) and was "above average" and played a "two-finger" style. Although her children did not play the banjo, her grand-son (Charles Rathbone's father, deceased) was an exceptional banjo player as is her great-grandson, Charles Rathbone. Both men retained aspects of the in-home folkway.

James Austin Bolden (1894–1977) was born in Haywood County. His family actively "made music," and he played the banjo "clawhammer" style (downstroking). A banjo player has been in every subsequent generation of James Austin Bolden's family. James Bolden's great-grandson, Jeremy Bolden, one of the banjo players in this book, is a fourth consecutive verifiable generation and his son, Jayden, and nephew, Riley, are, remarkably, fifth consecutive generation banjo players. It is quite likely that James Austin Bolden's father, James William Bolden (1857–1900) and grandfather, William Jackson Bolden (1824–1926), both born in Haywood County, also "made music," possibly on the banjo. Indeed, over the years, the Bolden family has felt that this was the case. Unfortunately, there are no surviving ancestors or definitive ancestral information to confirm this (see Appendix, Additional Demographics, The Banjo Players, The Great-Grandparents). I believe that it is quite likely that William Jackson Bolden could be the first, or one of the first, white banjo players in Haywood County and would, along with his son, have been a part of the developing in-home folkway. Jeremy Bolden, in that case, would be the sixth consecutive generation of Bolden family musicians who played the banjo, and his son, Jayden Bolden, and nephew, Riley Bolden, would be the seventh. Certainly, as will be seen, much of the in-home folkway has been retained in the Bolden family.

The three initial Haywood County reports noted above (1874–1880) refer to Waynesville and all three were African Americans. The writers were, quite possibly, not aware of the ongoing development of the in-home folkway, including the banjo, which was taking place in rural areas of Haywood County. While the in-home folkway was not the sole source of the banjo in Haywood County, the inaccessible and rural areas were certainly the major source.

MAJOR LATE NINETEENTH- TO EARLY TWENTIETH-CENTURY DEVELOPMENTS IN HAYWOOD COUNTY AND THEIR EFFECT ON THE BANJO

Five major developments occurred in the late 1800s and early 1900s in Haywood County. The advent of the railroad was the most important and was largely responsible for the others, including the development of the Clyde Stockyard, massive logging and lumber production, and nascent tourism. Major industrialization also occurred in Canton (Champion Paper and Fibre Company) and Waynesville/Hazelwood (tanneries and furniture manufacturing). There was mica and also kaolin mining, the latter a clay with multiple uses in the paper production industry. Many of these required massive amounts of investment from the outside and ultimately produced massive profits for the outside. They also "opened up" Haywood County, including, to a degree, "isolated" areas by creating new, "good-paying" jobs. These jobs decreased the major historic role of agriculture in the county.[90] Ultimately, these developments led to the dilution of the rural in-home folkway. However, they might also have facilitated Haywood County banjo and cultural interchanges outside the folkway.

The Railroads

The first train arrived in Waynesville in April 1883, having arrived in Canton in January 1882 and Clyde in April 1882.[91] Waynesville subsequently served as a rail hub for trains proceeding to the west toward Franklin and Murphy, North Carolina, and also to the northeast to Knoxville, Tennessee. Many "outsiders" passed through Haywood County or came to the county on business, vacation, or looking for employment.

Finally, regarding the railroads, it is well known that the great majority of laborers in the dangerous, and at times deadly, work of building the railroads in these mountains were African Americans, largely convicts. In a recent article about convict labor building the railroads, there is a photo of such laborers in a prison car. Outside, one of the apparent convicts is holding a guitar.[92] It has been suggested that railroad construction could have also been a source of banjo contact or introduction.[93]

Clyde Stockyard

The Clyde Stockyard opened in 1883 with the advent of the railroad, and for the next fifty years or so, it was a major stockyard in the Southeast. It was located about five miles east of Waynesville and, in many ways, replaced the Buncombe Turnpike. Farmers from East Tennessee and Western North Carolina drove livestock to Clyde, especially in the fall, where it was shipped by rail to South Carolina markets. Apples and chestnuts were also shipped from the stockyard.[94] This, too, as the Buncombe Turnpike did in the early 1800s, provided opportunities for intercultural and interpersonal exchanges, quite possibly including the banjo.

Logging

Logging in Haywood County occurred in two phases. The first began a few years before the railroad arrived and included the selective cutting of specific hardwoods, which were sold locally to small lumber mills. By the early twentieth century, large-scale logging operations were underway.

The largest logging consumer was Champion Paper and Fibre Company, now Canton North Carolina Mill, Evergreen Packaging, Inc.[95] There was, on the west fork of the Pigeon River, roughly east of Waynesville and south of Canton, a logging town, Sunburst (no longer present), with a peak population of several hundred people. It supplied logs for Champion. A small number of African Americans lived in Sunburst.[96] One of the African Americans, Fred Moore, who moved to the area from outside the county, was a banjo player and played for integrated Saturday night "hoe-downs" in Sunburst.[97] The Canton mill is, to this day, the major industrial manufacturing employer in Haywood County, with roughly a thousand employees.[98]

The logging and lumber operations were the major economic force in the county at the time. Workers came from all over the county, including from farms and from outside the county as well. Some of the lumber went to major local furniture factories. Oak and chestnut bark provided tannic acid for local tanneries. Most of the lumber was shipped out of the mountains. The large-scale logging operations had ceased by the 1930s.[99]

Logging Flume, Oconaluftee River, Jackson County. Note banjo player in the center of the photograph. The man to the banjo player's left is Amos Hunter, the father of Phil Hunter, one of the banjo players in this book. (Photo courtesy Haywood County Library)

A photograph from a logging operation on the Oconaluftee River in neighboring Jackson County shows several men and a woman standing on an elevated "flume" used to move logs. One of the men is holding a banjo. His identity is not known. However, the man to the banjo player's left is Amos Hunter, the father of Phil Hunter, a banjo player in this book. Amos Hunter could also play the banjo.

Apparently, a large logging operation near the White Oak area was well-known locally to have a significant number of fine musicians, including an excellent white banjo player, Henry Rogers (1909–1990).[100] It is reasonable to assume that other African Americans who worked in logging or lumber operations may well have played a role in the county's banjo history.

Sojourners and Tourism

From the early 1800s, summer sojourners and tourists have been important in these mountains. Beginning in 1828, as noted previously, the initial sojourners were wealthy Low-country South Carolinians, forming the Flat Rock Settlement in Henderson County.

> At the opening of summer the planter or merchant and his family, taking along the entire retinue of domestic servants, started for the cool, rural home in the highlands, where the luxurious living of the coast was maintained, to which additional gaiety and freedom was given by the invigorating climate and wildness of surroundings. Carriages and four, with liveried drivers, thronged the public highways. The Flat Rock Settlement brought the highest development of American civilization into the heart of one of the most picturesque regions of the American continent.[101]

Additional antebellum hotels and inns, initially catering largely to wealthy South Carolinians, were established in, but not limited to, Henderson County and Buncombe County, Asheville having the greatest number.[102] At least some of these sojourners probably brought slaves, who played the banjo and fiddle, with them.

Haywood County was not a significant part of this antebellum sojourner/tourism activity. Prior to 1879, its two best-known hotels were the Battle House and the Turnpike Hotel, the latter at the Buncombe-Haywood County line, but these were primarily for business travelers and drovers.[103]

The grand White Sulphur Springs Hotel was built in 1879, the first grand hotel in Haywood County, specifically catering to summer sojourners and tourists. In the years following the arrival of the railroad in Waynesville in 1883, the summer populations of sojourners and tourists in Waynesville, as well as Haywood County, increased. The "outside" had really arrived. Some stayed the entire summer. Over time, a small number of additional luxurious grand hotels, along with several smaller hotels, were built in and around Waynesville. There were also many boarding houses.[104] Some of the wealthy families who enjoyed the prestige and joy of having wealthy or distinguished visitors opened their homes to them.

It has been noted earlier that wealthy antebellum plantation owners often brought their African American servants with them when they came to the mountains. Reminiscent of those days, African American servants may have accompanied visitors to Waynesville. In addition, "turn-of-the-century" African Americans would come to Waynesville each summer from throughout the South to serve people in boarding houses, hotels, and restaurants.[105] People from Waynesville and the surrounding rural areas of the county, including local African Americans, were also "summer" service workers for the hotels and guesthouses, and county farmers provided meat and produce. Interracial interactions were no doubt important for cultural exchange, quite possibly including musical interchange among this group.

A brochure advertising the "luxurious" Gordon Hotel built in the early 1890s says, "Dancing is enjoyed every evening. There are frequent masquerades, fancy dress balls, summer dances of various types, including 'barn dances,' and many other variations of this most popular recreation. . . . The hotel orchestra of six pieces, all finished musicians, furnishes music not only for the dances but during meal hours."[106] A banjo player was likely present for the "barn dances."

In summary, tourism in Haywood County led to intercultural and interracial encounters. Many of the tourism workers came from rural areas of the county. The banjo must surely have played a role in the "barn dances." Perhaps banjo players were recruited from the local in-home folkway. These intercultural and interracial interchanges may have furnished other opportunities for sharing the banjo but also likely led to the dilution of some of the folkway.

POTENTIAL ADDITIONAL FACTORS IN THE SPREAD OF THE BANJO IN HAYWOOD COUNTY

There are, in addition to the major importance of the in-home folkway in Haywood County, several additional potential factors concerning the exposure to and spread of the banjo. Minstrelsy, the Civil War, and medicine shows have already been mentioned.

Manufactured Banjos

The massive commercial production of banjos in the late 1800s/early 1900s, as mentioned in the previous chapter, meant that banjos most likely became affordable for most people nationwide, including Haywood County.

"Isolation" Continues to Decrease

The isolated areas of the county, as noted, were historically at the periphery, or outside the periphery, of the county's contemporary culture. Several additional factors led to a decrease in cultural isolation in Haywood County.

Everyday life in the isolated areas was good, but it was also hard. Following World War I and especially World War II, returning soldiers had seen the "outside" and liked it. They brought new ideas and experiences home with them, and some of them ultimately chose a different life and moved away. Others moved away, looking for jobs. Further exposure to the "outside" also occurred with RFD (Rural Free Delivery) mail, including catalogs and newspapers, and of course, radio.[107]

Additional industrial jobs were created. These, too, decreased the agricultural focus of the county. The two major Waynesville factories, Dayco (Dayton Rubber Company) and Wellco, opened in 1941. Dayco closed in 1996, and Wellco moved its major manufacturing operation to Puerto Rico in 1999. There is no longer a major manufacturing facility in Waynesville.[108]

Radio, Phonographs, Television, Tapes, CDs, DVDs, and the Internet

Around the turn of the century, the phonograph and radio began to bring music, including Appalachian Mountain music with its banjo and fiddle, to the masses, many of whom wanted to learn more about it. This was, as noted in chapter 1, of major importance.[109] Along with television, CDs, DVDs, and the internet, these have played (as will be shown in part II) important roles in the lives of the banjo players in this book. At the same time, these changes steadily decreased cultural "isolation," leading to a "cultural dilution" of the in-home folkway.

Sears, Roebuck and Co. catalogue, 1908. (Photo courtesy Doug Trantham)

The Automobile and Automobile Tourism

The automobile brought increasing mobility to Americans. It was certainly true for Haywood County, especially the rural areas. The mobility of Haywood County banjo players, which provided access to other banjo players as well as other musicians, steadily increased. Indeed, as noted, musical "communities" in the county could be expanded and scattered by several miles, not always limited to the county. Similar to the radio and phonograph, automobiles also played a role in the "cultural dilution" in rural areas.

As early as the 1930s, Waynesville billed itself as the "Gateway to the Smokies." In the postwar 1940s, Haywood County, particularly Waynesville and Maggie Valley, began serving more and more tourists who were attracted by the nearby Great Smoky Mountains National Park and, subsequently, the Blue Ridge Parkway.

The Wild West theme park Ghost Town in the Sky, which opened in 1961 in Maggie Valley, led to an explosion in tourism.[110] Tourism continued to accelerate with road improvements and the arrival of Interstate Highway 40 in the early 1960s. The earlier Waynesville grand hotels and homes with their wealthy visitors had vanished. Middle and working-class tourists predominated. Maggie Valley, particularly, welcomed the automobile.[111]

Playing for the tourists, especially at roadside venues in Maggie Valley, as well as "Ghost Town in the Sky," became a huge source of banjo exposure, this time for the tourists. It was also, as will be seen, a "crucible" for a couple of the banjo players in this book. Locals, including some of the banjo players in this book, were also exposed to the banjo in Maggie Valley.

This tourist exposure ultimately led, beginning in the mid-1990s, to significant net migration into Haywood County, which will be discussed further in chapter 14.

EARL SCRUGGS

One of the great moments in the long history of the banjo, certainly for the banjo in Haywood County, occurred on December 8, 1945. Earl Scruggs (1924–2012), playing the banjo for Bill Monroe's band, "The Bluegrass Boys," made his first appearance on the Grand Ole Opry. He introduced a stunning style of three-finger banjo playing that ultimately became known as "Scruggs style."

Earlier, Jim Shumate, an excellent bluegrass fiddle player, had arranged an audition for Scruggs with Bill Monroe.

> Bill had never heard nothin' like that. I said, "What do you think?"
> Bill said, "Gosh, that's good, I'm gonna hire him." So, he went ahead
> and hired him. So that week I come back to North Carolina and I
> tuned in the Opry on Saturday night to see if he really hired him,
> and there he was, he hired him. When Earl hit the stage, he really
> tore that place up.[112]

Robert Cantwell, author of *Bluegrass Breakdown: The Making of the Old Southern Sound*, has described the sound: "What follows is a wildly accelerated, almost violently high-pitched frenzy of mountain music, one which while treading very close to the edge of the bizarre displays an incredible virtuosity which audiences in those days saw, and were plainly encouraged to see, as a prodigy."[113]

The audience, including the radio audience, was astonished and electrified. There was subsequently a tremendous effort by banjo players, as well as non-banjo players, including those in Haywood County, to understand and copy "what he's doing."

Scruggs had begun to develop his style at age ten (1934). He was influenced by other regional banjo players, including Smith Hammett, Junie Scruggs (his brother), Fisher Hendley, Rex Brooks, and Snuffy Jenkins, all of whom were also developing a three-finger style, but their styles were not quite what he was trying to achieve.[114] Ultimately, he retained "their strong rhythmic and melodic accent without sacrificing the smooth and melodic flow of notes."[115]

There is general agreement that Scruggs deserves the major credit for the three-finger style. John Hartford has said wryly, "Here's the way I feel about it. Everybody's all worried about who invented the style and it's obvious that three-finger banjo pickers have been around a long time . . . But my feeling about it is that if it wasn't for Earl Scruggs, you wouldn't be worried about who invented it."[116]

Scruggs, along with Pete Seeger, was responsible for a national and international proliferation of renewed interest in the banjo, particularly the five-string banjo. They actually "saved" the five-string banjo. In 1968, Scruggs released an instructional book, *Earl Scruggs and the 5-String Banjo* (Peer International Corporation, 1968). It was "revised and enhanced" in 2005. Both editions have been highly successful. Lester Flatt and Scruggs made cameo appearances, with Scruggs playing the banjo, on the sixties television sitcom *The Beverly Hillbillies* and, in 1963, recorded the "Ballad of Jed Clampett," which would serve as the program's theme song. In 1949, Scruggs recorded "Foggy Mountain Breakdown," which subsequently had tremendous exposure in the 1967 film *Bonnie and Clyde*. Later in his career, accompanied by his sons, Scruggs pressed forward in extending the banjo beyond its bluegrass roots.[117]

THE "SOUTHERN WHITE BANJO"

In the twentieth century, the banjo evolved from the "Southern Black Banjo" to the "Southern White Banjo." The banjo "elevation" fad of the late 1800s and early 1900s disappeared. The guitar replaced the banjo in jazz. Ultimately, the "sentimental" minstrel/plantation image of African Americans was, rightly, no longer tenable, and by the second half of the twentieth century, African Americans were no longer associated with the banjo.[118] Along with these changes, the popularity of hillbilly and then country music exploded in the 1920s and 1930s. Although it was an integral part of hillbilly and country music string bands, the banjo was not the featured instrument. The country music banjo player's often buffoon/clown persona replaced the bigoted blackface buffoon/clown of minstrelsy banjo players.

Bluegrass arose from "old-time" and country music. Earl Scruggs, as noted, first appeared with Bill Monroe's Bluegrass Boys in December 1945. His extraordinary ability and three-fingered "up-picking" style, followed by others, catapulted the banjo to the lead instrument and most-recognized feature of bluegrass music. Scruggs and Lester Flatt were inaccurately portrayed as country bumpkins on *The Beverly Hillbillies*, and, with the addition of "Foggy Mountain Breakdown," *The Andy Griffith Show*, and the movie *Deliverance*, the banjo and hillbilly stereotypes were embedded in the American public's mind.[119]

By the late 20th century, most Americans thought of the banjo as Southern, rural, and white, and many particularly associated it with the southern Appalachian Mountains. The plantation setting for the banjo had nearly disappeared in the popular media. . . . Historic metaphor allowed the Anglo-Americans of the Southern mountains to exist outside the official (societal) values: by placing them imaginatively in the past, poverty turned into pioneer simplicity, and cultural isolation into Anglo-Saxon cultural survival. . . . The traditional sentimental ideas of the banjo as pastoral, untamed, and antimodern certainly fit with prevailing notions of Appalachian otherness.[120]

The in-home folkway, which included a subsequent diluted and fragmented in-home folkway, was important in the developments that Karen Linn describes in her book *That Half-Barbaric Twang, The Banjo in American Popular Culture*. However, as she says, "along with positive conceptions of Appalachian potential, there developed strong negative stereotypes . . .

Mountaineer Inn, Asheville, North Carolina, 2018.

many depictions used the themes of poverty, ignorance, illicit moonshin-ing, and especially feuding."[121]

These stereotypes, like the minstrel stereotypes, were often biased and oversimplified. However, the lives of the banjo players in this book power-fully challenge these persistent negative stereotypes.

TWO CULTURAL EVENTS OUTSIDE THE AREAS OF "ISOLATION" IN HAYWOOD COUNTY

Two cultural events occurred outside most of the isolated areas of Haywood County and are mentioned here. Archival (1900–early 1950s) Waynesville newspaper accounts highlighting the words "banjo" and "minstrel" were obtained from the Haywood County Public Library's (https://www.hay-woodlibrary.org) online Community History Archive and were an invaluable resource.

The late nineteenth and early twentieth century efforts to "elevate" the banjo, as discussed in the previous chapter, also occurred in Waynesville. Waynesville newspaper reports in 1908 ("Society Event for August Seventh," *Waynesville Courier*, July 23, 1908) mention the presence of the Waynesville Banjo-Guitar Club, which had apparently provided entertainment at local club meetings and societal events "for years" (*Waynesville Courier*, August 6, 1908). This club also held fundraisers. The banjo is occasionally mentioned in the early 1900s as entertainment in other local social clubs and organization events. One of the members of the Banjo-Guitar Club, Margaret Stringfield (1879–1958), a member of a prominent Waynesville family, was a well-known and talented musician into the mid-twentieth century ("Chief J. L. Stringfield and Miss Margaret," *Waynesville Mountaineer*, January 13, 1958). She could play several instruments and gave music lessons, which included the banjo. She was also a composer. These mentions of the banjo are clearly not referring to the in-home folkway.

Minstrelsy, as shown in the previous chapter, was well known from its inception prior to the Civil War, but its popularity waned in the late 1800s. Fragments of minstrelsy persisted into the mid-twentieth century. A minstrel performer was first reported in Waynesville in January 1905. He was Billy Arlington, "an old time minstrel, a banjoist, and a dialectician of national reputation" (*Waynesville Courier*, January 12, 1905). The first Waynesville "minstrel show," a local production and fundraiser, was held on April 19, 1909 ("The Minstrel Show," *Western Carolina Enterprise*, April 21, 1909). Local, but rarely regional, minstrel shows were performed over the ensuing decades, again as fundraisers. The most popular and recurring one, beginning in 1939, was performed periodically over a few weeks in different small towns or rural communities in the county. It was abandoned in 1958 ("Lions Club Will Install 31-A Officers," *Waynesville Mountaineer*, July 14, 1958). Minstrel shows did not play a direct musical role in the lives of the banjo players in this book.

IN-HOME FOLKWAY

The most important foundational factor for the success of the banjo in Haywood County was the in-home folkway. It was, by the mid-late 1800s, widespread in remote and isolated rural areas of Haywood County. The songcatchers, while studying the ballads and songs, were among the first to recognize the prevalence of the banjo but mostly ignored it. The banjo and other instruments, particularly the fiddle, were also learned and played individually and in groups in the folkway's families, which included providing music for in-home as well as community dances.

Since the folkway largely developed historically at or outside the cultural periphery of the county, it inexorably became diluted as the twentieth century progressed and isolation decreased. Phonograph and radio exposure and the automobile were all pluses for the banjo in Haywood County but, at the same time, led to the dilution and modification of the folkway. In more recent years, the vast exposure of the banjo, including how-to-play instruction, has been remarkable. The media, CDs, DVDs, and the internet have been remarkable resources for anyone who is interested. Anyone can now easily hear and see Earl Scruggs and others play the banjo, albeit unfortunately lacking the important interpersonal relationships of one-on-one interaction.

SUMMARY

The banjo, as shown in the previous chapter, was initially taught to European Americans by enslaved African Americans, and it is the same process that occurred, directly or indirectly, in the mountains. Slavery in the mountains was different than slavery in the Deep South and eastern North Carolina. Considering the relatively small numbers of slaves in the county, slavery in the mountains allowed more interpersonal exchanges between mountain whites and African American slaves, likely including the banjo. There were also, almost surely, interchanges with the small numbers of free African Americans as well as mixed-race people.

The Scotch-Irish influences in the Southern Appalachians were certainly significant for interpersonal cultural transmission, including music, especially for the fiddle. This was true for other nationalities of settlers as well. The drover's roads, railroads, the Clyde Stockyard, logging, and major industrial expansion were also sources of intercultural/musical exchange. The role of sojourners and tourists was important. There were also cultural interchanges between local workers in the tourist industry and local and southeastern African American "summer people," including African American entertainers, which were likely significant. Interchanges with tourists' personal African American servants may have also been important. At the same time, many of these changes diluted the in-home folkway.

While the folkway has certainly been diluted, some of it has survived and has been important, to varying degrees, in the lives of all the banjo players in this book.

Finally, the impact of Earl Scruggs on all the banjo players here is beyond measure. Most play three-finger Scruggs style. He is known, loved, respected, and studied by the great majority of them and is known to them simply as "Earl."

Part II

MAKIN' MUSIC

Chapter 3

THE BANJO PLAYERS

INTRODUCTION

This chapter is drawn predominantly from transcriptions of audio/visual interviews (one to two and a half hours each) of thirty-two banjo players, which included twenty-nine men and three women, from Haywood County. The youngest participant was born in 1996 and was sixteen years old when interviewed. The oldest was born in 1934 and was eighty-two years old when interviewed. The mean age at interviews was 51.4 years old, and the median age was fifty-four years old. (I am not aware of any living African American banjo players in Haywood County.) The interviews were conducted from 2012 to 2016.

The participants are considered, by informed opinion, to be very good to excellent banjo players. A prerequisite for participation was that they were born and grew up in Haywood County. In a couple of instances, a participant was not born in Haywood County, but their banjo life began and was nurtured there. An additional small number (five or six), including one woman, were invited to participate but declined. There are obviously additional banjo players in Haywood County who did not meet the criteria for inclusion. The great majority of the banjo players in this study grew up in rural areas of the county. The locations of the banjo players' homes, where they learned to play the banjo, are on the map on page 46.

Several of the banjo players come from a subjectively defined "musical" family. None of the banjo players stated that they had "perfect pitch," but a third of them specifically said that they were "close" or had "a good ear." Two-thirds can read tablature. However, only a few of the banjo players who read tablature felt that it was important in their learning to play the banjo. Only roughly 20 percent read music. Several specifically noted that they also sing. A small number do at least some shaped-note singing.

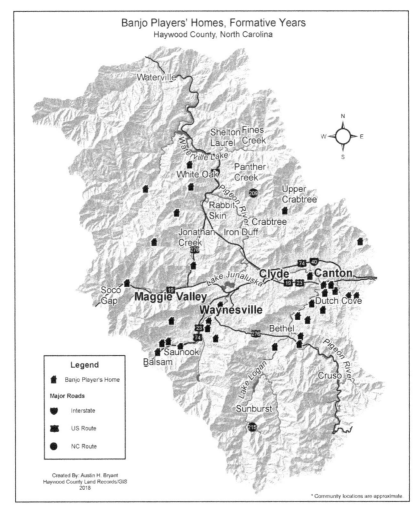

Haywood County. Banjo players' homes, formative years. (Created by Austin H. Bryant. Haywood County Land Records/GIS, used by permission)

Most of the banjo players play five-string resonator banjos. Five play five-string open-back banjos. The open-back banjos are usually played for old-time/mountain/folk music, down-picking "clawhammer" style. The great majority (twenty-seven of the thirty-two) play three-finger Scruggs style. The five who play open-back banjos play only clawhammer. An additional eight play, with varying skill, clawhammer. There has been, to varying degrees, an increased interest in melodic-style playing in about half of the banjo players.

Most play, in addition to the banjo, another instrument, usually (twenty-six of the thirty-two) the guitar. Almost two-thirds play three or more instruments.

Many of the banjo players at one time or another were members of a band that played music for Appalachian dancing, primarily square dancing and clog dancing, as well as dancing competitions.

All but five of the thirty-two banjo players in this study have at least one relative who, with varying ability, played the banjo. Twenty-one of the thirty-two banjo players had at least one first-degree relative (close blood relative including the individual's parents, full siblings, or children) who played the banjo, and eleven did not (see Appendix: Additional Demographics for additional information).

All but two of the banjo players took the musical aptitude test, "Advanced Measures of Music Audiation," developed by Edwin E. Gordon, PhD.[1] Subjective "above average" to "way above average" musical *achievement* was a prerequisite for participation in this study. "Musical *aptitude* is a measure of a person's musical potential. Briefly, the banjo players' mean (average) scores and median score (middle score, half of the scores above and half of the scores below) on the aptitude test were at roughly the test standard fiftieth percentile for high school students (see the Appendix: Additional Demographics, pages 224–26, for further analysis).

The banjo players' stories are told by the "first person" oral history technique used by Alessandro Portelli in his book *They Say in Harlan County: An Oral History* and also by William Ferris in *Give My Poor Heart Ease: Voices of the Mississippi Blues*.[2] The major portion consists largely of one or more selected verbatim paragraphs from interviews of the banjo players. The question-and-answer format of the interview transcriptions has been slightly modified into a first-person narrative. A few paragraphs in the book consist of one to three verbatim sentences from a banjo player's interview, usually along with one- to three-sentence comments by other banjo players. In addition, in the early chapters, the banjo players' comments are roughly separated into three age groups by dates of birth: 1939–1958, 1960–1977, and 1978–1996. It is helpful to consider ten to twelve banjo players in respective time frames rather than thinking about all thirty-two at once. Further, one is able to more clearly define changes in the banjo story in Haywood County over time. For example, one can easily recognize changes in the in-home folkway influences over the decades.

The weakness of this approach is that it is impossible to include important parts of any interpersonal interchange—body language, facial expressions, voice inflections, etc. In addition, compared to the written word, verbal communication, when transcribed verbatim, often seems choppy, with short, even one- or two-word interjections, which at times can be confusing. Occasionally, a word, phrase, or sentence to help clarify some of the words, persons, or places is included. In some instances, there are deletions of choppy words, phrases, or sentences, making the text more readable. Multiple paragraphs from interviews may be deleted. Finally, some sentences may not be in the original order of the interview transcripts. In all instances of editing, every effort has been made to ensure that the meaning is unaltered or even enhanced. The vast majority of the words of the banjo players are unedited from the original interview transcripts.

Photographs have been added where helpful and appropriate.

BRIEF BIOGRAPHIES OF THE BANJO PLAYERS IN ALPHABETICAL ORDER

The age of each of the banjo players at the time of their interview is included in this section.

Courtesy of Patti Best

JARED BEST

Jared Best is twenty-five years old. He lived in Crabtree until he was about ten years old and then lived in Canton until, at age twenty, he joined the Army. He was in the army for six years and had a tour in Iraq and a tour in Afghanistan.

He and his wife, following his military career, returned to Canton.

His sister is a concert pianist. His grandfather, Carroll Best, was, prior to his untimely death, an extraordinary banjo player and was one of the pioneers in three-finger "melodic banjo" techniques which are only relatively recently being recognized and further developed. His great-grandfather Best was also an excellent banjo player who utilized a melodic two-finger style.

Jared died tragically in 2016 at the age of twenty-six. At the time of his death, he was a student at Haywood Community College, beginning a welding course.

TRACY BEST

Tracy Best is fifty-three years old. He grew up in Upper Crabtree, a rural community north of Waynesville, where he has lived most of his life.

He graduated from Tuscola High School and subsequently earned degrees in welding and in the carpentry program at Haywood Community College.

He has lived in Montana, where he "worked as a stonemason and did a lot of fishing" and also has lived and worked as a homebuilder in Pennsylvania. Currently, he owns Best Builders Co. in Haywood County.

Tracy and his family live in a log cabin that he built. He, along with David Burnette (a participant in this book), also built a water-powered grist mill adjacent to his home. He has also enjoyed teaching and playing banjo with his stepdaughter, Helena, who is now in college and also participates in this book.

His mother has above-average musical ability, singing and playing piano, organ, and dulcimer. Tracy is also a distant relative of Carroll Best (chapter 12).

In his spare time, he is an avid bear hunter and also enjoys hunting wild turkeys. "My wife thinks that I bear hunt too much."

JEREMY BOLDEN

Jeremy Bolden is thirty-three years old. He has lived all his life in an area of Haywood County called Saunook.

He attended Hazelwood Elementary, Waynesville Middle School, and Tuscola High School. He is a stonemason. "I actually got started in Tuscola High School. I took it in high school for four years. That's where I got the interest in masonry." He subsequently started his own company, Bolden Masonry, which does excellent work and has been very successful.

He comes from a very musical family, particularly on his father's side of the family. Jeremy quite likely represents, remarkably, the sixth consecutive generation of banjo players descended from William Jackson Bolden (1824–1926), an early settler in Haywood County. His brothers are above average in musical ability, as are his uncle and three of his aunts. His paternal grandfather, Leon, had exceptional musical ability, including singing and playing the guitar, banjo, and mandolin. Leon's brother was also an exceptional musician (banjo and guitar) and, early on, helped introduce bluegrass in Washington State. Leon's brother's son is also an exceptional banjo player.

Jeremy is an intelligent man and has an easygoing personality. His steadiness and integrity are striking. He has a good sense of humor and laughs easily.

He is married and has two sons and a daughter, all with above-average musical ability. Jeremy's son Jayden is now taking banjo lessons, becoming probably the seventh consecutive generation of Bolden banjo players.

Jeremy also plays guitar and loves to sing bluegrass/gospel music.

In his spare time, Jeremy enjoys deer hunting and fishing.

TIM BRADLEY

Tim Bradley is fifty-five years old and was born in Haywood County Hospital in Waynesville ("That's where my mother was, and I wanted to be with her"). He grew up on the west end of Maggie Valley in a place called Mose Mountain. It was named after Mose Curtis, who lived there many years ago. "I don't know if I'm related to him or not. My great-great-grandmother was a Curtis."

He graduated from Tuscola High School and attended Haywood Tech for a while and took carpentry. "And it got to where I couldn't work and go to school at the same time, so I quit and got a job doing carpentry." For the past eight years, he has worked at the Evergreen Packaging Mill in Canton.

Tim is a soft-spoken, matter-of-fact man and has a kind face. He speaks slowly and deliberately and has a wry sense of humor.

He sings and plays the banjo, guitar, mandolin, and harmonica. He combines his banjo playing, at times, with storytelling and singing, his storytelling combining humor and history.

There is generally average musical ability in his family. However, his great-grandfather was an above-average banjo player, and his great-great-grandfather was apparently an excellent fiddle player.

He has enjoyed wood carving since he was a boy and also builds rifles.

DAVID BURNETTE

David Burnette is fifty-four years old. He has lived in Haywood County all his life, living in Burnette Cove, off Dutch Cove, since he was five years old.

He is married and has three sons and a daughter.

David graduated from Pisgah High School in Canton and has taken several courses of study (machinist, sawyer, saw filing, and welding) at the Haywood Community College and currently teaches hand-wrought metals there.

He is not a big man. He has piercing blue eyes. He seems perfectly at peace in his skin—steady and unflappable—and has an excellent, gentle sense of humor. He and his wife farm and pasture the land on which he grew up. They built, over a ten-year period, their two-story log cabin home, including the basement. They used logs, most of which they harvested from their land and most of which were cut from a farm sawmill that David had built. The ironmongery in the house was also built by David.

There are a couple of above-average musicians in his family tree, but there is not a strong prevalence of above-average musical ability. His son is an excellent banjo player (and is also in this book). His father, Albert Burnette, a larger-than-life character, loved square dancing and square dance calling.

David and his family also host a remarkable annual fall molasses-making event, "Molassee," on their farm (chapter 12).

JIMMY BURNETTE

Jimmy Burnette is twenty-six years old and has lived all his life on his family's farm in Burnette Cove, adjacent to Dutch Cove, just west of Canton. He is soft-spoken and has a wry sense of humor.

He is a high school graduate and works on his family's farm. He also works part-time with a friend in a home repair and plumbing business.

His father is an excellent clawhammer player and is also participating in this book. In addition, there are a couple of other above-average musicians in his family tree, but there is not a strong prevalence of above-average musical ability. He grew up listening to bluegrass/mountain music. But since middle school or high school, he listens to a variety of music, including country, rock, and pop.

He plays the banjo clawhammer style and plays very little three-finger (Scruggs) style. He enjoys singing. He does not read music.

He is very busy, but in his free time, he enjoys hunting and fishing.

Courtesy of Wilma Jean Burnette Chapman

SMILEY BURNETTE

Smiley Burnette was seventy-six years old when interviewed. He was born at home in Cruso, a rural community, one of twelve children. He grew up mostly in Bethel, an adjacent rural community, and graduated from Bethel High School. He did not go to college.

He was a soft-spoken, kind man. His nickname was certainly appropriate. A faint, calm, kind smile was always on his face, and that, in turn, often changed to a bright, cheerful smile. He had an excellent sense of humor.

His family farmed. "I always said when—you know, a lot of people like to grow gardens—I said when I left home, I had picked up the hoe for the last time, and I stuck to that."

Smiley worked for several years at the American Enka factory in Enka, North Carolina, and then worked for roughly twenty years at the Evergreen Paper Company in Canton until his retirement.

Extending all the way back to his grandparents, with the exception of a maternal first cousin, who was a way-above-average guitar player, there is no record of any above-average musical ability.

Smiley was an exceptional banjo player and guitar player. He learned to play the guitar before he learned to play the banjo. He also played the bass. His musical interests remained steadfast in country and bluegrass throughout his life.

He died in 2016.

LEWIN BURRELL

Lewin Burrell is just short of his seventy-third birthday. His hands are rough and strong. He is an intelligent and quietly confident man who is, at times, rather intense. When one gets to know him, he is very open and matter of fact. He speaks strongly and easily. He comes from a deeply Christian family, and his faith often shines through in his conversations. He speaks with a mountain accent and with mountain figures of speech. He has a good sense of humor.

Lewin was born in Waynesville and grew up in West Canton. He has lived all his life on a corner of the land that his parents owned. He graduated from Canton High School and did not have any further formal education, first working in a factory in Enka and subsequently, for twenty years, working as a stone mason and, finally, as a building contractor.

There is a remarkable amount of musical talent in his family coming from his father's side, including his father and paternal uncle and his brothers and sisters. All his brothers and sisters played the family piano and sang; some of them played other instruments as well—one of Lewin's brothers was left-handed and played the banjo upside down. Essentially, all the music in their home was Christian music. There was no classical music.

In addition to being a self-taught banjo player, Lewin plays the guitar, fiddle, bass, harmonica, piano, and bugle. He probably has perfect pitch or close to it. He reads neither music nor tablature.

SCOTT EVANS

Scott Evans is fifty years old. He grew up on Jonathan Creek in Evans Cove, where a number of his family members lived. After he was married, he moved to Fines Creek and has lived there ever since.

He graduated from Tuscola High School and took machinist and welding courses at Haywood Community College. He worked as a machinist at a local shoe manufacturing facility for sixteen years and, for the past fifteen years, has worked at Evergreen Packaging.

He has a paternal first cousin who is an exceptional guitar player. His paternal grandfather was an excellent banjo player who learned to play the banjo by ear. There is no above-average musical ability on his mother's side of the family.

He initially played predominantly bluegrass music, but in recent years, he has also become interested in melodic, contemporary Béla Fleck-like banjo.

He enjoys fly fishing for trout and also enjoys deer hunting.

ROGER FRADY

Roger Frady is fifty-five years old and, like Smiley Burnette, grew up in the Bethel community and has lived in this area "all my life."

He graduated from Pisgah High School in 1978 and attended Haywood Community College in 1979, and got a degree in welding. He was a construction worker for four or five years after he got his welding degree, working as a pipe welder and also with structural steel. "I wanted to do pipe welding the most. It paid the best." He has worked for the past thirty-two years at the paper mill in Canton.

He plays banjo and guitar and particularly enjoys singing. He was honored to be in the state chorus in high school. He can also play fiddle, bass, mandolin, and harmonica "a little bit."

His musical ability comes from his mother's side of the family. His mother is an above-average singer and pianist. His four sisters are also excellent musicians, predominately singers. Two of his mother's sisters are above-average musicians. One of them can "play anything," two of that sister's children are "way above average," and one of them can "play anything" as well. His maternal grandmother was also above average in musical ability and taught him songs by whistling the tunes to him.

In his spare time, in addition to banjo, he also enjoys hunting and fishing, particularly deer and squirrel hunting and trout fishing. He also enjoys metalworking and is now trying to learn blacksmithing.

"I've been told that I was born probably a hundred years too late because I like the old ways. Of course, I've got some grandkids, and that's my main thing right there, you know."

HAROLD HANNAH

Harold Hannah, eighty-two years old, was born at home in Little Cataloochee, at that time, part of an isolated (especially in the winter), self-sufficient mountain community roughly twenty miles north of Waynesville. "And times were tough." Little Cataloochee is now part of Great Smoky Mountains National Park. His father was subsequently a park ranger, and the family lived in the adjacent Big Cataloochee. "We became part of the Park Service as kids."

He attended high school in Waynesville, living with his sister during the school year in Maggie Valley near Waynesville. He is a graduate of North Carolina State University, where he received a degree in forestry. His thirty-one-year professional career was as a forester for the state of Virginia, predominantly in western Virginia, where he has lived to the present day.

He comes from a musical family with both paternal and maternal influences. His father was a musician, as were his brothers and sisters. In addition to banjo, he plays the guitar. He plays mountain, country, and bluegrass music, and his abilities are well-recognized in his area of Virginia.

Harold is a big, powerfully built man with blue eyes, white hair, and a beard. He is alert, intelligent, steady, knowledgeable, and affable.

Courtesy of Brandon Henson

BRANDON HENSON

Brandon Henson is thirty-six years old. He was born in nearby Asheville, North Carolina, but grew up in Bethel, a rural community near Waynesville. He is an only child.

He graduated from Pisgah High School in Canton and attended the local community college. He subsequently received an engineering degree from the University of North Carolina at Charlotte. He currently lives in Charlotte, where he works as an engineer.

He does not come from a particularly musical family, although he says that his maternal great-grandfather, who did not live in the mountains, could "play anything with strings."

He took violin lessons beginning in elementary school into high school until he discovered the banjo in his junior year. He can read music but has not used that skill in his banjo career. He is passionate about the banjo and has enjoyed forming friendships with a large number of banjo players, some nationally and internationally known.

He is an intelligent man. He is intense but not overly so and is very affable, comfortable, and poised in conversation.

HELENA HUNT

Helena Hunt, nineteen years old, was born in Piedmont, North Carolina. Her family moved to the Waynesville area when she was six years old. She now lives in a rural area north of Waynesville with her mother, her stepfather, and brother.

She has a winsome personality, speaking easily in a late-teen, contemporary vernacular. She is intelligent and enthusiastic.

She was, at the time of her interview, a student at the local community college but has subsequently entered East Tennessee State University, where she is majoring in biology.

Her father has above-average musical ability, singing and playing the guitar and the harmonica. Her brother also has above-average musical ability.

Her stepfather, Tracy Best, is an exceptional musician and is one of the participants in this book. He has been increasingly influential in Helena's development as a banjo and guitar player as well as a singer. They also perform together.

PHIL HUNTER

Phil Hunter is seventy-two years old. He has lived all his life in the White Oak section of Haywood County, north of Waynesville, less than a quarter of a mile from where he was born. He grew up on a farm that primarily grew tobacco. His mother's side of the family had above-average musical talent.

After graduating from high school and a short stint in the Army, he worked for twelve-and-a-half years in a textile plant in Asheville. He subsequently logged for roughly ten years. He then went to work for Powell Industry (logging and lumber) in Haywood County as a "timber cruiser" (timber appraiser and buyer), retiring after twenty-nine years. He says, "I'm still working. Well, I'm not going to call this work. I fish and I hunt. And when I'm not doing that, I'm doing something for a neighbor or working on lawn mowers, electric motors, or whatever."

Even though he was born in 1943, he is still a powerfully built man. He is intelligent, remarkably steady, and has a good sense of humor. He has a strong side-to-side handshake. As will be seen, he has some unusually introspective and incisive thoughts about what he has learned in his years of "makin' music." He and his wife, Peggy, have two sons, a daughter, and four grandchildren.

He plays banjo using a unique two-finger "drop thumb" style. He also plays the guitar.

ROY FRENCH KIRKPATRICK

French Kirkpatrick, who also goes by Roy Kirkpatrick, is seventy-four years old. Like Phil Hunter, he grew up in the White Oak area of Haywood County and comes from a remarkably musical family. As such, he has experienced "makin' music" his entire life.

He is a tall, thin, angular man with noticeably long fingers. He speaks softly and easily in a mild mountain vernacular, occasionally using words like "h'it" (it), "a'goin'" (going), etc. He has a good, gentle, somewhat self-effacing sense of humor and is a deeply religious man, always eager to share his faith.

French is intelligent and has an encyclopedic knowledge of music in Haywood County and has provided significant contributions, in addition to his interviews, to the writing of this book. He is an exceptional musician, playing the banjo, guitar, and dobro.

He is admired and well respected by those who know him. He and his wife, Judy, have a daughter and a son and two grandsons.

JOSEPH "JOEY" MASSIE

Joey Massie is sixty-three years old and, unlike most of the other partici-pants in this book, grew up in Waynesville, where his family owned and operated two movie theaters.

He is a friendly, easygoing man with a kind face and often a faint smile. He has a good, at times self-deprecating, sense of humor. He is intelligent and introspective.

As an adult, he has been involved in construction, at one time owning his own construction company, and in recent years worked as a project manager for Habitat for Humanity.

One of his aunts, in what he describes as a life-changing experience, introduced him to jazz, and he has been a devoted listener to jazz in all its forms to the present time. He also listens to rock and notes that when he listens to either rock or jazz, he is "blown away by so many unbelievable styles and techniques and genius."

Prior to nineteen years of age, he had no exposure to bluegrass, country, or mountain music. By chance, he heard a recording of Bobby Thompson playing the banjo and began pursuing banjo music and playing the banjo. He plays three-finger Scruggs style "with as much melodic as I can inte-grate." He occasionally expresses regret that he did not "work harder" and "do more" with the banjo.

His son, Patrick Massie, an excellent banjo player, is also in this book.

PATRICK MASSIE

Patrick Massie is thirty-five years old. He was born in Waynesville and lived in Waynesville until he went off to college. He is married and has three young children. He initially worked in his family's construction business but now is an insurance representative in Washington, North Carolina, on the Pamlico Sound, adjacent to the Atlantic Coast.

He is a calm, steady, intelligent, introspective man. He is well-spoken.

Both of his parents and one of his brothers have exceptional musical ability, as does he. His mother sings and may well have perfect pitch. There is above-average musical ability in his mother's family as well. His father is one of the participants in this book.

Patrick began seriously pursuing the banjo when he was nineteen years old. He learned primarily from tablature and the Earl Scruggs books. His father was also helpful. For about a six-year period that included his third and fourth years at North Carolina State University, he was consumed by the banjo. He became an excellent banjo player and plays three-finger Scruggs style and melodic.

After six years, he experienced severe burnout and only plays banjo now for his friends and at church. He seldom practices.

SCOTT MEHAFFEY

Scott Mehaffey is fifty years old.

He is a bright-eyed man who is intelligent and seems younger than his age. He converses easily and has a good sense of humor.

He attended Tuscola High School and subsequently attended Haywood Community College, where he became a machinist. He works at the Evergreen Paper factory in Canton. He is married and has three children.

Scott was an only child. His father, Wade Mehaffey, was a well-known banjo player. Consequently, Scott was exposed to music and banjo at a very young age, often accompanying his father to his performances. He has "been around the banjo all my life." He began to learn to play the banjo when he was seven or eight years old, intrigued by the "roll" (chapter 8) and thinking that it was more fun than strumming a guitar. His father helped him, and he says that he "just tried to copy what he heard." He practiced at least a couple of hours a day and has "played all night" many times, particularly at festivals but also at friends' homes. His mother was very supportive of his playing.

He performed with a couple of bands, The Bluegrass Drifters and Bluegrass Now, over a period of roughly ten years. They were well-known and popular local bands. One of the bands was the house band for square dance competitions at the Mountain State Fair. This required playing fast, and it also required stamina. He distinctly remembers the fatigue of playing for multiple square dance teams.

He agrees that "makin' music" was widespread throughout the county when he was growing up. Although not widespread now, he does not believe that "makin' music" is dead.

"I don't really ever remember any bad times a-playin.' It's all good."

STAN NICHOLS

Stan Nichols was fifty-seven years old when interviewed. He was a stocky, powerfully built man with a full, graying, rusty-red beard. His hands were strong and rough. He was intelligent, modest, and soft-spoken, although his voice was gravelly, and he seemed very steady and calm. He spoke with a slight mountain vernacular and had a wry sense of humor.

Stan grew up in the Plott Creek area of Haywood County, about five miles from downtown Waynesville. Upon graduation from Tuscola High School, he received a welding degree from the local community college and worked for two years as a welder at a nuclear power plant construction site in Missouri. He subsequently returned to Waynesville and established his own welding business. After a year, he went into the wood trade, including carpentry and furniture building and repair, but primarily as a log cabin builder.

He enjoyed hunting and fishing.

With the exception of his mother's brother, who was an exceptional musician who "could play anything," his family musical history is not particularly remarkable.

He died in 2018.

MIKE PRESSLEY

Mike Pressley, sixty-three years old, was born in Waynesville and grew up in Dutch Cove, northeast of Canton. He graduated from Canton High School and subsequently attended Haywood Tech and took electrical installation and maintenance. He worked in this occupation all his life and recently retired.

He is intelligent and speaks softly in a mountain vernacular. He has a kind face. He also has a good sense of humor and smiles easily. Occasionally, after relating an unusual or "different" story or occurrence, he will end it by saying softly, "How about that."

He taught himself to play the banjo using 45 or 78 rpm records, stopping and replaying short segments of a song until he could play it. "Then, I got it." He helped Marc Pruett learn to play the banjo, and the two of them, along with the Conard boys, spent many hours together "pickin." At age thirteen or fourteen, he, Marc Pruett, and Larry Conard formed a 4-H band that won some competitions. He also won other banjo competitions. He says that he did not have any interests other than his music.

He says, "Other than my wife and children, [the banjo] has been the greatest joy in my life—outside of the Lord, you know. Yes, it has. Wouldn't change a thing."

MARC PRUETT

Marc Pruett, sixty-one years old, grew up near Canton and graduated from Pisgah High School in 1969. He subsequently graduated from Western Carolina University, majoring in geology and minoring in biology.

He is an intelligent, soft-spoken man with a keen sense of humor. He has a wide range of interests and is a good conversationalist, looking at one intently during a conversation. At times, he illustrates a point by quoting a comment or a story.

His brother is an excellent musician, as is his wife, who plays guitar and also banjo and is a gifted singer.

His banjo career has been a remarkable success. He is a Grammy Award-winner and, for the past twelve years, has played banjo for the internationally famous bluegrass band, Balsam Range, all of whose members reside in Haywood County. He recently received an honorary Doctor of Arts degree from his alma mater, Western Carolina University, and has also received the prestigious North Carolina Heritage Award. He published a semi-autobiographical book, *Rascally Mountain Boy*, in 2019.

He has collaborated in the production of this book.

CHARLES RATHBONE

Charles Rathbone is sixty-one years old. He graduated from Tuscola High School and subsequently entered a body shop program at the local community college. He was a long-distance truck driver for over thirty years. He enjoyed the independence of his profession, being "outside," and going to different places.

Charles is intelligent and has an upbeat, but not overly so, personality, conversing easily and thoughtfully. One is struck by his steadiness. He is married and has two children and two grandchildren.

His band, Hill Country, is an excellent local and regional band that has been in existence for thirty years, he and mandolin player Bobby Allen being original members. The band continues to get together on Monday nights to "practice" for a couple of hours.

In a side business, he and his brother restore and sell old cars, including, among others, a 1929 Ford and a 1955 Chevrolet. He also enjoys trout fishing.

MITCHELL RATHBONE

Mitchell Rathbone is twenty-seven years old. He grew up in a rural area west of Waynesville called Saunook. He is an only child.

He is a big man. He is intelligent and steady and has a warm personality and a good sense of humor. He has been in law enforcement for several years and is now a patrol sergeant with the Haywood County Sheriff's Department.

Early in his life, he was exposed, through his grandmother, to mostly country music. He first learned to play guitar. He had a friend, Brady Price, who was also learning to play the guitar, and he learned along with him at age fourteen on a "$100 pawn shop special" that he had gotten for Christmas. His friend's father, Gary, was an excellent banjo player. Mitchell's grandfather bought him a better banjo a few months later.

Mitchell was largely self-taught, using books, CDs, and DVDs. He started listening to bluegrass. Gary Price was helpful, as were Marc Pruett and Smiley Burnette (both in this book). For the next two or three years, he (on banjo) and Brady (on guitar) were "consumed" by music, literally practicing for hours upon hours. He could play some of the CDs note for note but was not satisfied until he learned to play it the way "I heard it." Mitchell also began teaching banjo. He is an excellent teacher with several students.

His wife, Jade, is from a musical family and is a singer. She, her sister and brother, along with Mitchell, play guitar or banjo, have a bluegrass/gospel group, and perform regionally. He and his wife have two children.

THOMAS SMATHERS

Thomas Smathers, age sixty-one, was born in Waynesville and grew up in Saunook, a rural community a few miles west of Waynesville. He graduated from Tuscola High School and immediately began working at the Dayco factory in Waynesville. He subsequently worked with his cousin as a homebuilder until back and health issues forced him to retire.

He is an intelligent man with a good sense of humor. He often speaks in a mountain vernacular.

At a very early age, he began to learn to play the banjo, having been taught by his father, an older neighbor, and his great-grandfather. His great-grandfather was an excellent banjo player and took his banjo with him wherever he went. Thomas never took any formal lessons and plays "by ear."

His major interests are banjo, hunting, and fishing. Through connections at work, he was in a band that performed together (and also hunted, fished, and camped together) for twenty-six years. The band dissolved when two of the members became ill. Thomas has played his banjo very little since that time, although he has continued to play the guitar.

He enjoyed playing for people and particularly enjoyed bringing them pleasure or, in some cases, helping to raise money for them.

Thomas died in 2022.

JUNE SMATHERS-JOLLEY

June Smathers-Jolley, fifty-seven years old, was born in Haywood County and grew up in Dutch Cove, near Canton.

She graduated from Pisgah High School in Canton and studied horticulture at Haywood Community College, where she was awarded the 2017 Outstanding Alumna Award. She is the greenhouse manager at the North Carolina Arboretum in Asheville.

Her family, on both her father's and mother's sides, was strongly musical. Her father, her two sisters, a brother-in-law, and she became the highly successful regional band, the Dutch Cove Old Time String Band.

June is a petite woman. She is intelligent and has an outgoing, engaging, and insightful personality.

Her father, as noted in this book, was a major figure in shaped-note singing in this area, and she and her sister have recently begun, in his honor, an annual weekend shaped-note singing school.

TRAVIS STUART

Travis Stuart, forty-six years old, was born in Waynesville and grew up in the rural community of Bethel, east of Waynesville, "right in the middle of the valley." He graduated from Pisgah High School in Canton and attended Haywood Community College, where he studied in the Wood Products Department. Carpentry has been his trade since.

Travis is a steady, kind gentleman. He often speaks rapidly but softly, at times in short phrases, occasionally punctuated by an almost nervous chuckle. He has an excellent sense of humor and laughs easily.

Travis took formal banjo lessons for a couple of years, first in bluegrass and then in old-time clawhammer banjo, the latter most often. After that, he "picked up" anything that he could from friends, acquaintances, festivals, other bands, television, radio, and CDs. He "made music" almost every night as he was growing up. Early on, he practiced several hours a day. He also competed successfully in competitions. He emphasizes the support that he received from his parents.

He had a twin brother, Trevor (deceased 2016), who played the fiddle. Together they played fiddle and old-time clawhammer banjo, the banjo keeping up the rhythm. Travis can also play three-finger Scruggs style. Both brothers played guitar and bass as well, and Trevor also played the mandolin. They played nationally and internationally and made three CDs together. He has enjoyed the traveling.

He currently teaches in the Bluegrass, Old-Time, and Country Music Studies program at East Tennessee State University and has also been an active teacher in the local Junior Appalachian Music (JAM) Program in Haywood County. He says that he can tell the difference between his students who learned on YouTube and those who play with people. The latter "have more of an understanding and better rhythm."

PAM SUTTON

Pam Sutton, forty-nine years old, was born in Buncombe County. Her family moved to Haywood County when she was one year old. She grew up in Hannah Cove, near Dutch Cove, southeast of Canton. She graduated from Pisgah High School and had no further formal education.

She is intelligent, steady, and likable. At times, she has a "matter-of-fact" personality. She is interested in this project, and when I thanked her for her participation, she said, "My daddy would have wanted me to do it."

Her immediate family—her father and two uncles—were very musically talented. Otherwise, there is no striking family musical history.

Her father began to teach her to play the banjo when she was nine years old and required her to practice two to three hours every day. She says that she knew that she would be a good banjo player after her first lesson—her father taught her to play "Cripple Creek" one morning, and when he returned home that evening, she could play it as well as he could. She played in several banjo competitions at festivals in North Carolina and Virginia, and she and her brother and sister had a band, The Three Mountaineers, that performed regionally. The Three Mountaineers played on a variety program, the *Cas Walker Farm and Home Hour* television show, originating in Knoxville. She was ten years old.

Her father died in 2007, and she has played very little music since. "Yeah. my daddy was my backbone."

STEVE SUTTON

Steve Sutton was sixty years old when interviewed. He was born in 1956 and grew up in Waynesville. He graduated from Tuscola High School and subsequently attended Western Carolina University, graduating with a degree in business and marketing and a minor in trumpet.

He was an intelligent and alert man with a twinkle in his eyes. Two things about him were particularly striking. First, one was drawn to him personally. He was friendly, interested, informed, laughed easily, and had an excellent sense of humor. I have heard it said that "everybody liked 'Stevie.'" Second, he was a remarkable musician. Angie Messer, owner of Strains of Music (chapter 12), when asked if he played multiple instruments, replied, "He can play a chair!" He was, of course, also an extraordinary banjo player, certainly one of the greatest of his generation.

Steve started playing the banjo when he was seven years old and, not long after, began playing the banjo along the road at Ted Sutton's Hillbilly Campground in Maggie Valley, a Haywood County mountain tourist destination contiguous with Waynesville. When he was in seventh grade, he was invited to play in Gatlinburg, Tennessee, with Earl Scruggs. He played his first of many performances on the Grand Ole Opry when he was eighteen.

When he graduated from college, he played guitar for ten years with the Marc Pruett Band at Bill Stanley's Barbecue in Asheville. He subsequently played on the road with Rhonda Vincent for two and a half seasons and, later, with Alecia Nugent for three years. His final formal band was Whitewater Bluegrass Company. He also played internationally.

"And I don't know what I would have turned out as had it not been for the banjo. And, you know, I love it as much today as I ever did. . . . I want to be associated with 'We're going to have fun now.' I've been blessed to be able to make a living with it. Can't imagine anything else."

Steve died unexpectedly in 2017.

Courtesy of Thomas Tatham

THOMAS TATHAM

Thomas Tatham is sixteen years old and a junior at Pisgah High School in Canton.

He is a handsome young man, steady, unusually self-confident and at ease for his age. He is intelligent, interested, and has a good sense of humor.

Thomas has been actively exposed to music most of his life, beginning with Suzuki method piano lessons when he was two or three years old and continuing them until he was nine. He subsequently took formal guitar lessons for three years. His father began teaching him to play the banjo when he was twelve years old. He practiced hard and learned quickly.

For a couple of summers before seventh and eighth grades, he worked at the Biltmore Estate in Asheville, playing the banjo and guitar at one of the estate venues. He noticed that people were much more interested in hearing him play the banjo than the guitar.

Thomas states that he has, in addition to his homework, three major interests: basketball, baseball, and bluegrass. "The banjo is always there."

Thomas is currently a senior at Wofford University, where he plays baseball. He plans a career in optometry.

DOUG TRANTHAM

Doug Trantham is fifty years old. He grew up in the Bethel community near Canton and graduated from Pisgah High School. He is a graduate of Warren Wilson College with a degree in behavioral science. He initially worked in human services and mental health and subsequently received a Master of Social Work (MSW) degree from UNC-Chapel Hill. He currently works as a mental health professional at the Cherokee Reservation and seems very much involved in his work.

Doug is not a big man. He is alert and intelligent. In addition, when he speaks, it is clear that he has thought about what he is saying.

He has, literally and figuratively, followed in the footsteps of his father, a respected mountain music historian/performer. He initially learned to play the banjo from his father but also learned from exposure to other banjo players whom he met, and often recorded, at many festivals. He was somewhat of a banjo "prodigy," performing with his father at age nine or ten. He plays other instruments as well. He is also knowledgeable about mountain dance and is an excellent dancer. He is also a shaped-note singer.

Doug is an exceptional clawhammer banjo player. He has played banjo and sung old-time music since he was a little boy. He and his family have a band, The Trantham Family, playing and singing old-time music regionally.

Courtesy of Katherine Watson

LARRY WATSON

Larry Watson, sixty years old, came from a strongly musical family.

He was intelligent and had a great sense of humor. He enjoyed and excelled at telling "stories," particularly about events or about colorful characters whom he had known locally.

He was a remarkable musician and had played guitar since he was a boy. When he was a teenager, he played bass in a regional big band, The Hal Strain Orchestra. He also played piano and had an excellent knowledge of musical theory. His baritone voice was excellent.

Larry started to play the banjo when he was around twenty years old and excelled at it. In the 1980s, he played banjo with the nationally recognized Southern Railroad Lawmen, now the Norfolk Southern Lawmen Band. Weary of being on the road, he left the band after nine years. He taught guitar and banjo full-time and also created CDs as well as instructional videos. I was fortunate to be one of his students.

Larry died in 2014.

GARY WILEY

Gary Wiley is fifty-four years old.

Following graduation from high school, he attended Haywood Community College and has a degree in horticulture technology. He has worked for several years as a computer programmer and currently works in a blue-collar position at a distribution company.

Gary is an intelligent man and has an excellent sense of humor. He converses easily.

His father, an excellent guitarist, was Gary's single greatest musical influence. When he was thirteen, he went to a regional bluegrass festival with his father and heard Little Roy Lewis play "Foggy Mountain Breakdown"—he was hooked. He picked up the banjo very quickly and says that it came very naturally to him. He took lessons from Marc Pruett. Wade Mehaffey was a huge influence on his music. Early on, Gary started playing in local and regional bands. He also entered a number of banjo competitions and won some of them. He has taught banjo to a large number of students over the years. He plays three-finger style.

He subsequently learned to play the bass and, for several years, toured nationally and internationally with several groups playing the bass and occasionally the banjo.

His wife of thirty-five years died from leukemia a few months before this interview. They have three children.

The biographies of Marc Pruett, Steve Sutton, and Doug Trantham will be presented in additional detail in chapter 13, "Three Journeys."

SUMMARY

Learning to play the banjo is not an easy task. First, one had to be exposed to the banjo and develop a desire and commitment to play it. Then, one usually had to find someone to teach him/her to play. Remnants of the in-home folkway often provided these opportunities. One-on-one sessions among family members, or community friends and neighbors, often ensued. Several took formal banjo lessons. Currently, there is a plethora of "how-to-play" aids, including books, CDs, DVDs, and the internet. Much practice, over a considerable period of time, was required. The "novitiate" banjo players slowly began to participate in "makin' music," including "makin' music" for dancing.

It is unusual to find people who do not like to hear the "happy" sound of the banjo. So, while relatively few people learn to actually play the banjo, knowledge and enjoyment of it is widespread in Haywood County.

Chapter 4

"MAKIN' MUSIC"

The historical foundation of "makin' music" in Haywood County is the in-home folkway which has been discussed in chapter 2. Significant remnants of the folkway, as will be seen, have survived to the present.

Makin' music involves families, family friends and their friends, communities, and also even strangers whose connections are due to either being musicians or that they simply love music. It may, over time, take place at the same location or different locations, scattered widely around the county, and at times, outside of the county. It is primarily, but not totally, a rural phenomenon. The music is usually "made" within homes but also in churches, workplaces, hunting trips, fishing trips, dances, and campouts, including campouts at "fiddlers' conventions" and at "festivals." These were all, to varying degrees, social occasions as well. Learning to play the music is characteristically done "by ear."

The first Haywood County fiddlers' convention I am aware of occurred in 1908. It was a great success. A banjo and guitar contest was held with the winning banjo player receiving three dollars ("Old Fiddlers' Convention Here," *Waynesville Courier*, February 20, 1908).

Late spring through early fall, there are also weekly large public music venues including in Canton on Friday nights ("Pickin' in the Park") and also nearby Asheville ("Shindig on the Green") on Saturday nights. There are scheduled stage performances, including clog dancing, but also small clusters of people are scattered around the venue site "makin' music." This same is true for regional festivals, which are scheduled from springtime into the fall (see "Fiddlers' Conventions and Festivals," chapter 12). Friday night street dances are held in downtown Waynesville four or five times each summer.

Singing is also an important component of "Makin' Music." Many of the banjo players cite their relatives who are "above average" singers. Dancing can also be an important component.

The biographies of the banjo players at the beginning of part II above were listed in alphabetical order and included their ages at the time of the interview. However, the interviews were scattered randomly over a four-year period. The banjo players were ultimately separated by date of birth into three groups (1939–1958, 1960–1977, and 1978–1996). The banjo players are identified in the remainder of the book by birth year as well as age at the interview as follows: **Jim Banjo (b. 1947/68)**.

French Kirkpatrick (b. 1938/74) At our house, in the forties and fifties on any given Friday or Saturday night, Bill, you would have people that would come in—among others, the Setzers from Maggie Valley, the Swangers from Fines Creek, the Kingsmores from Fines Creek, the Hannahs from Suttontown—they were from all over. We were in White Oak—a little place called Laurel Branch. And what they'd do, they would come in to play. It was not structured like you'd go to a barn dance, but they'd still do it in a kind of a structure—they'd be four or five people playing for a while—they'd get tired of it—they'd go get some coffee or eat a piece of chicken or whatever—and somebody else would sit down and play for a thirty-five- or forty-five-minute set—that's the way we did it. Daddy was kind of restrictive of who would play or what they would play. He would not allow everybody to play at one time . . . And that was not trying to insult anybody, it was to make the music good. . . . H'it was not just a free-for-all. One of daddy's terms—he would say, if everybody was playing at one time, he'd say, "That ain't nothing but a rat race." Well, actually, when you start playing at five in the afternoon, you've got a full-fledged festival on your hands for that evening. Nobody can sit there from five and play till twelve, one or two o'clock in the morning.

In addition, on any given night, my brother Bill, who was older than me and who would usually do the drivin', would say, for instance, "Let's go up and see if Fred Hannah's at home" or "Let's go see if Wilford Messer. . . ." We could maybe go up there—well, there's no tellin' where them guys may be. If their mother was there, they'd say, "Well, they went up to the Setzers' in Maggie Valley." So, we'd go on to Maggie Valley and we'd get up with the gang ever where they were playin' and we'd play. Or we might wind up over at Carroll Best's house on Crabtree or Dexter Bumgarner's on the head of Allens Creek. They's no telling where we'd wind up playing music that night. Sometimes, we'd go and if we was a'havin' some good pickin', h'it would last a long time.

It was widespread. There were just some great musicians we hung around with when I was growing up. They were all over this county. It was just country folks getting together and singing, visiting, and playing music. Even before we had telephones, it was by postcards. . . . We would go to other people's homes. We would be all over the county. It was just a circle of friends is what done it. We'd be somewhere every Saturday night playing music—for years. It was just entertainment. It was something to do. It was who we were. It really was a remarkable legacy. And I can still remember some of the old songs that we'd sing.

The "community" aspect of the in-home folkway had rapidly expanded with the advent of the automobile. The big get-togethers described above began to wind down in the late 1950s.

Jeremy Bolden (b. 1982/33) Music was essential for our family. The great majority of "makin' music" in our family occurred at my Papaw's [grand-father's] house, just about every Friday and Saturday night and again on Sunday afternoon after church. My Papaw and I also picked [played] and sang at church that night. He and I, when I was in my teens and early twenties, picked all the time.

Papaw was an accomplished musician. During the Korean War, he provided entertainment on his troop ship on the way to Korea as well as on the return. In addition to playing the banjo [clawhammer, primarily], he was an excellent singer. He usually sang bluegrass gospel.

Makin' music would start around six or seven o'clock, and it was not unusual to play and sing until midnight. Forty or fifty people, family and friends, might come. I've seen fifteen or twenty pickers there. At times, people would dance, including clog dancing—it felt, occasionally, like the floor might fall in. Papaw didn't have any musical ability requirements for people to participate. That's one reason why people came—just the joy of it. That's what we done for enjoyment. People were a lot more happy then. This extensive "makin' music" began to decrease in 2000–2010.

That's right. It's got diluted. I've seen it decrease over the past ten to fifteen years insofar as togetherness or getting together. I don't see it coming back. There are still a lot of talented pickers, but not a lot of singing and harmonizing. They learn primarily on the internet and very little from the family these days.

Tracy Best (b. 1963/52) I mentioned earlier making music with high school friends. It was a big bond. There was a big thing with music when I was in high school. There were lots of kids that were interested in it. I know my next-door neighbor and I, as teenagers, if there was nothing else going on, got together every Friday, Saturday night. And he couldn't play anything other than "spoons," and we'd sit around and I'd play banjo and he'd play the "spoons" with me. [Playing "spoons" is done with two spoons that are held back-to-back with a finger separating the handles. With rapid wrist movements or tapping the spoons against a leg, chest, or arm, a clicking sound, at times quite complex, is made, providing rhythm.] And we done that, you know, lots of nights and had lots of others that were interested in the music.

There were also some people were a little more into the drinking crowd, and they made music every weekend somewhere . . . large gatherings. A lot of people could come. And you might have ten, fifteen musicians sitting around playing all at one time. When I was a teenager, I made [went to] a few of those along with some other kids that I went to school with in very similar situations. My parents didn't approve.

Even in church, we would have little groups that we would get together and play. It was just widespread, yeah.

Phil Hunter (b. 1943/72) I think that makin' music was very widespread because I got surprised many times. I'd go somewhere, and there'd be some-body playing, and I thought, well, this—this is great. I want to listen to this a minute. And you heard it in the Canton area, and you heard it all the way going into Tennessee and going out of Haywood County into Jackson County. There's even an overflow of it into Jackson County. When I worked at American Enka near Asheville, there was guys that I played with over there. We'd get off work and go—go and sit down and play for a couple hours and then we'd go on home.

"Well, the act of playing music is a wonderfully self-gratifying thing to hap-pen. It was a form of self-entertainment—before TV, video games. It was a great way to relax on the weekends." **(Marc Pruett b. 1951/61)** "There used to be a lot of Makin' Music going on. And it was very widespread—oh, any given weekend there was always somebody having a big pickin' party—somewhere, yeah." **(Charles Rathbone b. 1954/61)** "I think that the large number of banjo players in Haywood County has a lot to do with the old days—that's really the only entertainment that people had around here. And it was like people would gather at this house one weekend, and they would gather at this house the next weekend." **(Stan Nichols b. 1958/56)** "Music was just always around when I was young. Across the road, there was a cabinet shop. At night, the guys rolled back the tools and, you know, had jam sessions." **(Travis Stuart b. 1968/46)** "Insofar as community support, living in town, I was more kind of by myself. In other words, I didn't go over to Dutch Cove and play and I didn't go out to White Oak. Mine was more isolated, or solitary, however you want to call it. And I never really experienced, growing up, Makin' Music. When I got a little more comfortable on the banjo, I could occasionally go somewhere and be with people who were Makin' Music. I heard that expression all the time." **(Joey Massie b. 1952/63)** "Mr. Conner was just an old mountain man, and he could play about anything or make anything. A lot of people around the community would come to his house to play on Saturday night. There'd be a slew of people—there'd be at least eight to ten pickers, guitars and fiddles, in a circle. Oh, they'd just all jump in." **(Thomas Smathers b. 1957/59)**

◆ ◆ ◆

Larry Watson (b. 1952/60) People who came into these mountains years ago brought their instruments and music with them. Music was a way of life, like a conversation. People would walk for miles to play with someone and to hear someone play. Banjo players weren't that plentiful. Most of the people who migrated into these mountains were fiddle players and they brought with them fiddle songs from Scotland and Ireland.

In days past, musicians in this county were a closer-knit group. They knew each other. There were different venues for playing music, and one got to know the musicians.

David Burnette (b. 1961/53) Yeah. A lot of folks would get together, you know, depending on the community. Part of it was the community and then your family's background. If someone's father made music, everybody might come to their house and so he ended up as maybe a product of that. If they weren't involved in music, you know—and I know just growing up in my little community, there was people that lived around me that didn't have any musical aptitude or didn't really seem to care about music—those folks weren't exposed to that.

It wasn't a pan-cultural thing; it was more of a "here, here, and here" [scattered around]. I think it was. I think it was isolated somewhat and—of course you had, in these old mountain communities, you had different people that—you had a fellow over here and the whole family they made liquor, you know—and you had this family over here that was devout and went to church—and then you had this family over here that was renowned for doing something else. There's another thing about all this old-time music. In a lot of that history—there was a lot of stereotyping, and the banjo and the fiddle were instruments of the devil to a lot of the religious part. That's because at barn dances, a lot of drinking went on, you know. So, there was people that associated the banjo and the fiddle—and they wouldn't let them play in the church—stuff like that. So, I think there was probably an isolation for some families or for some people that didn't get exposed to it as much because of that—because of that strict religious influence.

And you know, the Scotch-Irish came, and they wanted to be left alone—make a little liquor and just scratch out a living. They had the fiddle—old fiddle tunes go back to Scotland and Ireland. There's a lot of history and a lot of background there that influenced the music, I think.

You know, the hardships that they had—they worked all day—but they had time to set on the porch and go visit (which we don't have today—and I think that takes away—but you always make time for what you love). I mean, you'll seek it out and you'll go—you'll make a point to go to this fellow's house every Friday night or whatever. Sometimes, people didn't have any other entertainment, so they may have sought to go to listen to music or whatever as an entertainment. Sometimes, they "made" music for their own entertainment, because there wasn't nothin' else to listen to. So, there was maybe families, that maybe weren't exposed to some of that—that kid might have made [become] a banjo player.

And then, we were so isolated that nothing else came in, so the language and the music and a lot of other things stayed the same when it was changing in other places. In my lifetime, there's been a big influx of people, and a lot has changed. And I felt like I got a view much further back than a lot of other people because my dad was fifty when I was born and then, you know, all of the ancestors that I lived around were older. I could count every family on one hand, and I knew every member of every family when I grew up there in the cove. And now, all them old people's dead and gone and that influence, that I was influenced by, is gone. You know, you can't go back and get that—and that's where part of that influence of the banjo comes from—you know, Quay Smathers and Ralph Putnam were positive influences on me. They kind of kept me playing more than I ever would have on my own.

"I don't know why there are so many banjo players in this area. One thing, it was more readily available in this area. There's probably a lot of people in our country that would have the ability, the natural abilities, but they're not exposed to it. In this area, you're exposed to it just a little bit more—not only in Haywood County but in the Southern Appalachians. And I think people want to hold onto the old ways, so it's a little bit more out there for you to access." **(Roger Frady b. 1960/55)** "And a lot of the—certain families, you know, everybody in the family played something. So, if you went to their house, you're going to hear music. It was really, really widespread. Yeah, I'd say so. And a lot of times it's like Tom T. Hall said, you know, they'd run the battery dead on the radio, and they'd get their instruments out and play then. So, they had music no matter what." **(Tim Bradley b. 1960/54)**

• • •

Thomas Smathers (b. 1957/59) We made music together and hunted, fished, and camped together, just as I had done with friends when I was young. Oh, we'd typically have the whole gang if we camped—everybody that played with us. There'd be many a night we'd play till two, three o'clock in the morning. Yeah, from six, seven o'clock that evening right after you'd eat supper. Stand and go. I never did sit down. It was always stand up. It was a special thing. So the wives would go camping with us. Oh, they'd cook for us, you know. Just have a good time with us and with the other women. And they'd dance. They went all the time. If we went, you know, they was there.

Some of the campgrounds had ten p. m. "cutoff times." But if you had everybody in the campground playing or listening, there wasn't no cutoff time. Nobody cared. So, it was pretty neat.

A lot of the boys who worked with me would hear me play, and they'd say at work, "Well, what are you doing in here?" And I'd say, "Well, you either be in here or you starve to death, whichever one you want."

"Oh gosh, yeah. I've had a lot of nights that I would start before the sun went down and still be going at it when it came up. I've heard of young people playing at Union Grove [fiddlers' convention]. Their parents would feel like they were safe, and they'd leave about eleven o'clock, and the young people would stay right there and play all night long. I've got up before, and I've held the banjo for so long—I used to have an old Baldwin C model, and those things were so very heavy—I've had big knots come up on my

shoulders from playing twenty-four hours, you know. What a load of fun."
(**Gary Wiley b. 1961/54**) "But now, see, a lot of people thought that they had
to drink when they played. They thought the drunker you got, the better you
played. There ain't nothing to that. You just can't tell the difference, is what
it amounts to. [laughs] I tell you, when we used to go to Union Grove, we'd
go camp out, my brothers with us. We'd start at dark that night playing, and
we'd be playing at daylight the next morning. All night." (**Lewin Burrell b.
1943/72**) "I would say that makin' music in these multiple local areas has
decreased, probably more than 50 percent in the thirty years that I have
been playing the banjo. Because it's not near what it used to be. I really
don't understand why. Well, you know, the younger generation, they've got
their little game [video] deals and all. And I guess there's just too much
for the younger generation to do." (**Charles Rathbone b. 1954/61**) "I've
been to a lot of people's houses and played a lot of music over the years. I
mean, it—it's pretty extensive. But I don't think it is any less extensive than
twenty years ago. I don't see it as much, but I've kind of been out of the
loop a little bit. I think it's still going on. And there's a whole new generation out there too that's coming along—they're doing the same things that
we did, gathering at people's houses and playing—and, you know, they're
just like a sponge. They're good musicians, really good." (**Scott Mehaffey
b. 1965/50**) "I know I used to go down to an old man [Ralph Putnam] that
lived just down the road from us—he was in his 80s. We'd go down there
once or twice a week and just sit in his living room and play music. It was
either there or other places. My dad would go some. I think it used to be
a lot better than it is now. Now probably it's just a few times a year. But it
seems like I used to do it a good bit more when I was in high school. Yeah."
(**Jimmy Burnette b. 1989/25**) "I just don't think there's as much interest in
the music as there was. I don't know if I know of any young kids that even
are interested in banjo now. Some older people have talked to me about
learning, but—there was one kid that I helped get started and he ended up
going to the Stuart boys with the Junior Appalachian Music Program and
finished it out. He's now at ETSU [East Tennessee State University] and
taking the bluegrass program [bachelor of arts in bluegrass, old-time, and
country music studies, the first degree of its kind in the world] up there."
(**Tracy Best b. 1963/63**)

◆ ◆ ◆

In summary, "makin' music," largely a rural phenomenon, is still widespread
in Haywood County. It has its roots in the in-home folkway, which came
into the mountains with the frontier settlers. While widespread, it was not

everywhere. It was not rare for "makin' music" to last into the wee hours of the morning and, at times, all night long. This was especially true for regional and local "fiddlers' convention" venues. There is a general consensus that "makin' music" is not currently as widespread as in the past. The big "get-togethers" are not as common. This, of course, has implications for the future, and this will be discussed further in the next chapter.

Chapter 5

EARLIEST MEMORIES OF MUSIC

The banjo players are divided, very roughly, into three age groups by date of birth (DOB 1934–1958, 1960–1977, and 1978–1996). The comments of Marc Pruett, Steve Sutton, and Doug Trantham will usually not be included with the comments of the other banjo players in the next eight chapters. Their comments will be included in their extended autobiographies in chapter 13, "Three Journeys."

The earliest memories of music among the banjo players date from early childhood. Hearing music on the family radio, TV, CDs, or LPs was the most common memory. The Grand Ole Opry was mentioned in the first group but not in the others. Families, as well as weekend "makin' music" gatherings of families and friends, were common. Church was prominent in all of the age groups. Others mentioned hearing a relative, usually a father, playing music and also sisters singing. Shaped-note singing was also mentioned. There is often an overlap between the earliest memories of music and the first memories of the banjo. Many of these memories represent remnants of the in-home folkway.

DOB 1934–1958

Family, as well as family and friend gatherings, along with the radio, particularly the *Grand Ole Opry*, and church formed the major earliest memories of music in this group. A local afternoon radio program, *Cornbread Matinee*, was also important. Television, as an early musical memory, appeared in the younger members of this age group. Several of the banjo players in this group were "immersed" in music in their families.

Weekly live in-home music at their home or at a friend's home was mentioned as a first musical memory by half of this group. A mother, or mothers and sisters, singing was mentioned by three. Singing at church was mentioned, as was the *Grand Ole Opry*. Memories extended as far back as ages three or four in some instances.

Harold Hannah (b. 1934/82) Well, the one thing I can remember for sure is they used to play music at somebody's house, and a lot of times it was ours, on Little Cataloochee. I was aware that my dad was always wanting to get people together to play music, and he had what he called The Cataloochee String Band even back in the thirties and before that, in fact. The Messers, going all the way back to my great grandfather, Elijah Messer, were the only musicians that I can remember hearing any stories about on Big Cataloochee. Almost all of them had musical ability.

Well, gospel music, of course, was the big one for all the people because that was the big thing on Little Cataloochee—a cappella singing in church— yeah, shaped-notes. I still have some of the old books that they used.
We had radio. We didn't have power, of course, but we had battery-operated radios, those big old things, big cabinets. And they had dry cell batteries that were humongous but didn't last very long. We used to be able to get the *Grand Ole Opry*. And that was one of the big things. It seems like we could get Charlotte or someplace, too.

So, the music that I was hearing as I grew up was basically mountain music, gospel music or the *Grand Ole Opry*. There was not any other music for us.

Smiley Burnette (b. 1937/76) Well, I listened just mostly to the *Grand Ole Opry*. And then they was a country song program that come on Waynesville radio every day called "Cornbread Matinee." You know, back then, they called it "hillbilly music." Of course, you don't do that no more without a fight. But we would listen to that in the evening [afternoon, four to five in the evening]. Most of the time, we would save the radio for Saturday night, the *Grand Ole Opry*. Everybody listened to that, you know. That was just it. Country and bluegrass were the same thing then—they went together, bluegrass and country. Then, about 1962, is when it separated. So it was all country—no classical, popular, or rock and roll. I just still listen to country and gospel music. I listen to bluegrass quite a bit. But as far as the other, I never really got interested in it.

French Kirkpatrick (b. 1938/74) My earliest remembrance of music is that many people would just be at our house on every Friday and Saturday night—friends, the best of friends. And I can remember that from the time

I was three or four years old and hearing what we called "hillbilly" music. I was immersed in music. My family went everywhere playing and played on the radio as well. I can remember sitting in the house with Momma listening at them on the radio on Saturday night, and I could never understand how they got in that radio! I was just a little old kid. I'd hear 'em—and I'd know it was them a'singin'—but I'd think, "How did they get them in that radio like that?"

We would also listen to Tommy Dorsey and Kay Kyser and some of them people on the big bands and I really enjoyed that. We listened to any kind of music except classical music.

Larry Watson (b. 1952/60) Well, I was interested in music because of what was going on in my family musically. My mother's side of the family sang this three-part harmony. They would often sing in different churches, and they would sing on the radio. They would not just sing hymns or gospel songs. They had the harmony of the Andrews Sisters—they could sing that stuff all day long. So, my awareness of music was brought about by that. Also, on my dad's side of the family—my dad played guitar in a local group called The Fiberville Ramblers. So that [his father's ability] led— that's when I first saw Chet Atkins. I was five years old and saw him on the Jimmy Dean TV show. I just couldn't believe what was coming out of that guitar. I thought, "Well, I've heard the guitar already, but I've never heard it played that way."

I also remember hearing, you know, hymns—I learned to sing a lot of the hymns in church. My memories are of hymns. Then, outside of that—you know, I think until I entered middle school—I think it was kind of limited, it was like I was looking through a limited screen here. Because there was— you either have to be around it, culturally, or you have to be introduced to it. And so, neither one of those options was available to me at that time. There wasn't any classical music. It was basically hillbilly music.

Thomas Smathers (b. 1957/59) I think every community had people that made music. And I think it was an entertainment and a pastime for this area because, you know, we were secluded years ago, and that was their entertainment. So, I know, every community had somebody a-pickin' on Sunday evening on the porch—Saturday nights, too. That's kind of the way all of us done, I guess.

Daddy would go and play on the weekend, and I just got interested in it. My dad was an average guitar player. He'd play a little bit. He would pitch in and sing a little. I just got interested in it, and I'd go and watch him and my neighbor play. I was four—three or four. I'd sit there until I went to sleep. I can remember going with him, falling asleep, and waking up at home. I'm sure it would be twelve, one o'clock in the morning when we'd come home. I would listen to it, and I thought it was great.

"My earliest memory of music was probably around 1947, listening to the *Grand Ole Opry*—on a battery radio. The whole family would listen." **(Phil Hunter b. 1943/72)** "Country music was in the house all the time. We listened to the *Grand Ole Opry*. I also watched the country music programs on network TV and also on local television on Saturday afternoons. I actually played on that local show later on." **(Mike Pressley b. 1949/63)** "Probably as early as I can remember back, live music was always in the house. And there were always people there, you know. There was always a Saturday night pickin' going on at the house. If not, we were always at somebody else's house. Music was always there, seemed like." **(Charles Rathbone b. 1954/61)** "My earliest remembrance of music was probably my Uncle Ben playing at family gatherings. And I was just really always impressed by his talents." **(Stan Nichols b. 1958/56)** "My earliest recollection of music was, I guess in school—chorus, or the teachers would teach us to sing. That was part of our curriculum—learning folk songs and things in school. . . . Daddy led the Christian Harmony singing, which was, you know, shaped-note singing." **(June Smathers-Jolley b. 1958/57)** "Well, I was raised in church, and the first thing I can remember about music is us singing—and singing harmony in church. My dad was a shaped-note singer." **(Lewin Burrell b. 1943/72)**

• • •

Mike Pressley (b. 1949/63) My mother and sister would sing out on the porch. They would do that. I loved the harmony. Yeah, it was pretty. It'd just kind of, what you'd say—get in your blood. We would get together and sing or play. We would go to other people's houses, and they would play the piano and sing. And talk. You'd have a thing like an ice cream party and stuff like that. Just to get together. I don't recall a lot of instruments playing, but I sure do recall the singing.

DOB 1960–1977

There are ten banjo players in this age group. Notably, only one of them, as compared to the older banjo players, specifically mentioned the *Grand Ole Opry* as an early musical remembrance. Playing music with family and friends was still a very strong influence: four specifically mentioned their fathers playing the banjo. Church was still an important musical memory. In addition to AM and FM radio, which by this time were widespread, recordings, including LPs and eight-tracks, were important. Music programs given by local musicians were also and well attended. One mentioned (as did June Smathers-Jolley in the 1934–1958 age group) musical programs at his local elementary school. Neighbors were also sources of early music exposure. One mentioned attending music festivals with his father as being important.

Roger Frady (b. 1960/55) My earliest remembrance of music is just singing at church—gospel music. We had an old Broadman Hymnal at church—and I remember one of the first things I ever done in front of the church, the first time I ever got up, and I'll never forget this song I sang, and my mama, she really—she really went over it with me. It's "Wherever He Leads, I'll Go." I was nine years old. My mama taught me that song. When I was a boy and growing up, we listened to mostly country music.

My daddy, he loved country music, the old country music. I listened to that. I can remember some of the fishing trips with my daddy. We'd go turn on the old AM radio and listen to Conway Twitty and Loretta Lynn and Merle Haggard. I loved it, and I still love it. I like to take some of those old country songs and turn them into bluegrass songs. I call it "grass 'em up." We also listened to a lot of gospel music, quartet gospel music.

Tim Bradley (b. 1960/54) My first memory of music was mostly going to church and also hearing country music. Sometimes, at church, we would have a piano player and sometimes not. And when we didn't, we would sing without any music. And I thought that's the way everybody did it.

And hearing country music. And then I got to hearing some bluegrass music along and liked it, yeah. So, before I was twenty, it was basically all country music [and] bluegrass music. No, not any classical, unless we saw it on TV or something. And everybody had Lawrence Welk. And we would listen to WLAC out of Nashville, music—primitive rock and blues.

We had an old radio, and it had an antenna, like an upside-down coat hanger. It was made out of Bakelite or something. You had to put your hand "inside" the antenna for it to pick up. And a lot of times, I'd go to sleep with my hand stuck in that radio antenna.

"My earliest memory of music was in the church. We went to Mt. Zion Baptist in Dixie Creek community. Music was just always around when I was young." **(Travis Stuart b. 1968/46)** "And then church, you know—we were always around music in church and stuff." **(Tracy Best b. 1963/52)** "My earliest remembrance of music is that my mom used to play LPs. She was a homemaker, and I was a kid, hadn't started school—and she loved those old country songs. She'd play 'em all day long." **(Scott Evans b. 1964/50)** "They used to have, a couple of times a year, at the old Crabtree School, which was our elementary school, little music programs and some of the local musicians would come in and do the programs. I was probably not even in school when we used to go to those. The whole family would go. It was kind of a community thing." **(Tracy Best b. 1963/52)**

• • •

Gary Wiley (b. 1961/54) My earliest remembrance of music would be watching my father, G. W. Wiley. He is an above-average musician and plays guitar. He was definitely, far and away, my biggest musical influence—not necessarily as a banjo picker, per se, but as an influence in music. There was a man named Buddy Davis, who my father worked with. About every other Friday night, Buddy and his family would come to our house. They'd have snacks and so forth, and my dad and Buddy would sit around and play music and sing country songs. And then the next time we would go to their house. Buddy and Dad both played guitars. Those were good classic country days. So, music in my home was just straight-up country.

"I guess the earliest thing I remember is, you know, my dad playing the banjo. That's probably the earliest memory of both music and the banjo." **(Scott Mehaffey, b. 1965/50)** "Oh, my first memory of music and of banjo was my daddy pickin' when I was just a little girl, probably four or five years old—having get-togethers. My dad and his two brothers had a band, and they had played together all their life. They were all good. My daddy was the best of the three." **(Pam Sutton, b. 1966/49)**

• • •

David Burnette (b. 1961/53) The first time, I guess, that I ever noticed music (and I've done this through my mind a bunch), I was fairly young, maybe eight years old or something, but I remember it like it was yesterday. My aunt used to pick me up from school. We pulled in her driveway, and she had the radio on. They played a bluegrass song of some type. And it just hit me as—I liked it—it was something that I liked. I can remember it just as plain as day—I don't know why. It was just something that just hit me. "Yeah, that's my kind of music." It excited me, I guess I'd been around it some, off and on, you know, growing up, but that's the first real remembrance I have. I don't know who the band was, but I remember that song on the radio. I remember it—yeah, real vividly that part.

DOB 1978–1997

The earliest memories of music in this age group included radio, records, tapes, and CDs for four musicians. The earliest memories of music for half of this group were the exposure to family members playing music or singing gospel music. One recalled listening to music segments on tapes when initially learning to play the piano by the Suzuki method. No one mentioned the *Grand Ole Opry*.

Mitchell Rathbone (b. 1987/27) I can remember riding in the vehicle with my grandmother, and she always had the country station on. I would listen to those things, you know, keep the beat, pat my foot or whatever. I remember thinking, "This is pretty neat." I don't know what it was striking in my head, but from age five or six, I remember that. I never really did grow up, to that point, listening to bluegrass, it was just country music. You know, I have never had any musicians or anything in my family. So the most I can remember, ever, in addition to the radio, is maybe hearing piano at church, or things like that.

"My earliest music remembrance is probably listening to 88.7 FM, bluegrass and old-time music, on the weekend. Dad used to tape it on cassette tapes, and we listened to that during the week." **(Jimmy Burnette b. 1989/25)** "The first thing I remember listening to musically, my dad had a record player, and I remember he had a Jerry Reed record, and it was the "East Bound and Down" record. I would have been three or four years old. And it's still just as good today as it was back then." **(Brandon Henson b. 1978/36)** "My earliest remembrance of music was probably singing, watching my mom and my aunts sing at Christmas parties and Thanksgiving. That's probably my earliest remembrance of music." **(Patrick Massie b. 1981/34)** "My father, mother, and brothers, we all sung at church—all hymns, but gospel music. But that's my earliest memories. I'd say five years old helping them sing." **(Jeremy Bolden b. 1982/33)** "My earliest remembrance of music, and of banjo, was probably when I was three, four years old, and I remember when Papaw [his grandfather, Carroll Best] would have people come over and play at his house. To me, it was just go and listen to music and run around like a screaming banshee and try and aggravate everybody; that's more of what I remember." **(Jared Best b. 1990/25)**

• • •

Helena Hunt (b. 1995/19) Well, I don't know my earliest remembrance of music—music has always been a really big part of our family because my dad always had a CD in all the time and was always dancing with me in the living room. I remember when we first moved to the mountains, he would always play a lot of bluegrass CDs, like Earl Scruggs and Lester Flatt—and that's what got me interested in it. I mean, not just bluegrass—my dad's more into like Prince and stuff like that, like Bruce Springsteen, folk stuff, but yeah, he did have a lot of bluegrass CDs.

Thomas Tatham (b. 1996/16) My earliest memory of music is laying in bed when I was very young and listening to tapes of short sequences [maximum of twenty notes] of piano music over and over and over again until I fell asleep. It was just basic rhythms and notes, not songs, played over and over again in sequence. I was trying to memorize them so that the next morning I could get up and try to pick them out on the piano. It was the Suzuki method, as taught by Elizabeth Price. I started when I was about two-and-a-half to three years old and did this with piano until I was around age ten, when I began guitar lessons with Miss Combs. Between age three and Miss Combs, I also listened to a lot of just basic country music.

Chapter 6

EARLIEST MEMORIES OF THE BANJO

There are a number of different "earliest memories" of the banjo. Certainly, radio, including the Grand Ole Opry, church, and family/community get-togethers, as well as the overall county musical milieu, played a role in the earliest memories of the banjo. Some of the banjo players were able to point to more specific instances of early banjo memories. The most common early memory of the banjo in the oldest age group was Earl Scruggs. This group was the first to be exposed to his astonishing ability. Having relatives or friends who played the banjo was also an important introduction. Many of these memories represent in-home folkway remnants.

DOB 1934–1958

The most common early memory of the banjo in this group was Earl Scruggs, either on the *Flatt and Scruggs* Saturday afternoon TV program or on *The Beverly Hillbillies*. Relatives or friends who played the banjo were also important. Two had a relative who carried the banjo with him "everywhere he went." Two of the banjo players remembered the banjo in their "musical" families. One mentioned the *Grand Ole Opry*, and another mentioned hearing Steve Sutton (also in this book) play. One "stumbled into" a recording of Bobby Thompson playing "Classical Gas." There are fragments of the in-home folkway in this group as well. Here the major introduction to Earl Scruggs was in-home, but "home" had expanded beyond its earlier roots.

Harold Hannah (b. 1934/82) The first time I ever really paid very much attention to a banjo was that Dad would play the banjo. He learned, partly on his own and partly from his half-brother Nick, who was the one that had that original ability to play the banjo. Nick carried a banjo around with him, you know, about all the time, and he was the one that played at all the gatherings and stuff like that. When they'd have big get-togethers and whooping it up and so on, dancing and stuff, why, he was the one. He didn't have a case for his banjo. He just threw it across his back and went on. It seems like he died around 1932–1935. I have his banjo now.

Thomas Smathers (b. 1957/59) My great-grandfather, John Sherrill, who lived in Jackson County, carried his banjo with him wherever he went. He would come and visit us and get off the bus carrying that banjo.

Smiley Burnette (b. 1937/76) They was a guy that I went to school with. His name was James Wilson [deceased 2012–2013] and he was the only guy around here who could pick the banjo Scruggs style. I don't remember exactly how I got to know him, but, you know, through music, we got to know each other. I'd go down to his house, and we'd pick [play, or to "pick" a guitar, mandolin, or banjo, or as in, "let's get together and 'pick' some"] all day, like from early in the morning to late in the evening. I was [in] about the fourth or fifth grade. Yeah, at that time, I played the guitar.

A lot of the other boys was playing ball—me and James, we was pickin'. I was friends with all of 'em, you know.

They used to have "Chapel" [student assembly] in school, and we would play in that, you know, sometimes. We played around everywhere. Later on, about the sixties, we was both married, but we had a bluegrass gospel band—we'd pick quite a bit. But he was the first—he got me interested in it.

"My earliest memory of banjo was probably Flatt and Scruggs on the 'The Beverly Hillbillies.'" **(Stan Nichols b. 1958/56)** "Daddy always played the fiddle (he could also play the banjo), but Homer Rathbone, which was his first cousin, played the banjo a lot. And that was probably in the late fifties, I'd say, probably in there when I can remember him playing it." **(Charles Rathbone b. 1954/61)** "I first noticed banjo when I was about twelve, but I could play other instruments, and when I finally got started on banjo, I was about twenty-three years old." **(Lewin Burrell b. 1943/72)**

• • •

Larry Watson (b. 1952/60) [Prior to becoming interested in the banjo, Larry Watson, a remarkable musician, was already an exceptional guitar player, beginning to try to play it at age five or six. He also played the bass and piano.] I didn't start foolin' with a banjo until 1971 or 1972, somewhere in there. I was just out of high school. I had the radio on in the car, and I heard a banjo tune, and it intrigued me. I don't remember who was even playing it. And then there was a timing factor. My dad had bought a Gibson banjo from a man over there. A couple of days after I had heard the banjo tune, I went by to see Mom and Dad. I saw this banjo case laying there, and I said, "Where did that come from?" and she said, "Ah, your dad come dragging a banjo in here." And so, I opened it up, and the first thing that leaped out about that instrument was the fact that it had that short fifth string on there. I thought, "Boy!" So, I got it out of the case and started foolin' with it. And I got to going by there about every day and dabbling with it. And I thought, "Boy, that's a unique sound."

I never took any formal guitar or banjo lessons. What I had was the good fortune of being around all these pickers in Haywood County and their willingness to show people things that they knew. It was something to feed off of for musicians who had the desire to learn to play something.

Joey Massie (b. 1952/63) My first exposure to music was through my aunt, who loved jazz. I came to absolutely love it as well. I also became interested in rock. I grew up in town. I had no exposure to bluegrass, country music, or mountain music—nothing that would even be close to local, regional, or indigenous music. I never listened to classical music. Never was exposed to it much. Never had friends or family that much listened to it. At about nineteen, I remember going to visit my sister in Chapel Hill. I walked into this record store looking for Pink Floyd. I was looking for every European version of their records that you couldn't get in America—and this music store had it all. I'm not even sure why, but I just all of a sudden gravitated to a bluegrass section. Thumbing through, there was an album, *Area Code 615*, by a bunch of Nashville studio musicians who were all world-class musicians. That was my life-changing introduction to Bobby Thompson and the banjo. I listened to him playing "Classical Gas" on the banjo. The man was throwing in blues licks, he was throwing in these melodic runs that started up here and ended up down here. I had heard of Earl Scruggs. I associated him with typical country music. But when I heard Bobby Thompson, I said, "I have got to find more of this. I've got to figure out what he's doing." That's when I said, "I've got to get a banjo."

DOB 1960–1977

The radio, along with tapes and TV shows, was mentioned by a third of the banjo players. *Grand Ole Opry* was mentioned only once. Two were introduced to the banjo by cousins and another by a father, who would play at family get-togethers. A couple mentioned festivals, and one mentioned hearing the banjo at musical programs at the local rural elementary school.

Scott Evans (b. 1964/50) My earliest memory of banjo was my cousin, Jimmy, who had a banjo, and they lived right next door to us—we all grew up pretty much right in the same little holler. And I'd go over there and stay all night with him. Jimmy could just plunk around on the banjo a little bit, and he'd end up ultimately playing the guitar. And I'll never forget how the strings felt—you know, I'd pick it up, and he'd say, "Here, try this"—I was just probably eight years old maybe. And the strings were big for an eight-year-old boy. And I can still remember how the strings felt under my fingers—they were kind of sharp and harsh—I can remember that feeling—I still remember it. But that's my first memory of, you know, actually looking at one and holding one.

Travis Stuart (b. 1968/46) I think my earliest memory of banjo was probably hearing it on Daddy's truck—on the tape or radio. He listened to country music on the radio and stuff like that. I can't remember exactly—it was just always around and often "live." There were some people up the road, I think I was about eight or nine, who would get together and play. C. J. Duckett played the banjo. I remember hearing it and thinking, "I've got to have one of them." And the Smathers family, Quay Smathers and his daughters, were playing around there too. The banjo player, June Smathers, was the prettiest one. [laughs] No, they were all beautiful. I heard June play the clawhammer style.

Across the road, there was a cabinet shop that people played music in. At night, the guys rolled back the tools and, you know, had jam sessions.

"My earliest remembrance of banjo—well, my earliest thing, we would watch music shows on our old 'rolling' TV—that thing sat there and the picture rolled all the time. My mom would also turn on the *Grand Ole Opry* on Saturday nights—and I absolutely hated it. I thought everybody sang through their nose." [Roger Frady was an All-State chorus singer in high school.] **(Roger Frady b. 1960/55)** "My first cousin gave me a banjo through the family. It was a long-neck banjo. I was small, maybe seven or eight years old, and I couldn't reach the frets real easily. I guess that was about the first memory of the banjo that I had. I tried to learn a little bit, but I really didn't pursue it, didn't keep practicing—or I wasn't really drawn to really want to try to learn it, I guess." (**David Burnette b. 1961/53**)

• • •

Tim Bradley (b. 1960/54) My earliest memories of banjo. Well, my great-granddaddy, Mark Rich, had an old banjo that he had bought for twelve dollars from Sears and gave to Blind Sam Sutton. And when Blind Sam died, his widow gave it back to him, and I remember seeing it hanging on the wall. I now have that banjo. And then, I think I was probably thirteen or so when somebody had gave us an LP of bluegrass music. It had the Stanley Brothers, Flatt and Scruggs, and the Osborne Brothers. And I got to listen to it and liked it.

DOB 1978–1996

Half of the early banjo memories in this group came from in-home fathers or grandfathers who could play the banjo. One first recalled seeing/hearing a banjo on a television kid's cartoon, *Doug*. Radio, television, records, and CDs were also mentioned. Grand Ole Opry was not mentioned.

Brandon Henson (b. 1978/36) You know, I think I heard banjo, as a matter of fact, on that record "East Bound and Down." But I really didn't know what it was. I knew I liked the sound of it, and it wasn't anything that was very prominent in the music. It was more of a background thing. And I recognized it when I saw it on TV, you know, but I just didn't know much about it.

Mitchell Rathbone (b. 1987/27) Whenever I was a kid, probably somewhere between ages nine and twelve, there was a cartoon that came on called *Doug*. It came on Nickelodeon or whatever, and the kid on there played a banjo. And whenever they had the intro to the show, it would show him playing the banjo, and he would play it every now and then, and I thought, "You know, that's pretty cool, that's really something. This cartoon is playing this banjo." I think he was picking it. That's been years ago. I don't know what it was I thought was neat. In the cartoon, he had the banjo hanging on his wall, and I was like, "That's really neat to be able to take one down and play it," but I never did think much more about it. But as far as I can remember back, that's just the one thing that I can remember.

I started playing the guitar when I was fourteen. I started playing with my friend, Brady Price. He was just starting to learn himself, so we were learning together. We were learning all kinds of old rock songs and stuff like that. We would go over to his house, and his dad played the banjo, and so we played along. I really got into listening to bluegrass at that time because I would hear Brady's dad play that banjo. He played sort of a modified Scruggs/Don Reno style—he did a lot of single string and stuff like that. His name was Gary Price, and he had a bluegrass band that was called Alive. He was an excellent banjo player.

So later, I was talking to my granddad, and I mentioned that I would like to try the banjo because Gary played really well, and I thought it was really neat how he did it. My granddad's mother, Sally Naillon Gates [1899–1990], who lived just outside Haywood County in Tennessee, played the banjo very well. So, whenever I mentioned to him that I would like to learn to play one, he wanted to get me one. So, we had the classifieds out, and finally, we found one in the *I Wanna* paper. It had a '75 Fender "Leo" banjo with a hard-shell case for $500. My granddad ran a [fishing] bait shop. He would also go dig ginseng—he loved to do that. He'd save all his money, so he gave me the money, and we went and bought it. That was in probably June of the year of getting the guitar. I would still have been fourteen at the time.

"My earliest remembrance of banjo was probably just listening to Dad playing. We had records, and Dad had a bunch of old records of, you know, different artists: Grandpa Jones, Lester Flatt, and Earl Scruggs—I always listened to those on the record player. I've already mentioned listening to FM 88.7." (**Jimmy Burnette b. 1989/25**) "My earliest memory of banjo as well as music was listening at my Papaw's [grandfather's] house." (**Jared Best b. 1990/25**) "My earliest remembrance of banjo was probably watching my dad play. I don't have a lot of memories of him playing, but I do remember he would play occasionally around the house when I was younger." (**Patrick Massie b. 1981/34**) "I was nine years old when I started getting interested in the banjo . . . from watching my grandpa." (**Jeremy Bolden b. 1982/33**) "Well, my first memory of banjo was—well, I remember my dad showed me the CDs—Earl Scruggs and the three-finger banjo style. It was probably when I was around six or seven. When I was eight, my grandma bought me my first banjo." (**Helena Hunt b. 1995/19**)

• • •

Thomas Tatham (b. 1996/16) My first real memory of hearing a banjo was with country music. I remember coming home one day, and I had always seen a banjo out behind the TV, kind of out of sight, out of mind, back in the corner. I had asked my dad a couple of times before, "Can I see it?" And of course, he would let me look at it and hold it, but at the time, I was very young, six, seven, or eight, and there wasn't just a whole lot that I could do with it.

Chapter 7

THE APPEAL OF THE BANJO

It was not easy for the banjo players to describe what about the banjo appealed to them. All of them loved the "sound," but the "sound" was not defined the same by everyone. I mentioned to some of them the title of Karen Linn's book, *That Half-Barbaric Twang*, and they all thought that was a good description. A third pointed out that "there is a lot going on" when playing the banjo, and that appealed to them. Others also mentioned the rhythmic qualities of the banjo, particularly its "driving" rhythm. A few liked the fact that it often played the lead. One said that it is a "commanding" instrument, another described it as a "fun" instrument, and another said that it "grabs" you.

French Kirkpatrick (b. 1938/74) Just the sound of a banjo appealed to me. It was one of these sounds that you get in your head, and if it ever starts crawling in, it's like a disease. It won't go away. I mean, when you go to bed of a night, and you've played—and, you know, you get that in your head. It would just keep ringing. I think you learned it in your sleep. You have to physically learn how to make it work, but I think it just creeps in on you.

Phil Hunter (b. 1943/72) But I liked/loved the banjo from the first time I heard it, really. I was intrigued by the banjo sound. And I hear sweet notes on a banjo and can sit and listen to it all day. But if it's not sweet, I don't want to listen at all. I had heard it on the *Grand Ole Opry*. I want it to be in tune, and it needs to be in time.

Well, for one thing, the sounds and how the sounds so readily coordinated theirself when I first heard it. You didn't hear that on a piano, or I didn't. I mean, maybe I wasn't listening for it. But I didn't hear it like I did on a banjo. So I guess the way the sounds of a banjo comes together.

✤

"The sound of the banjo was different. And that's about all I can tell you about it. You'd hear somebody like Flatt & Scruggs, and Scruggs would put some of them hot licks in there, you know, and that would stick out. I mean, you'd really hear that." (**Thomas Smathers b. 1957/59**) "And then when the movie *Deliverance* come out, that song ['Dueling Banjos'] just— you know, it just intrigued me—the rhythm, the sound, more or less just the 'ringing' in the individual notes. And that's when I decided I wanted to try the banjo. I was probably fourteen years old, something like that." (**Stan Nichols b. 1958/56**) "And I can say that clawhammer banjo appeals to me much more than bluegrass style, three-finger style. That's what I liked, you know. I like the sound." (**June Smathers-Jolley b. 1958/57**) "I liked the sound of the banjo. And then, I just liked the way they fit in the music and everything. Yeah. It's that twang to it, you know. Back in the early days, they'd say, 'A man who's got a hound dog with a banjo, he ain't worth a hoot.'" [laughs] (**Smiley Burnette b. 1937/76**) "I guess just the way that my father's first cousin moved his fingers appealed to me. He picked the three-finger style, you know, early three-finger style—just the looks of it. The big round head with all the inlay up the neck and the head on it. The sound, I always loved the sound of it. 'That half-barbaric twang' pretty well covers it." (**Charles Rathbone b. 1954/61**) "Well, the appeal of the banjo wasn't just its particular kind of sound. The banjo was leading, and you could tell what song they were playing because they played notes. I was wanting to play the part where you could identify what you were playing instead of just playing chords." (**Harold Hannah b. 1934/82**)

• • •

Joey Massie (b. 1952/63) I'm not sure what about the banjo appealed to me. I think what got me was partly the melodic aspect of Bobby Thompson's playing style as well as the rhythmic aspect of it. So, you had almost a perfect combination of melody and rhythm. I know you get that in other instruments, but there's something about the banjo and maybe the fact that it's so staccato. There's not a lot of sustained. And it allows for the rhythm to really shine and show through.

Roger Frady (b. 1960/55) I don't really know what about the banjo appealed to me. My uncle had one, and it was just shiny, and it was loud. It was a Kay, a little old cheap Kay—no tone ring, nothing. I was so enthused by watching his fingers and his hand on the neck, and I thought, "I'd just love to be able to do that." I wasn't thinking about wanting to be famous or anything.

I wanted to be able to do it for my own satisfaction. That Kay is the banjo that I learned on—I learned to play. I absolutely played the strings off that thing for about a year.

Tim Bradley (b. 1960/54) It's hard to describe the appeal of the banjo. You know, somebody that's really good on one, it just seems like if you walk by where they're playing—if they're getting the right tone and the right lick on that, it's like it reaches out and gets ahold of you. And it's like somebody that can sing real good or something; people will stop and listen to them. That's the way it was with me for the banjo. I'd stop and listen to it because I liked it. And it's kind of an old-time sound, too. Even the bluegrass has got the old-time sound. And the bluegrass gospel, I really like that. And usually, somebody that can play a banjo a little or a guitar a little bit, you can put up with them. Somebody that can just play a fiddle a little bit or a dobro, they've got to get good pretty fast to be able to stand theirself.

Gary Wiley (b. 1961/54) I know exactly what turned me on to the banjo. With my father being a guitar player, I thought I wanted to play guitar. We went to a bluegrass festival, and the Osborne Brothers were on stage. I heard Little Roy Lewis play "Foggy Mountain Breakdown." I heard that, and at break time, I went out in the parking lot and found a guy who was selling instruments. And I said, "Hey, could I see one of those banjos? I've never actually held one. Do you mind if I look at one?" And so, I held it, and the guy showed me a C chord and a D chord. I bugged my parents and bugged them, and that Christmas, they got me a banjo. I was twelve or thirteen years old.

I like the fact of how loud and how many notes you can get out of just three fingers on a banjo. Of course, Earl Scruggs was one of the most famous banjo players around. But then you think of somebody like Alison Brown or Béla Fleck. Listen to some of the notes—it's amazing. You can do any type of music with a banjo. It can be used as a classical instrument. As a matter of fact, Béla Fleck has done a couple of things with orchestras. I just love the sound of it all the way around. "That half-barbaric twang" is very fitting.

"It's just something that I enjoy. I don't know exactly how to explain it but it's an exciting feeling. The older style—the clawhammer banjo and a lot of the old bluegrass stuff, old, old, country music—just speaks to me. It just draws me in, kind of like a moth to a flame, I guess. That's the only way I can tell you." (**David Burnette b. 1961/53**) "The first banjo I picked up was a resonator five-string banjo. It was really sharp and keen, and my ears hadn't really experienced that before. I was just making noise on it then, but I really liked it. I still like it. That sound still gets me." (**Scott Evans b. 1964/50**) "I just liked the sound of it always, and I guess I just gravitated toward it more than any other instrument. The three-finger kind of intrigued me. It was different than just strumming on a guitar. I guess it just kind of drew me in." (**Scott Mehaffey b. 1965/50**) "I was nine years old when I started to learn to play the banjo. I just liked the sound of it. It just looked fun to play. I just sat down one day and told my daddy that I wanted to play, and that was it. He had a banjo, and that was my first instrument." (**Pam Sutton b. 1966/49**) "Just the drive of the banjo appealed to me. It seemed like the banjo always had the drive. You've got the sound all the way through the tune. And it's a little bit percussive, too. I loved it from the first time I picked it up." (**Travis Stuart b. 1968/46**)

◆ ◆ ◆

Tracy Best (b. 1963/52) I'm not really sure why I liked the banjo. I liked the sound. And to me, it was kind of an exciting little sound, and that just appealed to me. I had, growing up, some great musicians to listen to. I've mentioned the musical programs at our local elementary school. I can remember French Kirkpatrick [in this book] and Carroll Best playing. They just made it so lively and that was—that was what I wanted—the sound and the rhythm. It just had a happy sound to it. I guess that I realized that I liked, even loved, playing the banjo right away.

Patrick Massie (b. 1981/34) A few things about the banjo appealed to me: the soul of it, the sound, the depth, the rhythm of it. I think what it provides to music is that rhythm that gives it the, not necessarily the foundation, but it gives it the motivation. There's one thing that I don't like. I don't like really to play by myself. I think the banjo can get monotonous and the tone of it can get kind of dull if it's just by itself, but that's just me.

"I've always liked the sound of the banjo. It relaxes me, it really does, listening to it and playing." (**Jeremy Bolden b. 1982/33**) "When somebody can really play it in a bluegrass setting—it's just 'drive.' I don't know if it's the 'drive' or the sound of it. But I just thought that it was the coolest thing going." (**Mitchell Rathbone b. 1987/27**) "I always liked the sound of the banjo. And listening to other people play it, like my dad, just made me want to learn it. Once I got the basics down, I could kind of mess around on it a little bit—make up kind of my own way of playing." **(Jimmy Burnette b. 1989/25)** "Papaw [Carroll Best, an extraordinary 'melodic' banjo pioneer, who will be discussed in chapter 12] had died when I was five years old, so it was just kind of a way of experiencing something that he had experienced. It was kind of a connection that we could make, even though he was gone." **(Jared Best b. 1990/25)** "The sound appealed to me. That's basically it. It's loud. Anytime you hear banjo in a song, you can hear it over all the other instruments, and also, there's always a lot going on—it's not just strumming." **(Helena Hunt b. 1995/19)** "One day, my father started playing a really quick, fast song that sounded pretty difficult. And I just was mesmerized. I looked right at him, and I said, 'What's the name of this song?' And he said, 'It's called "Foggy Mountain Breakdown." I said, 'I want to learn how to play that. That sounds really cool. I like how that sounds.' I was about twelve years old." **(Thomas Tatham b. 1996/16)**

• • •

Brandon Henson (b. 1978/36) You know, I guess it would be hard to say what appealed to me because there's so many things about it that I like, but I guess the thing that got me the first time, when I really once started to learn to play, was the first time I heard Earl Scruggs play "Foggy Mountain Breakdown," that original cut from 1948, and that—that ruined [overwhelmed] me. I played that over and over and over. And I said, "You know what, I want to be able to do that." And I said, "I'm going to be able to do that." And I just—something about that sound that he had that's just so magical, it just took me and it took me away from here. I can't explain it.

"That half-barbaric twang." I guess that's a good way to describe that. I guess it's just the way that the banjo has—it has a lot more emotion than a lot of people think. It's more of a "commanding" instrument. And, you know, it can be used to drive a band, and then at the same time, you can play slow stuff on it and bring out sounds that you don't really associate with a banjo. You can do steel guitar licks on it.

Chapter 8

BEGINNING TO LEARN TO PLAY THE BANJO

Learning to play the banjo well is not an easy task. It is critical, therefore, that the aspiring banjo player strongly wants to learn. This has been true since the early 1800s when African Americans began to teach European Americans to play the banjo. This is the same "want" that African Americans, who wanted to learn to play the Celtic-American fiddle, experienced. The in-home folkway nurtured that "want."

Most of the banjo players in this book do not read music, and the few who do have not used it in learning to play. Tablature, noting left-hand positions on the banjo neck, along with strings to be plucked (picked) with the right hand, is available but has not been widely used. The great majority of early banjo learning/teaching among the banjo players in this book occurred "by ear" in person-to-person encounters, usually involving a family member or friends/acquaintances. French Kirkpatrick (also in this book) was mentioned by a number of banjo players as having a significant role in their learning to play the banjo.

All the banjo players have good musical "ears," and at least a couple of them probably have perfect pitch or very close to it. The great majority also play other instruments, particularly the guitar. All of them listened to other banjo players, recorded or live, to try to "pick up something" that they didn't know and would work hard to "figure out what they were doing." They would often pick up "licks" (see below). A few had formal (person-to-person) teachers. A very small number initially "learned" from banjo recordings or "how-to-play" books. Currently, "how-to-play" videos, which are, in effect, "interpersonal," yet not "interpersonal," instruction, are available on the internet and as DVDs.

In initial efforts at "by ear" learning, a short musical segment consisting of only a few notes is commonly played, and the student attempts to imitate it and play it.

Any succinct definition of a playing style is invariably an oversimplifi-
cation. The majority of the banjo players in this book play the up-picking
Scruggs style. It involves the thumb, index, and middle fingers—downward
with the thumb and upward with the index and middle fingers, all three
with finger picks. The left-hand fingers press (fret) the appropriate string,
or strings, at the appropriate location on the fretted banjo neck, helping
create the song being played. The great majority of the strings picked do
not require fretting and are simply played "open." Right-hand "rolls" are
added. The "roll" is, in its simplest form, rapidly, usually very rapidly (at
times described as "machine gun-like"), picking three strings in sequence—
rapidly and repeatedly. These are not played as "triplets" but as a long series
of evenly spaced plucks. There are many variations on plucking sequences
in the roll. The left-hand techniques of "pull-off" and "hammer-on" are
frequently used in Scruggs style as well as the clawhammer style (see below)
to produce multiple notes in quick succession.

"Clawhammer" is the term used by the banjo players in this book to
denote "down-picking." It has a characteristic "bum-diddy" rhythm. The
first note ("bum") is struck down on a bottom string with the nail of a finger.
Subsequently, "did" is struck down with the nail on one of the lower strings,
or all the strings are brushed, and "dy" is subsequently struck down with
the thumb on the fifth (top or "drone") string. The tune is usually carried
by a finger strike down on one of the bottom four strings, often combined
with a left-hand "pull-off" or "hammer-on," with the fifth string serving as
a drone. An advanced feature includes "drop thumb," or "double thumb,"
in which the third finger strikes down with the nail on the first string, the
thumb strikes down on the second string, the third finger strikes down with
the nail on the first string, then the thumb strikes down on the fifth string.
This creates a clawhammer "roll." Strings are "fretted" by the left hand, as
in the Scruggs style.[1]

The beginning banjo player tries to get the tune in its simplest ("skeletal")
form, slowly playing it on his/her banjo and then filling in the rest (adding
to, or covering, the "skeleton") with varying rolls as well as licks. Licks are
short, colorful, often complex segments that can be inserted to complement
the tune or at the end of a phrase.

The great majority of the banjo players in this book play three-finger
Scruggs style. Some can play the older clawhammer (down-stroking) style
and its variants, five playing clawhammer only. Several have become "interested" in melodic-style banjo playing. A bedrock principle of banjo playing
is to be "in tune" and "in time."

All the banjo players practiced diligently, many being "consumed" by the
banjo. Practice will be discussed in the following chapter.

DOB 1934–1958

There are fourteen banjo players in this age group. Most were less than fifteen years old when they began learning to play the banjo. Some of them initially began learning to play on very old banjos, which were in very poor condition. Four were eleven years old or less. The oldest were seventeen, eighteen, nineteen, and twenty-three years old. A few in this group, at least initially, learned from a parent, usually their father, or a friend or relative, and one from a sister. Outside these informal lessons, the major source of learning the banjo was "picked up" from other musicians, either through personal contact, the radio, records, or books. One used tablature "a lot." There were no CDs or videos. French Kirkpatrick and Carroll Best (see below) played an important role in the development of a few of the banjo players in this group, and Carroll Best played an important role for French Kirkpatrick. Ultimately, all of them learned "by ear." Five of the banjo players were essentially self-taught. Only three of them had formal lessons. Most played Scruggs style, one two-finger and one clawhammer. Essentially all of them were, at some point in their playing careers, "consumed" by the banjo. Two ultimately had "burnout."

Harold Hannah (b. 1934/82) Once I got into wanting to play, why, then I started working on it. Then the problem was getting a banjo that you could do anything with. And so I played on my Uncle Nick's banjo that he had carried around all over the Cataloochee area and the Mount Sterling area. [Uncle Nick was the resident banjo player in the area. It was a major part of his life. He apparently carried his banjo with him "everywhere he went."] You know, we whittled the bridges out of a piece of dry lumber. To hold the strings at the base, you know, all of that kind of stuff was just all rigged up on that old banjo.

On Christmas Eve, 1951, my dad bought me a Gibson RB-150 banjo. I opened that up, and that was the biggest thrill you could imagine anybody would ever have. An RB-150, it's not like a Gibson Mastertone, but compared to what I was playing, it was better than that. It was like a Ferrari.

Smiley Burnette (b. 1937/76) When I was around sixteen, James Wilson began to teach me the banjo. I still practiced a lot learning the banjo, too. When I first started—of course, now this is back in the old days—the hardest thing was getting the Scruggs roll. I'd get aggravated 'cause I couldn't get that roll, and I'd quit—then one day I picked it up, and I had it, you know.

Phil Hunter (b. 1943/72) My brother and a friend of his could play the banjo a little bit—the old-time way—clawhammer. And they came to our house two or three times. They also had an old banjo that had the head busted on it, and they left it there. It had a crack in a corner above the bridge. I played it anyway. It wasn't no Mastertone Gibson, but it did have a banjo sound. I didn't fix the crack. If I remember right, there was two or three of these old Black Diamond strings on the banjo. I put fishing leader on the two broke ones. I was about ten or eleven years old. I couldn't tune one then. My mother had to tune it for me. But then, if you pick a banjo, you'll learn how to tune it. So, I did.

I played that original broken banjo for years. I finally got strings and then finally got a head put on. And one of the old gentlemen there that I was telling you about earlier, Mr. Rogers, who played the banjo, he took a cat, cured the skin, and helped me put a head on that banjo. It was hard to do. He put a cat skin head on it. Well, that's what they all used to—I mean, they didn't go out to the store and buy them. If they busted the head, they'd make a head.

Mike Pressley (b. 1949/63) My daddy bought me my first banjo—I had never seen one prior to that. The picks—daddy bought me the thumb pick—because we didn't have nothing to make one of these. I made my first two-finger picks out of beer cans. I seen them before in a drugstore, but I couldn't afford to buy them—so I looked at 'em, looked at 'em, and looked at 'em, and I had in my mind how to cut them things out. And they were stiff aluminum back then, not like now. I made me a set like that, and I used them. Smoothed them down with a fingernail emery board. I'd smooth it down on the bottom side. It didn't matter about up here, but on the bottom, it had to be smooth, or it wouldn't pull the strings.

The influence of Earl Scruggs on most of the banjo players was immense, particularly among the older banjo players.

Harold Hannah (b. 1934/82) And then one day—one day along came Earl Scruggs. And I don't remember where I heard it, but I think it was at the jukebox down at the Edgewood Cafe, right down near where my sister lived in Maggie Valley—and here came that sound. Oh my gosh! It blew my mind. It blew my mind. I would go by there when I'd get off from school. I'd go by there on the way to school because people were playing that record all the time. All you had to do was go there and wait because somebody was going to put a nickel in there and play that thing.

Mike Pressley is an example of initially learning to play the banjo by listening to 45 and 78 records. Most of the banjo players did not learn this way.

Mike Pressley (b. 1947/63) I learned to play the banjo by listening to 45 and 78 rpm records. My Aunt Nellie, who lived just down the road, had a whole stack of them things—the old thick 78 records—had Ralph and Carter Stanley on it, Earl Scruggs, Lester Flatt, and Bill Monroe. I got to listening, and I'd play a little bit—I want to learn that. And I would try it—couldn't do it. One of the 78s was a recording of "Cripple Creek." I played it over and over and over. Until I come to a part that I wanted to really learn—I'd back it up, go through it—back it up, go through it, until it hit me that I'd try it myself—until I learned that one part. After I played the records over and over, I would go home and practice. That was the first one I ever learned. It was hard, but I kept driving—until I learned it. It would take me about two weeks to get to—to note it out and pick it. Not so good.

A number of banjo players said that if they could "hear" it, they could figure out how to play it.

Larry Watson (b. 1952/60) Several persons helped me when I began to play the banjo. Tom McKinney knew a lot about the banjo and was an excellent banjo player. I have already mentioned French Kirkpatrick and Wade Mehaffey. Despite the help and effort, I became frustrated after a year or so and sold my banjo. A few months later, I started again. I was playing the bass for a band that was performing at a festival near Reidsville, North Carolina. I heard J. D. Crowe and The New South play. It was a clinic in what could be done—and they executed that on stage—and they did it very well. I couldn't believe it—I couldn't believe what I'd heard—and that really, that really jerked me up by the nap [sic] of the neck. It hypnotized me. It was smooth singing, and it was smooth playing—it was innovative playing. It wasn't a I, IV, and V chord at all. It was a lot deeper than that. So, they sort of put a jazz spin on it. You know, it was extremely syncopated, which you hear a lot in jazz and blues, different type things. So, I really became interested in the banjo at that point, and I just stayed with it. I stayed with it. [Sadly, Larry Watson died a few months later before we could complete his interview detailing his banjo career.]

"During this time, Carroll [Best] kept insisting, 'You've got long fingers, and you really need to work on the banjo some.' He would sit down with me and drill it into me, and I just thank the Lord every day for him. He was tremendously influential for me." **(French Kirkpatrick b. 1938/74)** "Anybody that was picking, I would be there watching and seeing what I could pick up from everybody. 'Show me how to do that.' Then, 'Okay, put your hands here, here, and hit that string here, and hit that string here.' And I would say, 'Okay, I've got it,' and then I'd pray till I got home that I'd still have it. Right. Exactly. Then I'd play it till I got tired of hearing it." **(Charles Rathbone b. 1954/61)** "I grew up in town and had no exposure to bluegrass, country, old-time music. One of the difficulties with me starting out was that, at first, there were very few people who were willing to sit down and show me something." **(Joey Massie b. 1952/63)** "Every time I got the opportunity to listen to a banjo, I did, and I tried to play what I heard." **(Phil Hunter b. 1943/72)** "I found out later that I could play by ear, and I could hear it in my head and play it better than if somebody tried to teach me anything. And that helped, but still yet, I had to go home and practice. And I found that I could play the same sequence of notes, but I would use my left hand and my right hand different than he did. I kind of put my own spin on it. I could hear it. And then I would spend my time learning it the way I wanted to play it." **(Stan Nichols b. 1958/56)** "My sister Liz taught me how to basically play it. And so, Daddy would sit with me every night in the living room, and we'd practice. He would encourage me along, and he would whistle the tune to me. And the tunes were familiar, most of them, because I had heard them, and so I learned them by ear." **(June Smathers-Jolley b. 1958/57)** "I could play multiple instruments before I started playing the banjo. A band at work needed a bass player. I worked in the welding shop, and I made a bass fiddle out of a tub. Out of necessity, I moved from the bass to the guitar and finally to the banjo. I used the Earl Scruggs book to look at the basics. But then I just listened to the records. I taught myself. I don't know whether you'd call it 'perfect pitch'—I'm sort of hesitant about that. I don't use electronic tuning." [His brother was left-handed and learned, remarkably, to play two-finger upside down.] **(Lewin Burrell b. 1943/72)**

• • •

Thomas Smathers (b. 1957/59) I guess I'd pick up the banjo when I was five or six, you know. I really couldn't play nothing, but I tried. And then I'd get a little help along the way, and you'd learn a little bit. I'd try to plunk on something, you know, but I guess when I really got where I could make a song out or something, I was eight or nine, somewhere in there. Daddy would help me, and then Mr. Conner, who lived above [up the hill] from us, he would help me.

My teachers were just Mr. Conner and Daddy. That's all there was. Well, they didn't really teach me. They just let me do on my own. They'd show me a note or two, you know. "Put your finger here and hit that." Yeah. They didn't tell me what note it was. They'd just say, "Well, right here is your next two notes." You'd do that for a week or two, and then you'd go back and try to get you another one. You was trying to piece that song together. And that's how I learned, just by piecing it together. Just a few little notes. You knowed how it sounded. You knowed the song. So they'd give you them little notes and you'd work on it and work on it. And then when you got done, you could put it all together. And they encouraged you—in their own way.

I'd also listened to all of the records and wished I could do that, you know. But insofar as learning, initially, I learned it just a few notes at a time—a few hand positions.

DOB 1960–1977

There are ten banjo players in this age group. All but one of the banjo play-ers in this group began learning to play the banjo when they were fourteen years old or less, the youngest seven to eight years old. Four of them play clawhammer, three of the four clawhammer only, and the remainder play three-finger Scruggs style. Most were initially taught by a relative, usually their father. Again, imitation of short segments with left-hand positions and right-hand Scruggs style or clawhammer, along with remembering and practicing them, were the foundations of learning. Half also learned from formal teachers. A couple had more than one teacher. Learning by listening to and mimicking others—either live, recorded, on television, or on radio—was also very important. Three were "consumed" by the banjo.

Roger Frady (b. 1960/55) I started learning to play the banjo when I was thirteen years old. My uncle Robert Justice taught me to play. Everything about his and my aunt Lillian's lives revolved around music. She could play anything. They had a car full of instruments, and they played every one of them, and they sang. I won't ever forget them. The first song I learned to play was "Cripple Creek." My uncle showed me the "Cripple Creek" roll and the pinch, sliding from the second to the fifth fret. It came to me pretty easy. And I was playing "Cripple Creek" before he left that night. It set me on fire!

Every chance I could, I would get together with my uncle—I'd say once every month or two, and sometimes it would be quicker than that. They had a place at Fontana Lake, and I'd get to go out there with them on the weekends. And they'd have a cookout, and thirty or forty of their friends would come over, and we'd just sit around and play music outside. If it was cold, we'd play inside. And we'd stay up half the night, maybe sleep for two or three hours, get up the next morning and eat breakfast, start again, and play all weekend like that. And I kind of enjoyed it. My mom made me go to church every Sunday, but when they were out there at the lake, we just picked all weekend. I was really absorbed in it.

"I picked up on banjo very quickly. That's not a bragging thing, that's just the way it was. It just came very natural to me." **(Gary Wiley b. 1961/54)** "He [his father] would show me some stuff, and it would stick in my mind, and I'd go get my banjo out and try to copy it—stuff like that." **(Scott Mehaffey b. 1965/50)** "I knew I was going to play the banjo probably the first day because my daddy showed me how to play 'Cripple Creek,' and I was playing it pretty much as good as he was when he got home that day from work. I knew, 'This is it! I can do this. Yes.'" **(Pam Sutton b. 1966/49)**

• • •

Tim Bradley (b. 1960) I started to learn to play the banjo when I was about thirteen. My great-granddaddy used to play on his old banjo. He played the old two-finger style. Well, he didn't really instruct me too much on it. He'd just say, "You play it with this hand and note it with that hand." Well, I'd go out and sit on the porch and play. Yeah, try to remember, and tried to focus on and remember that same sound. I kept a-tryin' and beating on it and trying to make it sound like the way my granddaddy played it.

I didn't have any other teachers. Nobody else in particular helped me personally. No, just what I could hear and watch people play. Just anywhere. Usually, if I found out somebody was playing somewhere, you know, I'd go and see them, watch them, listen to them. And then you would come back and try to remember it. In addition to the radio, TV programs, I would listen to eight-tracks and cassettes.

Gary Wiley (b. 1961/54) My daddy was, far and away, my biggest musical influence—not necessarily as a banjo picker per se, but as an influence in music. Well, I took some lessons from Marc Pruett, from a lot of people around here, actually. Marc was a big influence.

I also listened over and over to recordings.

David Burnette (b. 1961/53) I must have been about twelve or fourteen years old when I began getting serious about the banjo. Quay Smathers's daughter, Liz, started giving old-time music lessons, clawhammer banjo. I got interested in taking some lessons and learning. So, I would go to her house over in Dutch Cove maybe one afternoon a week for a music lesson, and sometimes I would walk, sometimes Mom and Dad would take me—I have driven a farm tractor over there.

I just learned where to put my fingers, more or less. And they would teach you that way, you know. They'd play a little segment of the song and then let you play from that. It just would stick in my head. I could just remember it at that time, I remember it stuck pretty good. It kind of came a little bit natural to me, I guess you might say. I started out picking out, real roughly, simple tunes, maybe "John Henry" or something that I could just hear that song in my head and then kind of play it from that. I just worked away at it. Yeah. Worked.

But I gradually continued to play more and more—just kept continuing to play. Learning songs and mostly—all I know were the old-time, really old-time songs that were taught. Quay Smathers, Liz's father, was kind of an icon as far as keeping the old mountain music alive. He kept it straight as he had learned it. He stayed with that, you know—just exactly like it had been played probably for a hundred years or something. I liked that.

And then, you know, I had, as any kid would, a whole bunch of other interests, you know. So, I didn't just sit and play. I mean, I was out possum hunting—you know, everything else. Didn't just really set and practice.

Tracy Best (b. 1963/52) I started to learn to play the banjo when I was in my early [to] mid-teens. I wanted to play. I couldn't get anything going on my own and I didn't have anybody to help me. And then I guess I just kept aggravating my parents enough till they got me with a young lady named June Smathers [June Smathers-Jolley, one of the banjo players in this book] over in Dutch Cove. Her family all played. All of them were very talented. And she was teaching me clawhammer.

Then, things started clicking, and it kind of was easier to figure things out—I just fell in love with it right away. I also realized that I was pretty good. I took lessons for maybe a year.

I never took any more lessons. I just continued on my own and playing with whoever was out there to play with. I was also influenced by several of the older banjo players, including, among others, Carroll Best, French Kirkpatrick, Marc Pruett, and David Holt. I also played with Scott Evans.

Makin' Music. (L) 1979–80. Tracy Best (banjo) and his mother (dulcimer), Mack Snodderly (fiddle), Chuck Russell (guitar). (Photo courtesy of Tracy Best)

(R) 2012. Tracy Best and his mother, both playing dulcimers. (Photo courtesy of Tracy Best)

I still like to have some accompaniment when I'm playing. That adds to it. There's just something about the old-time songs, I still love the old sounds. And my mother was, and still is today, real big on some of those old, old ballads and songs and singing them. She plays a dulcimer and would play them with me. I love bluegrass music, but you just don't get that feeling like with some of those old ballads and songs.

Scott Evans (b. 1964/50) I was twelve years old when I started to learn to play the banjo. My dad loved it and wanted me to learn to play. I came home from school one day, and there was a banjo laying on the couch in a case—opened up. My dad said, "If you'll learn to play 'John Henry,' I'll give that to you." He had arranged for me to go down and see French Kirkpatrick. It was just me and Daddy and French. Of course, I wasn't—I couldn't make any noise hardly, for a long time. We'd go on Friday night. We was taking up a lot of French's Friday nights, not every Friday night, but he welcomed me in, you know, and he just sat down with me and taught me sort of how to hold it and all that stuff. That's when I tried to learn to play. I'm still trying to learn to play! [Chuckles] I didn't write down a lot of stuff. You know, he'd go over it with me and see that I got it. Sometimes it would take a lot of "over and over"—it still does for me. And sometimes, I would go straight home and go in my room and do what he showed me—I'd get

Scott Evans, Makin' Music, Evans Cove, early teens. Left to right, Shelia Evans (sister), Elaine Greene (first cousin), Vicky Evans (first cousin), Scott Evans (banjo), Gary Greene (first cousin, deceased). (Photo courtesy of Scott Evans)

it hammered into my brain. While it was fresh. That night. That's when it was freshest, and I'd just try to get it remembered and then, like the next day and your next practice session, try to perfect it.

French showed me how to do a forward roll and a thumb in and out roll (I think it's what a lot of people call it). And you know [he demonstrates] over and over again until I got the, guess you'd call it, "muscle memory." It took me a long time to make those rolls sound like they should. I can remember when that happened—the school bus come pretty early at our house. I'd get ready for school, have breakfast, you know, get everything ready—and I'd get that banjo and set on the couch and watch for the school bus for maybe ten to fifteen minutes. I would just struggle with those rolls, you know, do them over and over—I wasn't even fretting any notes. One day, I was just setting there trying to hold my hand in the correct position when all of a sudden, it just came together. I got the roll! I asked my mother, I said, "Did you hear that?" She just smiled and said, "Yeah." But that's when I thought, "Man, I like this!"

The banjo substituted for baseball, football, and basketball for me. It was banjo and not ball.

Scott Mehaffey (b. 1965/50) My grandfather gave me his old banjo probably when I was about five. I still have that banjo. I've had a banjo pretty much all of my life.

My dad taught me to play the banjo. I can remember the first song that my dad ever showed me, and I sat around and used to fool with. I was probably seven, eight years old, maybe. He'd show me a couple of songs and a few things, you know. We didn't really have what you'd call formal lessons. So, what I picked up in the beginning came from my daddy. He also had a band, and they'd go to different places and play. And a lot of times, I'd go with him and I'd hear this stuff. And at the time, I didn't think I was really paying attention, I was pretty young, but, you know, it kind of sticks in your mind.

The banjo substituted for football, baseball, and basketball for me. I guess pretty much. I never was into much of that stuff.

Pam Sutton (b. 1966/49) I was nine years old when I started to learn to play the banjo. I just sat down one day and told my daddy that I wanted to play, and that was it. He had a banjo, and that was my first instrument.

My daddy taught me to play. He would play a new song in segments. He just had his banjo out in front of me, and he'd show me, and I'd pick it. It was very easy for me.

Travis Stuart (b. 1968/46) My daddy got me my first banjo for Christmas— I think I was eleven. You remember it. Yeah. It was a sacrifice for my dad. I'm sure he had to work overtime a lot. Earlier, I think my daddy brought home the Smathers Family record, and we had a couple of Bill Monroe and the Bluegrass Boys records.

I started out with lessons playing the three-finger style. Cindy Green and then Pam Sutton were my teachers for about a year. Then, kind of shortly after I'd been playing for a while, I switched over to the old-time banjo. June Smathers [June Smathers-Jolley] was my teacher then. After that, I kind of visited somebody I wanted to learn from and spent a little time playing with them. I tried to do that as much as I could and tried to pick up anything I could.

The Smathers family was the most significant in my development as a banjo player.

DOB 1978–1996

There are eight people in this group. Two of them, Helena Hunt and Jimmy Burnette, participated in the local Junior Appalachian Musician Program (see chapter 12), both playing clawhammer. Helena subsequently learned three-finger Scruggs style. Seven play three-finger Scruggs style, one incorporating a melodic style. All but one were less than fifteen years old, and six were twelve years old or less when they began to learn to play the banjo. Three were "consumed" by the banjo. Three were basically self-taught, one using the Scruggs book and tapes and two others with only occasional help from a friend, father, or grandfather. Three had formal teachers for a time.

Brandon Henson (b. 1978/36) I was in the "strings" program at Bethel Elementary for several years and, along with private instruction, learned to play the violin. When I was a junior in high school, a good friend's father, Eric Clark, suggested that I consider learning to play the banjo and loaned me a banjo. My neighbor, Roger Frady [also in this book], loaned me the Earl Scruggs book. I sat down with that book and read through it, and I worked on it for a couple months. Then I borrowed the tape that goes along with the book, and as soon as I heard Earl playing it and heard the way that it was supposed to sound, that's when the light bulb came on. It's been a forward progression ever since then.

Patrick Massie (b. 1981/34) I tried, unsuccessfully, to learn to play the banjo when I was probably seven or eight years old. I was probably nineteen when I really started playing again. I was in Haywood Community College and was living back at home. I kept looking at Dad's [his father, Joey Massie, a banjo player in this book] banjos. And I got into bluegrass a little bit, listening to bluegrass, knowing that people from here do that, and I decided, "I'm going to start playing." My dad handed me the Earl Scruggs book, and there I go.

I learned from tablature books, including the Earl Scruggs books. I was self-taught. Also, there was a program that would slow a song down and maintain the pitch and that helped me. Now, don't get me wrong. My dad—you know, when I would stumble or really get stuck on something—would say, "Now, do it like this," or "Keep your hands like this," or "Keep your thumb behind the neck," just the fundamental stuff that is hard to get from a book till you watch somebody do it.

It was easier for my generation to learn compared to the older generation. We had CDs. You could put the CD player in and hear the song and the timing of it. I often wonder how the old-timers did pick it up and learn it.

Jeremy Bolden (b. 1982/33) I began learning to play the banjo when I was nine years old. My grandpa was my major teacher and a guy named Larry Watson in Canton. I took lessons from Larry for over a year, probably in my early teenage years. And even my father, he helped me some.

Bill Allsbrook: And how did it work with your daddy and your grand-daddy "teaching" you?

J: We had a lot of living room experience, I mean, as far as Papaw [his grandfather] coming over, and Dad. And they would pretty much just—just showing me, you know, some chords and rolls and—

B: And said, "This is the chord. Put your fingers here, here, here. That's a D, and here's an A."

J: That's exactly the way I learned. That's right.

B: And then maybe make a sound. Then he would say, "Now, this is how you do that."

J: That's right. He would try to show me, and I would take off from there.

B: And then you could practice and fine-tune—not the banjo, your playing. If you needed to come back and talk to them to clarify something, you could.

J: That's right. It was definitely hands-on and no tablature or nothing like that.

Jeremy Bolden and his great uncle Frank Bolden. (Photo courtesy of Jeremy Bolden)

I drove my parents crazy learning the roll. That's—that's what I first started on. I practiced on my roll for probably six months

Earl Scruggs has been a great influence on me. Also, my grandfather's brother, Frank Bolden, was a big influence. He moved to the state of Washington when he was a young man. He introduced bluegrass in that area and was known as the "father of bluegrass" in the area where he lived. He taught me a lot—we'd pick till 3:30–4:00 in the morning—several times. He was a great teacher, and he was very strict. When I say "strict," when he would show you how to do something, he wanted you to do it exactly right—not almost right, but exactly. And that brings back smiles. He was so concerned about you doing it correctly. He was a great teacher.

Mitchell Rathbone (b. 1987/27) My granddaddy gave me my first banjo, a '75 Fender Leo Banjo, when I was fourteen years old. I went to Strains of Music [an iconic music store in Waynesville; see chapter 12] and got just a banjo primer, you know, with a book and a CD and a VHS. And that's how I learned, with books and CDs and VHSs. I never had a formal teacher. My grandmother would carry me back and forth—and she paid for the books because she really wanted to invest in me doing that. I probably had one of every banjo book that Strains of Music ever sold.

So, I had played the banjo just a little bit. But whenever I had that one of my own, it's just like it took off—from the word "go." My friend Brady

Price's father, Gary Price, helped me. As I was going along, he would show me things. He was always about playing like yourself, not just playing like Ralph Stanley or Earl Scruggs or Sonny Osborne. I also listened to a lot of CDs. Marc Pruett helped me some too.

About a year after I began learning to play the banjo, I met Smiley Burnette [also in this book]. He came over, and my friend Brady and I kind of picked around a little bit with him. We were just amazed at what he did. He was a very strict Scruggs player—and was excellent at it. He gave me a set of old National picks. He said whenever he started playing the banjo, he bought two sets of picks, and he had played with the one and had never used the other ones, and he gave them to me. And so, I've still got those two metal National picks.

Jimmy Burnette (b. 1989/25) I was in middle school when I started to learn to play the banjo in the Junior Appalachian Music Program [see chapter 12].

I switched over from playing the bass and started taking lessons on the banjo. Dad would also teach me, and then there were the things you pick up over time.

The banjo is fun to play—I could kind of mess around on it a little bit, make up kind of my own way of playing. I think that's when I really enjoyed it. I especially liked the clawhammer—it didn't seem like there was as many rules to it, you know. You could kind of "get wild with it." [laughs] Sometimes, I'll throw in a long strum on all of the strings or a drop-thumb. I don't think I ever play a song the same every time.

Some people concentrate too hard on getting everything perfect instead of focusing more on just having fun with it and enjoying the music. The new ones, I mean nothing against them, but I listen to them on the radio, and every one of them sounds the exact same to me. It sounds like the same banjo player on every song. It's like they just copied it too much or something, I don't know. I heard Earl Scruggs said that he likes to listen to other people play his songs because they put his mistakes in there. They were copying it so close that they wasn't even trying to do something on their own, you know. They just were copying him, and he was making mistakes the whole time, and they were thinking that—they were playing his mistakes! You've got to learn from somebody, but, I think, everybody's got a little something they can add—not try to be like somebody else, you know.

Most of the time when I'm playing, I don't even, you know, think about what my fingers are doing—that's the last—I'm just listening to the music more than anything. I don't think music's supposed to be perfect; I don't. If it was, it'd be something wrong. [chuckles] I also enjoy playing with a group.

Jared Best (b. 1990/25) I was about ten years old when I told my mom I didn't want to play piano anymore, and I started to learn to play the banjo. I took lessons from Flave Hart for probably a year and a half, two years, off and on. Flave's grandfather, Danny Johnson, played guitar with my grandfather. [His grandfather, Carroll Best, was a remarkable melodic banjo player and one of the major pioneers of melodic banjo. See chapter 12.] So Flave kind of got me started in how Papaw played and showed me the basics. I play a three-finger and melodic style. And really, after I learned how my grandfather played, I just realized that there's—you know, there's no patterns. There's nothing the same. Whatever you have to do to play the melody, that's how it's played. But I learned everything that I've learned by ear. And so, if somebody played something, I would be able to play it back to them, as long as it's a few notes at a time.

My grandfather was smart enough to record all his practice sessions. So, I've got boxes and boxes and boxes upon boxes of cassette tapes of him playing banjo. So, when I would want to learn something, I would just go through there, find a tune I wanted to learn, and just listen to it. I don't learn new songs easily. The more you play, I mean, the easier it gets because a lot of the songs [in the key of D] use the same positions. But it's still not easy for me to be able to play them note for note. Usually, what I end up doing is playing the melody one note at a time and then just kind of filling in the gaps. That's about the only way I can do it.

Helena Hunt (b. 1995/19) I started to play the banjo when I was nine. I started out with the Junior Appalachian Musician Program here in Haywood County. It's basically just an after-school program to teach younger kids to learn fiddle, banjo, guitar, and bass. It was once a week. We would go and all sit in a circle, and they would teach all the song[s] at one time. They would just go through each part of the song, and we would have to repeat after them. We'd go over and over and over again until we all got it. But it was a really, really awesome program. It was mostly by ear, focused listening. Travis Stuart [also a banjo player in this book] was the main teacher. It was clawhammer. And so I went home and had to remember what I had learned that day. And I wouldn't remember all the time. A lot of times, I would remember bits and pieces, but not the whole thing. But then, when we would go back the next week, they would go over again what we learned the week before just to refresh us. I was in that program for two to three years.

I was probably around eleven or twelve when I started lessons with Mitchell Rathbone [in this book] and took three-finger lessons from him

Makin' Music. Helena Hunt, in this photo playing guitar, and stepfather Tracy Best. (Photo courtesy of Tracy Best)

for probably two to three years. I started really liking it after I started with Mitchell. Compared to clawhammer, there's a lot more going on with picks and moving all three of my fingers. When I started taking three-finger lessons, I noticed I'm picking these songs up pretty fast. I would learn a song in class that day and then come home and just play it—everybody was like, "You learned that today?" They didn't believe me. [Her teacher, Mitchell Rathbone, says that she was excellent when she was in sixth grade.] My stepdad taught me a couple of songs as well. I just built on what I had learned.

When everybody else was at their sports and stuff and art, I was playing my banjo. A lot of the time, I would tell people I played the banjo, and they would say, "Oh, wow, you play banjo. Banjo is a hillbilly instrument." It's weird how things change, because now I tell people, and they say, "Wow, you play banjo!" in a different way. So, yeah, besides tennis in high school—I never got into sports and stuff and art. I just liked to be on my own, playing my instrument.

Thomas Tatham (b. 1996/16) One day, my dad played "Foggy Mountain Breakdown" on the banjo. And I just was mesmerized—by all the moving parts—how fast his three fingers were moving and also the wide range of the movement—he used the whole neck, coming down the neck, up the neck, in between, just flying all over the place. It was just like a big puzzle to me, and I wanted to figure out how to do it. It looked very hard to do. I was about twelve years old. From age two and a half to ten, I had taken Suzuki method piano and then guitar lessons.

So, my dad taught me three-finger Scruggs style. He began by teaching me forward rolls, backward rolls, and different sequences of rolls, and subsequently, he taught me chording. We started the chording real slow, and I would just ask him to play it over and over and over, and I would listen and listen because that's all I knew. Learning the Suzuki method on the piano as a young child trained me to be able to hear something, then translate it, and make the same sound.

My interest in bluegrass came not long after I began playing the banjo—not long at all. "Foggy Mountain Breakdown" came fairly well. Still, it was a challenge. I really liked it, and I realized pretty early that I could be pretty good at it. I just kept going and kept trying to polish everything. In music, I'm very much a perfectionist—in other things, not so much. But when it comes—when I pick up a banjo, I become a perfectionist.

In learning new songs, I would have to listen to it to distinguish what he's doing and then being able to play it in my brain without actually hearing it again. And then, after I am at that point, I can go with it. After I would get it, I could remember it. I get the simple melody, and then I play that on the banjo, and I fill in with different breaks, slides, rolls, and pull-offs. I know the chords by finger placement.

You know, none of my friends play the banjo or even listen to bluegrass music. That's thought of as a thing of the past now. Nobody's interested in it—very few even listen to it. At school, everybody calls me "Papaw" because I listen to bluegrass music, seem old-fashioned, and play the banjo. They just see that as who I am, and they're fine with it.

I have not been consumed by the banjo, wanting to practice all the time. I would just say it's the third piece of the puzzle. During basketball season, from about November till February, I'm pretty much die-hard into basketball and homework. And then the rest of the year, it's baseball and homework. But the banjo is always there. It's always just the third piece of the puzzle.

In summary of these three age groups, the great majority of the banjo players were less than fifteen years old when they began learning to play the banjo, and they learned by ear. Roughly half were initially taught or helped in-home by a father, grandfather, or other relatives. In addition, "picking something up" from others was important, particularly in the oldest age group. Radio, recordings, books, and particularly interpersonal contacts were important in learning for the oldest group and were supplemented by television and recordings in the second age group and by CDs and the internet in the youngest. Two-thirds of the banjo players, including all in the oldest age group, were "consumed" by the banjo. In addition, roughly half of the banjo players in the second and third age groups had, at some point, formal teachers. Roughly a third of the banjo players were "self-taught." Two in the youngest age group were products of the local JAM program. The greatest opportunity for interpersonal musical contact was in the oldest age group, where remnants of the in-home folkway were most prominent.

Chapter 9

PRACTICE

Obviously, every banjo player in this book practiced diligently. Roughly two-thirds of the banjo players, as noted previously, including all in the oldest age group, were, at least initially, "single-minded" or "consumed" by the banjo, some practicing almost every spare minute. A few of them reported "muting" their banjo late at night so that their parents would not hear them practicing and make them go to bed. With one exception, none were forced to practice. Watching someone play the banjo or listening to music, trying to "pick up what they were doing," was, in a sense, also a form of practice.

Occasionally, when practicing a technically demanding portion of a song, often a "roll" variant, there would be a "eureka!" moment, and the difficulty would suddenly fall into place. A few of the banjo players reported "drooling" on their banjos or going to sleep while practicing on the banjo. (Author's note—I have drooled on my banjo twice!) A small number also mentioned that they would dream of a technical problem or a tune, wake up, and get up and play it while it was in their mind.

Stories of playing the banjo "all night" or into the wee hours of the morning were not uncommon. This occurred when playing with a friend or with a few friends and also at festivals (see chapter 4, "Makin' Music").

This enthusiasm for practicing the banjo was usually, but not always, long-lived. At times, it waxed and waned. At other times, the banjo player, for different reasons, might stop playing completely. The latter instance occurred in a few cases where a close "picking" friend or a fellow member of a band became incapacitated or died. A small number also had "burnout."

David Burnette (b. 1961/53) You've got to have talent, but you've got to work at it, too. Yes sir. A friend of mine said, "You'll take something as far as your love for it will take you." You know how deep your love is for it. You know, that's the same way with anything, whether it's race car driving or playing the piano, painting, or whatever. You'll take it as far as your love for it—there's got to be some ability there—and some people are gifted more than others—but you'll work at it if you love it.

Smiley Burnette (b. 1937/76) Then it's more, and you've probably found this out—practice—you work out the practice yourself—they can't no one teach you that, you've just got to work it out yourself. This part up here [on the neck] is simple, you know; it's all in your fingers. Well, yeah, I'd get into it pretty good.

Mike Pressley (b. 1949/63) After I played the records over and over, I would go home and practice. Yes, I sure would. We lived in a two-story house—we were on the second-floor bedroom, and I'd play late into the night. Momma and them would holler at me to go to bed. I'd mute my banjo. Back on the strings at the bridge, you could mute it down where you could hear it, but nobody else could hear it. I would use a bobby pin, right in behind the bridge or up in front of the bridge and cross them strings and you could play it and hear it—you had to listen good to hear it—but nobody else could hear it.

But I kept practicing, and finally, it just smoothed over, and I learned it. I got it. I did it just by listening over and over and over. Yes. By ear. That's what I done it by. And that's hard to do. Starting with something that you don't know nothing about. I couldn't afford books. Nowadays, they've got tablature, sheet music, all that.

I would say after school, after homework was done and chores—I'd say I practiced a couple of hours a night, sometimes more, sometimes less. Well, a lot of weekends, I'd have free time outside of chores and stuff I had to do. But when I got that one minute or one hour or whatever, I was right on it, because I didn't want to lose out. 'Cause my mind—I had one of these minds where I could learn something, and two days later, I had forgotten it. Then, I could start remembering by practicing. Had to stay with it.

I get my banjo out now at least one to one-and-a-half hours every two or three days—at least. When I feel like it. When I work, I don't feel like foolin' with it. But when I'm off, I get it out and practice. It's by myself. I have drooled on my banjo. I done it one time. And, well, I thought that I was concentrating so hard, you know, you lose what you're doing.

Stan Nichols (b. 1958/56) I mean, I "wanted" to play. There was nobody in my family that played, so nobody taught me nothin'. And everything that I learned, it took me twice as long to learn it because I had nobody to show it, you know. But I had the "want." I had the "want," the "yearn," to play. And I think everybody has got that. It just comes out more in some people than it does others.

When I was fourteen to eighteen, I practiced every spare minute I had. Yeah, they'd run—Mother and Dad would run me out on the porch, and then the neighbors would run me back in the house! Oh yeah, I would play late into the night by myself. There was no doubt in my mind that I was going to be a banjo player forever. I practiced at least two to three hours every evening—I liked it.

I would sit in school with my hand on my leg like that [mimics the finger motions of a roll] and sit there and do that constantly—just to learn that Earl Scruggs roll. And even when I started out, this [ring] finger wanted to move. [Most three-finger banjo pickers anchor their ring and little fingers to the banjo head.] I would tape these two fingers [the fourth and fifth fingers of the right hand] together and set them on my leg and practice. When I had my banjo, I taped them together, and then I locked them right in behind the bridge. And that's the way I broke myself from that—keeping them taped together and keeping them anchored.

I now practice a couple hours—at least an hour a day. Yeah. Like I said, I just recently picked it back up. I had laid it down, hadn't touched it, for four years. And a lot of the people I picked with had passed away. I just kind of got out of the—just kind of got out of it. About a year ago, I picked it back up—I just play by myself now.

Yes, I have drooled on my banjo—thousands of times—in several different capacities, I'd say!

Roger Frady (b. 1960/55) Since I started playing and was able, there's always a tune in my head. I've actually dreamed songs at night and got up and played them. That's when I was really practicing hard. I'd get up and play them. Now I don't really dream that much. That's not happened in a long, long time. But there's always a tune.

I would just struggle with those rolls, you know, do them over and over—I wasn't even fretting any notes, just setting there trying to hold your hand in the correct position and then all of a sudden it just came together, and I made it flow, I guess you could say. But that's when I thought, "Man, I like this!"

Banjo took the place of baseball, but it wasn't no big deal for me to give things up to play the banjo. Actually, it really didn't take the place of hunting and fishing.

Travis Stuart (b. 1968/46) When I first started, I probably played six to seven, up to eight hours a day—when I first started out. Not every day. I'd have to get out and mow or do something like that. I maintained that pace for a couple of years, maybe two. The first two years, any chance I had to play, I would. A lot of times, I didn't do my homework. [laughs] I stopped for a while when I was seventeen or eighteen and started back up when I was nineteen. In my mid-late teens, I practiced probably two to three hours per day. Now, I'd be doing good to get an hour to an hour and a half a day. I enjoy practicing. Nobody ever encouraged me to practice or made me practice. I loved it from the first time I picked it up. I was single-minded in my pursuit of banjo—banjo was not completely my life, but it was really, really important to me, and has been all of my life.

Patrick Massie (b. 1981/34) When I was playing heavily, I would wake up at night and hear a song in my head. I'd get out of bed and play it. That's how I wrote some of my songs. I would wake up with something in my head and play it. And I would have to record it because I wouldn't remember it in the morning. Then I'd play it back, and that's how I made some of the songs that we actually wrote, me and a couple other guys.

Chasing women and drinking is basically what I gave up. Because instead of hitting the bars on Thursday night at North Carolina State, I was playing banjo in my room. That's the truth.

Jeremy Bolden (b. 1982/33) I liked the banjo from the day I started. Early on, I would practice say two hours a day. At least once a week, I would practice more than two hours, like on the weekend—probably four to six hours a day sometimes on Friday and Saturday and Sunday evening. Well, working, and with a family, it's very few now. I would say less than an hour a week, and sometimes now, not even that. So it's really cut back. I still like to practice. I practice, you know, very much on my own. I really enjoyed it and I did, like I say, practice a lot, but no, it didn't—it didn't really get ahold of me as far as that. It didn't consume me at all.

I learned new songs easily when I was younger. I can hear and reproduce a tune pretty quickly on the banjo. I can, but it's harder as—the older I get. Most of the time it would take me two or three evenings and I'd have it pretty close. I had the tune in my mind. I could tell when I was making a mistake and try to fix it. Yes. I did. You know, I can store tunes in my mind and then I can replay it. Sure can. Like you was talking, it's a God's gift.

Mitchell Rathbone and Brady Price. (Photo courtesy of Mitchell Rathbone)

Mitchell Rathbone (b. 1987/27) So really, between fourteen and seventeen, I learned everything I know on the banjo right now. Because, whenever I was at home, my buddy, Brady, would come over all the time and that's all we did. That is all we did—was play the banjo. We didn't mess around with video games, we didn't do anything else, except for—I played the banjo and he played the guitar. And that's all we did. And so, from daylight to dark, especially in the summertime, I mean, it wasn't unusual for us to sit in the room right there where we do our lessons and play—and we'd come out and maybe grab a bite to eat or whatever and we'd go back in and play some more. We'd get on the internet and find more tablature or this or that. But we really stayed with it.

Brady and I still try to get together and play. He now lives in Landrum, South Carolina, and we both have families, but we'll get together every now and then. He hasn't kept up with it like I have.

Chapter 10

WHAT DOES IT FEEL LIKE?

Playing the banjo is a complex experience, and the great majority of times, it is a great experience. The banjo players in this book use words like *peace, happy, joy, freedom, fulfillment, delight,* etc., to describe feelings when playing the banjo. I agree with them. These feelings can be experienced individually, including while practicing, and also in playing with others or in a band. Playing with a band, the interaction with the audience is very important and potentially tremendously fulfilling.

Finally, all the banjo players have experienced moments when everything was perfect. Such moments are well recognized as a "flow state." It occurs in musical performance, usually individually, but also in playing music with others. At times, the audience can be swept up in the performance.[1] It is "a sense that one's skills are adequate to cope with the challenges at hand, in a goal-oriented, rule-bound action system that provides clear clues as to how well one is performing. Concentration is so intense that there is no attention left over to think about anything irrelevant or to worry about problems. Self-consciousness disappears, and the sense of time becomes distorted."[2]

"Flow" is not limited to music but can also be seen in, among others, rock-climbing, athletic competitions, and surgery. When it occurs, it pushes "the person to higher levels of performance and leads to previously undreamed-of states of consciousness."[3] In the following comments, there are often manifestations of "flow." More detailed descriptions of "flow state" in some of the banjo players will be presented at the end of this chapter.

Mike Pressley (b. 1949/63) It's pure. Playing a banjo brightens you. I mean, it does.

Music's calming. I feel like, when I'm playing, that I'm a'doin' somethin' that's real good for me and putting out the clarity of sound to somebody that really enjoys it. And it feels like I'm on top of the world. It's a mighty thing.

It is to me. It might not be to nobody else that does it. It feels so deep. It's got deep roots. You know, and it's in my blood. And—I feel like, if I couldn't do it, I don't know what would happen. I've done it so long. It's precious.

Phil Hunter (b. 1943/72) Playing the banjo has been a deep thrill to me. It's a satisfaction that I've never been able to find in nothing else that I've done. But that's the way it's always been with me. And even—I can hear different banjo tunes that really set me off. I mean, you know, a lot of people say, "Do you like all banjo?" No, I don't like all banjo. There's some tunes that wasn't made for a banjo, but there's some that really fits. I love to hear big band music played on a banjo. There's nothing intrigues me any more. And I learned to pick some of it. But I rather hear basically any bluegrass tune.

It really has been an incredible thing in my life. The most incredible thing about it that I wouldn't leave out of this interview is I've been able to meet some of the nicest people—and encouraging people all over the country, wherever I've been. And the one thing that I've noticed myself in it is they're very ready to help you in any way in the world they can. I've seen that out of 99 percent that I've met. I've never met but one or two that just—was just a dog. That's the only way I know to say it.

Stan Nichols (b. 1958/56) What does it feel like when I'm playing the banjo? Sometimes I like to refer to it as "gettin' the 'all overs.'" And it just— you get consumed in it. You just feel the rhythm, and you just feel good all over. Like you said, when you hit that one certain lick—that's what I call "getting the 'all overs.'" You know you're doing that, and you're a part of that. And it just fills you up. No, not every time.

Tracy Best (b. 1963/52) I guess it's joy. I just—I like playing and getting it right. You know, it's the striving to get it as perfect as I can get it; not to say that that's anywhere near perfect—but to my ability, the best I can. My mind is totally on that, nothing else, and it's just a focus into that. And if I was to sum it up in one word, just joy. And a lot of people probably go through life and never know what joy is, you know.

Mitchell Rathbone (b. 1987/27) You know, when I'm playing a banjo, it's kind of like it's part of me—it's like it's an extension of what I am. What-ever mood I'm in, it doesn't matter at that point in time because I'm sitting here with this banjo and having a good time. The world could be crashing down, you know. But I've got this—I've got my banjo—just going with it. Like I was telling you, it gives me a happy feeling. I don't know what it is about—whether it's the tone or the drive or just the ability to play. I enjoy sitting down and playing—it brings me joy, you know. It just makes you feel like everything's okay.

I think that it's a happy instrument. To me, it is. And you know, if you think about it, if you're sitting with someone and you hear people playing and then it's time for a banjo break, and somebody takes off—they just burn it down—you can't help but grin a little bit when they get finished. I don't know what it is about it but it just—it's like a kid when somebody's driving fast—whenever you roll into that throttle, you can just feel the car, you can feel the engine, you can feel it just kind of push you back in the seat—and it makes you smile. Maybe it's something like that.

Travis Stuart (b. 1968/46) Playing the banjo kind of makes you forget everything else, you know—like anything you're worried about—that's the biggest thing with the banjo, I think. And I don't always feel like I've got to be "perfect" on it. Sometimes, I'll just pick it up and bang around on it just for fun, you know. Just do what I come up with. You can just focus on one thing—one thing you like and not think about anything else.

It makes you feel happy just to play it—in a good mood, you know. It brings me joy. It is also relaxing. It seems like if you have a bad day, you can just go home, pick up a few notes, and feel better. It's very important. I just don't know if I can go a day or two without playing music—I just get "tense" or something. I feel like I have to play it. It's almost sacred to me.

I don't know—just the discipline it takes to play an instrument is kind of good for me. Because I'm kind of a lazy person, pretty much. I just feel like I'm achieving something when I learn something new, you know. It gives me satisfaction. Sometimes, just the simplest little things you learn—like you might learn a little part to a song that's hard—and when you get it, that's kind of satisfying. I still don't think of myself as too musical. You know, some people can just pick up an instrument and play any kind of music or they can play—I know people who hear something on the radio and come back and play it—the lead—and know all of the harmony parts. I never felt like that. But I felt like I achieved a little bit by keep working at it—keep working at it.

Patrick Massie (b. 1981/34) Peace is what I feel when I'm playing a banjo—peace, release. A lot of it for me was just releasing emotion, you know, maybe pent-up emotion, I don't know, but it was peace. It was release. It was—yeah, just tranquility. "Pure" is a good word. When I was playing with the boys in the Brickyard at North Carolina State—happiness. It was that expression of myself. It really was. It was just the peace that came with that—after sitting down and having a good session. I mean, there wasn't a bad session, you know. That was the beautiful thing that it finally got to. There wasn't a bad session. It was all good. So, yeah, if I had to sum it up, for me, it would be just a release or peace.

Helena Hunt (b. 1995/19) When I play the banjo, it's such a bright and happy sound, I can't be sad. I feel—this is going to sound kind of stupid—it's like being filled with joy. Every song that I know on the banjo is a happy song. They're all upbeat, and they make me want to tap my foot while I'm playing. I'm just so happy when I play the banjo. It's just the perfect moment, very fulfilling. Well, if I'm playing like one of my favorite songs on the banjo and I'm just playing it perfect, I'm not messing up at all, I'm really satisfied with myself, I guess. You earn that. For the time being, I don't think about all the stuff that stresses me out. I'm only listening to the music and letting it go through me—it just kind of makes everything else go away for the moment.

French Kirkpatrick (b. 1938/74) I think I feel fulfilled when I'm playing the banjo. Because it's something that I feel like is a God gift. Whether it's the best gift of anybody else or not, it's my best gift, and it's what I can do better than any other one thing. It gives me an attitude of thankfulness. Because I do believe—and I'm not trying to preach to anybody—I do believe that God gives certain gifts. And I think that they can do good with them. It doesn't necessarily mean that they are going to go out and do Carnegie Hall. But they can do good for people with them. They can enhance other people's lives. You can play for the box supper, you can go play for the church social, you can go play for somebody in a rest home, you can sit down and show some twelve-year-old boy what you've learned, and you can share—and it's fulfilling, it's very fulfilling.

You get a peace out of it, I do. Even when I practice, I'm at ease. It's ease, you know. And it's more than that. You have all this opportunity of the comradery that you can develop with other people and share what they have learned. And it's a network of understanding people. Musicians are a rare breed of people. I have seen it too many times, like Carroll Best—you'll never meet another Carroll Best, there's only one of them. There's only one Raymond Fairchild. And that's what musicians are. They are unique in what they do.

Well, I don't know where passion comes from, do you? I don't know where that passion comes from. You just have that—it's a love that you have for it. You can't explain it. You might think, well, I'm not going to do this much more. I'm going to quit it, and you'll find, no, you're just getting ready to do something with it that you never did before. It's an inward thing with you. It's something that's motivated from somewhere you don't know about.

Scott Evans (b. 1964/50) But that "electricity"—that's a pretty good description—especially when you're playing a little passage over and over again and when you finally get it. That's a good way to describe it—but I sort of get lost in it. Everything—all the outside world disappears and it's just you and that sound, maybe. Probably not every time—but especially if you're trying to do something that you really like—maybe a little "lick" or getting a note clear that you really want to hear—to make it sound like you want it to sound—you know, I get chill bumps. That's when it comes back to "electricity"—might be a pretty good description. You just play it over and over and over again, just because you've figured it out and you've been wanting to hear it like that—coming from your banjo, from your hands, and your brain. The time would just cease to exist till you realized how much time had passed and thought, "Wow, where have I been?" I have felt that as a teenager, but maybe more as an adult—more here lately.

Jeremy Bolden (b. 1982/33) When I play a banjo, I feel happiness, joy. And it does, it strengthens me—just to sit down and pick, it does something for you. It's happiness. It's happy to sit down and pick and play. It really does me good, you know, to sit down and play. It relieves stress a lot of times. It's just enjoyment. Oh, it's—from one to ten, it would be a ten. It is really important. I guess that's one of the reasons why I practiced four to six hours a day. Yeah.

Doug Trantham (b. 1963/50) I think that "delightful" is a great word for playing the banjo. I feel joy, and I feel very comfortable playing the banjo. It feels like, just an extension of my body—energy just flows right through it, in a very comfortable way, in a way that I don't feel with any other instrument that I play.

Well, for whatever reason, I like the banjo best—the characteristics of the instrument are captivating to people and certainly they were to me. I got started so young—I just have lots of positive associations with it. It just was always a very positive thing for me—it's like some things that one learns so early and so well that they're just part of your makeup. It's not something contrived, it's not something that I have to work real hard to do. It's just a part of who I am.

"Playing a banjo was delightful. Yeah, it was." (**June Smathers-Jolley b. 1958/57**) "Playing a banjo is a joy. It's delightful." (**Charles Rathbone b. 1954/61**) "Well, you know when I was talking about feeling grounded and connected playing the banjo? I think that it has been with me forever." (**Joey Massie b. 1952/63**) "When I'm playing, I feel a sense of calmness. It makes me feel alive. Achievement. I feel achievement. I feel my daddy when I'm playing with drive. I feel my daddy with me." (**Pam Sutton b. 1966/49**) "Playing a banjo is a 'rush.' It's true, it's 'pure.' I don't remember any bad times a-playing. It's all good." (**Scott Mehaffey b. 1965/50**) "It's just an awesome feeling. It's really indescribable to me. It's a good feeling, but there's a lot of levels. It's just hard to put into words." (**Brandon Henson b. 1978/36**)

• • •

As noted earlier, the banjo is often played with other musicians, including in a formal band. These times are enjoyable and often seem to be very special for many of the banjo players. The interactions or feedback from the audience is an important part of the band experience. At times, positive feedback from the audience can become a part of flow.

Harold Hannah (b. 1934/82) Well, I guess the result is just a great satisfaction. Another thing, well, it rested me. I could be tired, but I actually rested playing. If you get through it and you make it sound the way it sounds in your head, and if you can make it come out through the banjo, that is one heck of a satisfaction. But the other satisfaction is to sit down with somebody that is playing good rhythm, and you hit it—the whole things is sounding so good—and it just multiplies that same feeling—because it's you. Then the other one, I guess, is whenever you step out there or sit in a group and they just love what you're doing. And playing for a crowd—when you played it right, that was the darndest feeling you ever saw. When they just keep on applauding, that is a satisfaction that I can't even describe, yeah, to know that somebody enjoyed what you were doing that much—as much as you were enjoying it. And it was not like playing for a party where everybody is talking. They were listening to everything and you had to get it right.

Thomas Smathers (b. 1957/59) Well, when you were playing the banjo, you just—you just felt it—down in your soul. It was just something that you was a'doin'. And if you was a'playin' in front of somebody and they was liking it, it just gave you an uplift. That's the only way I could describe it. Oh, I loved it, yeah. Well, it was just your time, you know. Nobody could interfere with that. It was your little box. It was yours. You just wanted to do it. That's the best I could describe it.

Gary Wiley (b. 1961/54) When I'm playing, it's a freedom. It's a freedom of my expression of that particular song. That's why, to me, going back to playing with a good vocal group, you can make just beautiful sounds on a banjo. It doesn't have to be that screaming, hard-driving banjo thing. So, it gives me a freedom of playing what's in my heart and soul for that particular time. A lot of my slow backups that I do are actually taken from what Floyd Cramer used to do on a piano [makes a sound]—a real country sound. And I just sort of applied that to a banjo. So just freedom. Freedom to express yourself, yeah.

Jimmy Burnette (b. 1989/25) What do I feel, or what does it feel like, when I am playing the banjo? Ah. I don't know. It just feels good to play the banjo. I'm happy, I guess. It just makes you feel good. Not all the time, though. I mean, there are just certain times, you know, you play and everything is just right, it makes you feel good. "Joy" would be a good word.

Steve Sutton (b. 1956/60) The banjo player, of all the other people in a band, gets the most response from the audience. There's a lot of intrigue, I think. A lot of people seeing all this coming out of this hand, just missing strings by literally a millimeter to go from a first to a second string. And I remember Steve Martin, a comedian, just saying, "You just can't be sad playing the banjo."

Thomas Tatham (b. 1996/16) I think that the enjoyment that people get out of listening to the banjo is a mixture of factors. It's just the mixture of the high tempo, the adrenaline rush that you get from listening to it. Just sitting there—you know, it's going along, and it has the bouncy tune—and you start going, and your toes start tapping, and then you start wanting to dance, and it just has that feel that puts movement into you. It just kind of captures you—it's just a blend of sounds going at the same time that gets you. If you're sitting there and listening to a good bluegrass song, you're going to look down and think, "Oh, my foot's tapping to the beat." And then watch whoever is playing, and you'll be kind of captivated by all the moving parts—you know, these fingers, you can't really distinguish which finger is which because they're moving so fast—it's just a blur—and then the other hand is running up the neck and down the neck and in the middle—all kinds of chords and positions. I've experienced that as a listener and a performer.

Smiley Burnette (b. 1937/76) I've noticed especially, the best feeling I have is when, like on a PA system, I'm hearing myself play—it's like it's someone else, and I'm a'gettin' to notice it. It feels good to know that's me a'playin.' It's coming back to me. It's hard to describe. It's like I'm a'playin' here, it's coming back to me, really sounds good, you know, that's my best feeling.

It's just a happy feeling when you're pickin,' the sound's good and everybody's together—ain't nothing like it—just a joy to pick. I feel free. You've got a bass, a mandolin, and a guitar—everything going right in time—it's a good feeling, a precious feeling. It is. You hate to quit, you know.

Then I have been at—at times, when you couldn't do nothing right and it didn't sound right, you know. I've picked at times, and the banjer didn't sound right or something—I reckon everybody has days like that.

Some people it touches, and some it don't. Yeah. You can tell when the audience is affected. You can tell when they're gettin' into it and when they ain't. I found out if you picked an hour or if you pick fifteen minutes, if you lose the audience, you might as well quit. You get a feeling back from them, you know—how they're liking it, you know. You can tell it, too. And when you lose 'em, you might as well quit right then.

Lewin Burrell (b. 1943/72) What does it feel like when I'm playing my banjo? Well, it's better than eating to me—if there's a band, if there's a band where you're getting all up. Playing it by itself is not fulfilling, but taking a part in a band, or even singing, when somebody is singing, whether it's me or not, you know, but all of it is fulfilling to me. At peace. Mike Pressley said it was "pure." Yeah, there is. There's a purity to it. Yeah, there is.

David Burnette (b. 1961/53) The feeling I have when I play a banjo is complex. But I don't know, there's just something about the beat, and I love to sit and listen when people are playing—like at molasses makin.' The thing I look most forward to when we make molasses is that a few folks, that sometimes I don't see but once or twice a year, will come and make music. And I can set really close and have that music just bouncing, booming in my head. We don't use any amplifiers or anything, just natural.

There's some folks that come, that usually I'll coax them into singing a song or two. You know, it's a "family" group, and they'll sing an a cappella gospel tune or something. There's just something about that—I don't know, it just makes—it makes you tingle all over, makes the hair stand up on the back of your head. I don't know exactly how to explain it, but it's an exciting feeling.

More detailed descriptions of "flow" are presented below.

French Kirkpatrick (b. 1938/74) Sometimes, everything is just right. A couple of years ago, Harry Robbins and I were working on an old song, "A Minute of Your Time." And we sat there and played about ten or twelve songs that night. And when we got through, I said, "Harry, you know what I wish? I wish we had had somebody in here recording it because I think that's the most perfect music I've ever played." I don't know where it came from or why it came. But I know exactly what people who experience this are talking about—the trouble with that type of picking is you can't capture it—it's fleeting. It comes and goes, you know. And you don't know why the banjo is in perfect tune, you don't know why everything, just the timing was perfect. You don't know that. You can get this "high" more times than one, and I've had it more times than one. But it's not every time that you play that you're going to do that. It's just something you feel. You're just like, "Man, that is perfect, that is cooking, that is the way I like music to sound." But don't count on it being there the next time you go play—it may not be.

Patrick Massie (b. 1981/34) I've had that exact "flow state" moment. We had just—it was me and two guitar players. One of them, Edward Dalton, from Winston-Salem, was just exceptional. We had a rhythm guy. We would sit there and play, and it was one of those days where we had been playing and playing and playing and playing, and we just hit this song. It was—we just made it up. We couldn't even have stopped and started playing that song again. But when we got done, we looked at each other and said, "Now that right there was amazing," because we knew, you know, we could never play it like that again, whatever it was we were playing. You have those moments, and they are rare.

When I said it was perfect, it was just like—it was euphoric. You get there—you know what you're going to play before you play it. You can hear what you're getting ready to play. You know, that never had happened to me, but I knew—it's like, "Okay, I want to do this," and I would just start doing it. It's like I was just playing it, something that I was thinking or feeling. You knew you had done something special in that one moment. And there's only maybe one or two times in my entire banjo playing that I felt like "that right there was amazing!" It's just special.

Well, I can tell you that both times I had been playing for hours and hours. I had been playing continually, and then, all of a sudden, it just started clicking. I can remember the feeling, but I can't remember what I was doing or playing, but I can remember the feeling and how it felt to get in that kind of groove. I was playing stuff that I didn't know how to play—that I didn't know how to play. I didn't know that that would make that sound when I was playing it at the time. If I stopped and tried to do it the next day, I couldn't do it, wouldn't know how I did it, what I did at that point.

It was like that feeling, you know, of first love—it's like love, almost. It was like a feeling down in your gut, in your soul, kind of, like a warming feeling that would come over me. I mean, it's something I'll never forget.

Phil Hunter (b. 1943/72) Yes. Yes. There have been a few—a few times in life that I've—in playing with somebody, or even playing by myself, that I knew that I'd never play it that good again. How did it feel? Well, that's what kept me a-going. And, I mean, it's—it's probably something you can't explain to somebody. Well, I'll tell you. Sort of like salvation. The only way you can explain it is to have it. To me, I mean, that's the best analogy that I have of it. I agree with Mike Pressley that "it is pure." And I finally realized I wasn't going to learn it all. But I was very thankful for what I was able to learn and accomplish in my life.

Thomas Smathers (b. 1957/59) Oh, yeah, I've experienced playing when everything was just perfect. Well, you'll be playing, and everything would be just, I mean, every note was right on, no miss, nothing—and also your ending, that's where it's at, anyway. When you end, it has to be together to make your music. But you know when you do something like that, it's just a—it's a different feeling. It's just an uplifting feeling. I mean, you know that you've—you've pegged it out, and you know you probably can't do it again. It took a whole team to do it. There ain't just one up there. It's everybody, and everybody makes it gel. So, they knowed too. So, I think I've done that before. It was great when it happened. It is special. Right, it just happens. I think we've been there a time or two.

Scott Mehaffey (b. 1965/50) Yeah, I've had that experience, especially playing with certain people. Maybe it's—I don't know. Maybe when everything gets just right, there you'll be playing, and it just—it meshes just like no other time. And you know that the best it will ever be. I don't know how to explain it. It just seems like when everything just lines up perfect and everybody is meshing together. It feels good when it does that, you know, but it's not something that happens all the time. I know when it happens, it seems like you can just play all night. I mean, it just—you know, it's like you don't want to stop.

Stan Nichols (b. 1958/56) Sometimes, it's perfect. And I've done that. Knowing that you couldn't—the rhythm of the guitar, the rhythm of this and the bass, and everything just all at once hits—hits a sweet spot, and you couldn't go back and do it again if you—you couldn't put your finger on it. I mean, just everything hits together all at once. Everything lines up and everything just becomes one, you know.

"There are times when everything is perfect. Oh, yeah. It feels good when I can just pick it up and go through a tune and not miss a lick, you know. It's not every time. But when it's there, it's there. Sometimes I just don't even feel it. So, I'll just lay it back in the case. But if I'm feeling it, I pick good. It's precious. It feels good." **(Pam Sutton b. 1966/49)** "I have played with somebody at times when everything is perfect. It just works out where it's just easy to play. It's like you're not even trying—it's just coming out. There are moments when, 'Boy, that was it right there. That's as good as it gets.' It makes you feel good, you know." **(Travis Stuart b. 1968/46)** "But those moments, for me, were those times where there was nothing else in the world but the banjo and me right then, and I was putting in 100 percent focus and doing exactly what was inside me, and it was coming out." **(Brandon Henson b. 1978/36)**

◆ ◆ ◆

Roger Frady (b. 1960/55) The last time I actually played "Shindig on the Green" in Asheville, we had a jam afterwards, and everybody—everybody that was in that place that night came around us. And it was one of those things you didn't want to stop. And everybody that—there was like two or three fiddle players, two or three mandolin players, and Paul playing the bass. But the singing, the harmonies, and maybe another banjo player or two jumped in on it. An old friend of mine, Don Ledford, was a great influence on my playing. He would say, "That was celestial." It's just a feeling that you don't want to stop. That's hard to put into words. I mean, you can actually—you can play things that you've never played before, and they're perfect. Really good.

Jimmy Burnette (b. 1989/25) I guess "everything is just right" is not as often as it should be. It happens a lot more when you're playing with other instruments, I think. Whenever everybody is getting the licks and everything just right, it really sounds good. Joy. And it happens occasionally. Yeah. It's worth playing all night, just for the one time when everything is just right, I think. Yeah.

Tim Bradley (b. 1960/54) Have I ever played when everything just seemed perfect? Yeah. And too, on the other end of the scale—when no matter what you tried, it didn't come out right. That's like work. I carve wood and stone and build muzzle-loading rifles and do woodwork and stuff like that. Sometimes, it's almost like you don't even have to think about what you're doing. It all just flows. And like I say, and other times no matter how hard you try, it don't work right. The times that flow are a great minority of times. And when you're working on something, it seems like everything just falls into place and works right. And the music's the same way. A lot of times, it's easier and almost to the point you don't even have to think about it. Can't do nothing wrong.

David Burnette (b. 1961/53) I remember one particular time. You know, I mean, this was thirty years ago. But a friend of mine, Trevor Stuart, who's a fiddle player, was there—we played a song there at Shindig, and it was just like everything was exact—it all meshed, the whole beat was there, you know. It was like the fiddle was in my head and—you know, that stands out—that one time stands out more than any other time I can remember as far as me playing. I wanted to keep on playing. Yeah. I wished it would never end. I've thought about it a bunch since then. It's been a long, long time ago. But it just all clicked, you know, the fiddle beat, the bow strokes, were exact with the banjo.

Marc Pruett (b. 1951/61) I was on stage at Bill Stanley's BBQ with the great band I'd been with for several years. The room had over three hundred bluegrass fans that night, and the dance floor was full of people enjoying the night. It was as if no one had a care in the world, and it began to feel like I was insulated from any attention. As the band played, it started to feel as if every person in the room was part of a fine-tuned machine moving effort-lessly. It was almost as if I could step back from myself and enjoy everything as I played the banjo without even trying. My hands worked independently of my mind, and it was a strange but wonderful few moments. (I should add that I was sober.)

Steve Sutton (b. 1956/60) It doesn't happen often. I played a show over in Cashiers one time with Doc Watson—but it was me and Darren Nicholson and Buddy Melton and Milan Miller. We also had a bass player and a drum-mer. And my sister was up, and she was in tears when we got finished. She said, "That was the most awesome set of music I've ever seen." We didn't rehearse. We didn't know what we were going to do. We just got out there and it—things started happening. And, boy, once they start, you better look out, you know. When that happens, it's not just one person in the band that just says, "God, that was awesome." You find everybody in the band goes, "God, that was awesome." It's certainly a team effort, you know.

Chapter 11

WHAT HAS THE BANJO MEANT TO ME?

The banjo has been very important in the lives of all the banjo players. Not all emphasize the same things that have been particularly important to them. Many mention the people that they have met and the relationships that they have formed through playing the banjo. Some specifically mention the importance of playing with their fathers or children.

Scott Mehaffey (b. 1965/50) To me, the banjo has been a source of enjoyment and relaxation, as well as carrying on the legacy and heritage of my father and grandfather and the people of this region.

Brandon Henson (b. 1978/36) "What has the banjo meant to me?" One would think that's an easy question, but I'm finding a little difficulty putting the answer into words. It's almost like someone asking you, "What does breathing mean to you?" The banjo has been a part of my life for twenty-three years, and not many days of that time have went by that I didn't play the banjo or at least listen to the banjo. The banjo has given me endless hours of entertainment, including entertaining others, entertainment by listening to others play, entertainment by physically learning, and entertainment in the sense of it being something to feed my imagination. The banjo has been a tool that's aided me to make a lot of connections with people I would have probably never met or become friends with, and it's been a key factor in helping me learn and build self-confidence and focus. I suppose I could go on, but in short, the banjo is an extension of myself.

Patrick Massie (b. 1981/34) The banjo has meant a great deal in my life. It gave me my wife, which inevitably gave me my children. It's a huge part of my life, an extension of me. I hope that one day my children can look back and say, like I did, "My dad played the banjo." Hopefully, I can play more in front of them.

The banjo has allowed me to have friends that I might not have otherwise met—just meet people, talk to people. I don't know what it is about the banjo. I played with a man who played the fiddle. I mean, he could just—he'd wear it out—it was gorgeous. But, after the shows and stuff, people would come over to me and start talking to me— but not to this guy on the fiddle even though they couldn't even fathom how difficult what he just pulled off was. They wanted to hear that banjo, and that has continued to this day. Maybe you can one day explain that mystery. But yeah, it's been huge—and it's shown me that, for the most part, I can do something if I put my mind to it. For me, it wasn't a lot of talent. I had a decent ear, you know, but it was more of a drive to accomplish something. And it showed me that I can—once I set my mind to something, I can achieve it.

Joey Massie (b. 1952/63) The banjo is one of the most positive experiences in my life—one of the most positive periods and endeavors of my life. And that's among a lot of negative endeavors and negative times. And so that, in and of itself, has to be worth everything.

The other thing is, I think that my kids look back and say, "Some of the best memories I have of Dad is when he was practicing or playing banjo." My son, Patrick, said, "You're the greatest influence I've ever had in banjo." And to hear someone say that—that makes everything worthwhile. It's one of the most important and best things I've ever done. It's right there in the top five of the good things I've done in this life.

"The banjo opened up a world to me that I would not have had otherwise. It helped me to meet people and places that I never would have been exposed to." **(June Smathers-Jolley b. 1958/57)** "It's been a joy in my life. Other than my wife and children, it has been the greatest joy in my life—outside of the Lord, you know. Yes, it has. Wouldn't change a thing." **(Mike Pressley b. 1949/63)** "I mean, I don't know how to answer this. The banjo means everything to me, and it's been a part of my life for many, many years." **(Pam Sutton b. 1966/49)** "In summary, the banjo has given me a lot of enjoyment. And I met—I guess one thing—I've made a lot of good friends with my music and enjoyed entertaining people. But I enjoyed it. So, oh, yeah, it's meant a lot to me for a long, long time." **(Stan Nichols b. 1958/56)** "Oh, yeah, it has meant a tremendous amount to me, over my lifetime—all of the music, just participating. Yeah, doing it for my own enjoyment because when it come down to the fact of did I want to make a living at it, I did not want to make a living at it because I just knew you had to put your heart and your soul in it. And in that amount of participation, you about lose your family." **(Lewin Burrell b. 1943/72)** "If somebody reads this, one hundred years from now, the biggest thing is the thrill that I got when I was trying to learn a specific tune—or a part of a specific tune. But just to hear the banjo and certain songs has just been a great thing to me all my life. And I hope that I've left a little something in this life concerning the banjo." **(Phil Hunter b. 1943/72)** "It's meant good times, closeness, and even worship, you know, at church. It really has, in some senses, been formative. It's been very helpful to me. It sure has." **(Jeremy Bolden b. 1982/33)** "Banjo gives me a peace of mind. It's hard to put into words, and it's hard even for me to understand. I love it." **(Roger Frady b. 1960/55)**

◆ ◆ ◆

Charles Rathbone (b. 1954/61) The banjo to me has been, I don't know, maybe a way to try to express through the songs and the pickin,' how you feel. And it takes you to a different place to where a lot of your troubles and anything like that, you forget. It takes you to a better place. And, I don't know, it's calming. It just seems to make you a better person if you pick.

Harold Hannah (b. 1934/82) Oh, gosh. It's been a tremendous part of my life, there's no doubt about that. No matter what I would do, I would have it with me even though there's periods of time that it wasn't convenient.

But it's a relief valve, I guess you would call it. You can be tired and you can be frustrated and sit down and play like that, and you just—you just knock out all the other things that might be on your mind. And it's been so important for my overall health—it's been that satisfying to me. I used to come in, no matter what I had been doing; if I was there before the kids went to bed, I still had to sit down and play a few tunes. I might not play long.

Jared Best (b. 1990/25) It's like I was explaining earlier. My grandfather died when I was so young. You know, it's always been kind of that con- nection that, you know, something or some skill that he's passed down to me. It's been a way to meet a lot of great people that I wouldn't have met otherwise. It's also been an out for frustrations. When I used to play a lot, it was almost like a friend, something that you could communicate with through how you played it. But more than anything, I think it was a way for me to kind of express my individuality and be good at something because I wasn't, you know, a great ball player. Music was my thing. And so, when you finally did get to get together with a bunch of musicians, and people were just, you know, dumbstruck, that I was this eleven-year-old kid playing a banjo that good, it was very rewarding. It was very challenging, too—but it was a very rewarding experience.

Thomas Smathers (b. 1957/59) The best things that we've done is where we—we helped all them people, both financially and otherwise. That's my philosophy of it. We brought them joy. That's what you done. I mean, really, it helped you, and it helped them. That's the way I see it.

Well, I'm just glad I learned how to peck around on it. It's my entertainment. We just all had a—we had a good time. Well, the banjo also kept me out of trouble, I guess. You had something you could do. And you forgot about the other things. So, I guess that's an achievement. Wouldn't you think so? It's also social—it helped you with other people. Of course, I had help along the way on that.

Tracy Best (b. 1963/52) As a young kid, I would hear the banjo. It had an exciting sound that instilled in me a desire to learn how to play it. I spent a lot of frustrating hours trying to make it make some resemblance of music. It was only after getting instruction from a young lady that I finally began to get a little music in it. I have been playing now for forty-plus years and have enjoyed it very much. It has been a large part of my life. I've had a lot of frustration at times with the banjo, but it always seems to work out. I don't think I will ever get tired of learning and listening to others play the banjo. I know that I will never know as much about the banjo as some do, but it gives me pleasure to continue trying to make this instrument make the sweetest sound within my power.

French Kirkpatrick (b. 1938/74) As I look back on my career, it's hard to summarize. I never did achieve much playing a banjo, but I did achieve what I wanted to do with it. Because, like I said, learning to play tunes like "Somewhere Over the Rainbow," "Lady of Spain," "Up a Lazy River" was what I was noted for doing—if I was ever noted for anything. Nobody else did what I did. So, to be an individual in your own makings of something, to be unique, or, let me be honest with you, at least feel like you're unique in what you have accomplished—that gives you some satisfaction about it.

Smiley Burnette (b. 1937/76) Well, I've enjoyed playing the banjo over the years. It's been a good pastime, you know. I love to do it, but I never did think I'd like to do it for a living. 'Cause it's fun, you know—'cause I know guys that do it, and it's just a job to them. Yeah. I like to really enjoy it, play when I want to.

No, I don't think I would change anything about the way I've gone about playing the banjo. I've enjoyed what I've done. I figure I've done pretty well—with work and everything—having the time to do it—what time I could, I done it, you know. I'm glad I never done it to where it got boring to me. I might have wished I had done it a little more, but—it's come out pretty good.

Tim Bradley (b. 1960/54) Well, what does the banjo mean to me? It's—I think it's like a lot of things that people do. You're not really that cognizant of the decision to go in that direction—when you first say, "I like that. I want to hear more of it." And then the next you know, you're hearing more of it, and you say, "I'd like to learn to do that," and then you're going down that road. Well, it's made a lot of friends. And like I say, some people enjoy hearing it. I also use it to accompany my storytelling and singing, which I enjoy.

Thomas Tatham (b. 1996/16) My greatest happiness with banjo would be, as of right now, I've not run into a song that I've had to throw in the towel. I've had some that took a lot longer to learn than others, but as of right now, when I have set my mind and sat down and said, "This is what I'm going to learn how to play," there's not been anything, to this point, that has shown me that I'm not that good yet—or that I'm not capable of accomplishing. And I would have to say that that is my greatest satisfaction so far.

David Burnette (b. 1961/53) I've enjoyed it [the interview], and I'm glad you're interested in the culture—a lot of people want to come and help us poor old people out. We've lived here—we could have lived in Boston or New York or wherever, just as well as we've lived here, you know. We just wanted to live here and, you know—we was happy here—that's why we've stayed here.

Chapter 12

THE BANDS, THE PEOPLE, THE PLACES, THE EVENTS

Most of the banjo players in this book were, at least at some point, members of a "band(s)." Many established lifelong friendships with other musicians. In some instances, the very early development of some of the banjo players led to the formation of a few small "novitiate" bands. One of the "tasks" for many of the banjo players was playing in a group of musicians for square dances, clog dancers, or competitions. There were a couple of local venues as well as regional festivals and fiddlers' conventions where some of the banjo players, in addition to "makin' music" with other attendees on-site, played either in solo competitions or as members of a band. Singing was important to and enjoyed by essentially all of the banjo players. Remnants of the in-home folkway are recognizable. In summary, there was and still remains a vibrant musical tradition in Haywood County.

GETTING STARTED

Mike Pressley (b. 1949/63) There were three Conard brothers—Charles, who was a gifted guitar player and singer, Larry, who played mandolin and sang lead, and Jim, who played guitar and sang tenor. I was in my early to mid-teens and went up to Stamey Cove to their house and made music with them. And then, they brought Marc [Pruett, also in this book] in somehow. I don't remember how he come in—but they knowed him, I reckon—through the 4-H or whatever. He'd come over, and we got to talking and playing, and he was trying to learn, you know. I was already playing pretty good. He got to wanting me to teach him, so I taught him a couple of songs. I believe that it was "Earl's Breakdown" and "Foggy Mountain Breakdown."

He told me that he kept that in his mind when I learned [taught] him. He went downtown to what they called The Old Community Store, and he said that he didn't go in the store because he wanted to keep the songs in his mind. And he did.

Later, Marc used to come to my house all the time. Eat with us. And we'd play and talk and spend a lot of time together. Everybody into music like that goes to somebody's house—they think they wear their welcome out—but people like listening and enjoys it. You know, they do.

Marc Pruett (b. 1951/61) Larry and Jim Conard and I were all in the 4-H club in Bethel School together. It was called the Starlight 4-H Club, and we named our band The Starlight Ramblers. Mike Pressley played with us sometime. That was our first band. We won some competitions. And that's the little group that we used in 1967, in May, a Wednesday night I think— Flatt and Scruggs came to Canton. Our 4-H Club leader, Ann Brackett, knew how much we loved it, and she got Louise Scruggs to let us open up for Flatt and Scruggs at the Canton Junior High School. The only time that I ever got to open for Flatt and Scruggs was at that show. And my old friend, Lane Worley, played bass with us, so we had a four-piece band that night. Mike Pressley was not in the band at that time.

Jeremy Bolden (b. 1982/33) When I was around sixteen, me and my brother Cameron [guitar] would go to Allens Creek and make music with Charlie Deaver [guitar], Mark Austin [guitar and mandolin], and Nathan Ashe [bass], and we kind of got us a band started. Charlie's grandma had a small "can house" building [used to store homemade canned goods] adjacent to her home. But we kind of got us a band started, and that's where we always sat up and picked. So we started calling ourselves The Can House Boys. We played a good bit at local functions.

Phil Hunter (b. 1943/72) Well, earlier, when Boone Messer and I were kids, he was one of the first ones I ever played with in playing backup with the banjo. And, as I said earlier, we'd play at school. Well, we played for five or six years like that, and then we got separated. He moved down to Charlotte. And then, in the seventies, we'd visit back and forth from here down to there, and that was a long way for me then. He used to come up from Charlotte, and we'd start after dinner in the evening, maybe it might be five or six o'clock, seven o'clock, depending on what time of the year it was. We'd be playing at four o'clock the next morning. Now, he's one of these guys that could sit down and start at six o'clock in the afternoon and

Phil Hunter and Boone Messer. (Photo courtesy of Phil Hunter)

six o'clock the next morning still be a-singing and never sing the same song. Yeah, I have played all night, and all day, too.

Tracy Best (b. 1963/52) Early on, for four or five years, I played a lot, just a tremendous amount. When I was about sixteen, I met a young girl named Ashley Osment [deceased]. Her mother owned a music store in Sylva. Ashley played guitar and, along with her two brothers, we formed a band and made a lot of old-time music. We spent a lot of time traveling around different places playing. We played in a Junior Band Competition at Union Grove in the mid-seventies. We played together no more than a year, and I lost track of them after that. And then just the friends and all, we would get together quite a bit, too.

Scott Evans (b. 1964/50) In high school, there was a boy named Kirk Sandlin who rode the school bus with me. He was older than me. He said, "I hear you play the banjo." I said, "Well, I try to play." His dad had bought him one—he'd come down to my house, and we would try to play together—and, of course, it was a mess because neither one of us had ever sat down and tried to play with anybody—try to keep in time and all that stuff. But he knew these other guys that lived down on Rabbit Skin—Chuck Russell, Steve Parker, who had been jamming together since they were small—and they'd get together at Chuck's daddy's house. They had a bass player. It was really something. And, we'd get together with them boys on Friday or Saturday night and play way up into the night—or try to play. They were really good. Richard Caldwell's son, Darren, was playing bass. That's when I first, I guess, started branching out a little bit besides sitting on the couch and playing. I think I was sixteen, maybe, when I started—still in school—and I played with those guys for two or three years. We had us a little band later, after a couple of years, called The J Creek [short for Jonathan Creek] Bluegrass Boys. And we'd go play for these square dancers—went to a campground or two and played—you know, had a PA system and all that stuff—sort of, I guess sort of semi-professionally [laughs]—and it was fun.

David Burnette (b. 1961/53) An old man named Ralph Putnam was an influence on me. He played the guitar and mandolin and would play for barn dances when he was younger. I'd go and visit Ralph every now and then—I'd take an evening or something and go down to his house. His wife loved music, but she didn't make music—but she loved music. They had an old ledger, a store ledger, that contained the words to many songs. Ralph sometimes couldn't remember the songs, but his wife, Irene, would find a song in the ledger and hum it a little bit. He would remember it and would then play it. You know, they'd just play old, old songs, you know, that went way back. [David Burnette's son, Jimmy, also in this book, visited Ralph Putnam from time to time as well.]

THE BANDS

There have been, over the years, a number of bands in Haywood County. Following are descriptions of a few of them.

Hill Country

Charles Rathbone's band, Hill Country, has played together for thirty years. It is an excellent regional band. There are two original members, Charles and Bobby Allen, along with Gary Downs and James Stinnett. The band gets together on Monday evenings for practice. They have played at Pickin' in the Park in Canton many times over the years. They have also played in Florida and Georgia.

"Hill Country." Left to right, Bobby Allen, Charles Rathbone, Gary Downs, and James Stinnett. (Photo courtesy of Charles Rathbone)

The Carolina Country Boys

Lewin Burrell (b. 1943/72) Well, there was three guys down there [at the factory where he worked], and they had a band—a mandolin, a guitar, and a fiddle. But they didn't have a bass fiddle. So, I worked in the welding shop, and I made a bass fiddle out of a foot tub. [A foot tub is turned upside down and a single string is attached to the center of the bottom and to the end of the neck of a three- to four-foot "L-necked" or curved piece of natural wood, which is attached to the side of the tub. The neck could be moved backward and forward, tightening and loosening the tension and, consequently, the tone on the string. When plucked, the single string plays effectively as a bass.]

Well, it wasn't too long until I could pick lead on that string bass. A guy in the electric shop had a big, old "doghouse bass" [big enough for a dog to live in], and he loaned that to me and I learned to pick it. At lunch, we ate for fifteen minutes and played for fifteen minutes. And they'd all gather in all over the plant and listen for that fifteen minutes and then, you know, go back to their jobs. Then, we'd play some more after work.

The way I got to the banjo was that the guitar picker got to where he couldn't be there all the time. So, I got somebody else to pick the bass, and I started playing the guitar. Then Smiley Burnette [also in this book] had to spend more time with his family. And so, I started learning to pick a banjo.

String (tub) bass. Bassist not identified.

It was a little bit out of necessity. But now, it was also love of—the ear for the sound of it, you know.

And then we started going out to different places where they'd want us to go. We formed the Midway Quartet [Midway Baptist Church]. And there was one other old guy in there that went with us to sing bass. He was in the welding shop. But anyway, we done that for two or three years—go to different churches, you know. We later formed a band, the Carolina Country Boys. And all of that sort of come out of that "shop corner," we called it.

Our band, the Carolina Country Boys, was well known. We occasionally played nationally, including once at Notre Dame University. We also played on radio and TV. Jim Sisk, James Birchfield, Ned Smathers, and myself played together, with occasional substitutions, including Smiley Burnette, for seventeen years.

We went to Sidmouth, England, in 1973, as the band for a Haywood County clogging team, which participated in the Sidmouth International Folk Festival. We were over there three weeks, and it was a paid deal. They didn't pay us for time. They just paid the way, you know.

And we stayed in a little hotel in Sidmouth—that's the only hotel. And this was 1973. And there was one bathroom for four floors, and there was no refrigerators. The coldest thing you could get to drink was wine, and they got it out of the wine cellar, and it was naturally cool. And we played twice a day. The stadium [venue] was a mile away. In this hotel, they had little ol' maids who'd come and work for the summer, and they were about sixteen years old, fifteen or sixteen. But anyway, them maids wouldn't let me carry my banjo that mile to the place every day. One of them carried it there, and one of them carried it back. And it weighs thirty-eight pounds. But it was just something that stuck out in my memory, you know. But if we went to play—and I wouldn't have thought about bluegrass being that popular—but we could start to the school over there and go downtown, and you'd stop anywhere on the street corner, and the whole street would fill up and listen to you play. How many times you'd do that, they'd just stop and listen. They loved the sound of a banjo—I wouldn't have thought about them doing that, but they did. They really loved the sound of a banjo.

The Three Mountaineers

Pam Sutton (1966/49) My brother, sister, and I ultimately joined the band with my daddy and his brothers. My mother went everywhere with us when we were performing. She was right there. My sister played the guitar, and my brother played the bass. I've picked everywhere. My brother [age thirteen], sister [age twelve] and I [age ten] subsequently had a band, the Three Mountaineers. We cut a record, a little 45 record. So, it was us three. Yeah, Daddy was focused on us three. We played in Florida, Kentucky, Virginia, Tennessee—all over. We played on the *Cas Walker Farm and Home Hour* television show. We never did any special preparations. We just went and done it. My brother and sister kind of drifted away from it as they got older. They just didn't have the interest like I did.

The Dutch Cove Old Time String Band

June Smathers-Jolley (b. 1957/57) Probably in the early to mid-seventies, my daddy, Quay Smathers, bought an upright bass fiddle for my sister, Cynthia, and started teaching her how to play that. They, along with my sister, Liz, started getting together with some other musicians and formed a band.

Daddy wanted to ultimately have his band made up of his children. So finally, the band consisted of my father, my sisters, Cynthia, and Liz, myself, and Liz's recent husband, Lynn, who played the fiddle. We were The Dutch

The Three Mountaineers. Pam Sutton (banjo), Linda Sutton (guitar), Jimmy Sutton (bass). (Photo courtesy of Pam Sutton)

The Dutch Cove Old Time String Band. Album cover. Left to right, Cynthia Smathers-White, Liz Smathers-Shaw, June Smathers-Jolley, Lynn Shaw. Front, Quay Smathers. (Photo courtesy of June Smathers-Jolley)

Cove Old Time String Band. And so, it was the five of us for years. That's who's on the cover of the album. Then, along came my husband, Zeb, and Cynthia's husband, Ted, and they started playing some with us.

But at the performance, on stage, it was usually always the five of us. Then, because of my father's age and loss of stamina, Zeb [her husband] began to play with us on stage.

I think the first time I ever played on stage was maybe the Bascom Lamar Lunsford Festival. I don't really remember, but I remember being nervous but getting out there and playing and how everybody was congratulating me, and the friends we were beginning to make in that realm were all excited about me playing.

We won the Smoky Mountain Festival one year. I think the same year, we won the Asheville Folk Festival as the best band. And I competed a couple of years, I guess, down at Fiddler's Grove in the old-time banjo category, and we also competed as a band down there. Instead of having a summer job of working at Hardee's or whatever, that was how we earned our money. And Daddy was pretty well retired as a carpenter by that point, and so he was free to pick up and go at any time. And so we traveled and played music, and we also played for dance teams.

Well, we played old-time mountain music, and we were successful, winning several festival competitions, and we were nationally recognized. We did an album and sold a lot of them. It was my daddy's dream.

David Burnette (b. 1961/53) There was a branch of them Smathers's that was all musical—banjo, fiddle, guitar players, and they were into the shaped-note singing also. Quay [Smathers] led that for years and years—music was something that they sought out and then kept alive. A lot of people came to his home to jam and also to learn the old-time mountain music. The Smathers family carried me around to a lot of places that I would probably have never gone if it hadn't have been for them.

SHAPED-NOTE SINGING

William Little and William Smith, in the early 1800s, developed and patented a method for "reading" music based on assigned geometric "shapes" for each note.[1] This was originally a four-note "do-re-mi-fa" system, and subsequently, a seven-note "do-re-mi-fa-sol-la-ti" system was developed. This proved important for early inhabitants of the Blue Ridge Mountains or deep South, most of whom could not read music. Both systems are still employed today. There are, among others, two major "shaped-note" song-books. Benjamin White's *The Sacred Harp*, a four-note songbook used par-ticularly in the Deep South and William Walker's *The Christian Harmony*, a seven-note songbook used in the Blue Ridge Mountains, where it is also known as "Blue Ridge style" because of the influence of ballad singers and the isolation of many of the mountain people. "Sacred Heart" tends to be loud and sung rapidly, while "Christian Harmony" is sung more slowly, and no one voice stands out above the others. The singing is a cappella. There is a shaped-note musical staff for each voice part. A leader first "pitches" the song and then the group sings it—first, in the case of seven-note, singing the sounds "do-re-mi-fa-sol-la-ti" and subsequently singing the lyrics. Due to the unusual arrangement of the voices with the tenor switching with the usual soprano for the lead, the sound is remarkably beautiful, almost "otherworldly."

QUAY SMATHERS

When his family, The Dutch Cove Old Time String Band (see above), appeared at music festivals, Quay Smathers also taught shaped-note singing. He taught shaped-note workshops and for years, was an adjunct instructor in Appalachian Studies at Warren Wilson College, where, on Sunday afternoons, he taught Christian Harmony. In 1990, he received the prestigious North Carolina Folk Heritage Award, which honors the state's most eminent folk artists, for his efforts in preserving Christian Harmony Shaped-Note Singing. For more than one hundred twenty-five years, his church in Dutch Cove, Morning Star United Methodist Church, has held "Old Folks Day" on the second Sunday in September, including a worship service, followed by "dinner on the grounds" and shaped-note singing. The Annual Quay Smathers Memorial Singing School, a workshop for shaped-note singing, is held in Waynesville each spring. It is led by Quay Smathers's daughters, June [June Smathers-Jolley] and Liz [Liz Smathers-Shaw].

Quay Smathers, as a teenager, taught himself to play tenor banjo and tenor guitar. He and four of his cousins traveled to the 1937 Folk Festival in Chicago, where they were the band for the Champion [Champion Paper Mill in Canton] Cloggers but also performed as a band. Upon getting mar-ried, he quit playing music, turning his attention to his family. Subsequently, his daughter, Liz, began to learn to play violin in the Canton Junior High Orchestra. However, her teacher retired in the middle of the school year. Recognizing his daughter's exceptional musical aptitude, Quay reconnected

Quay Smathers. (Photo courtesy of June Smathers-Jolley)

with his cousins so that she could learn to play the fiddle. He subsequently formed The Dutch Cove Old Time String Band (see above), composed of him and his children. He enjoyed playing music and invited people to his home to "make music." He mentored a lot of young people who were learning to play.[2] He died in 1997.

JAMES TRANTHAM

Jim Trantham was born in Haywood County. He was an excellent musician, ballad singer, and storyteller. He later performed mountain music across the Southeast with his son, Doug (in this book), and his grandchildren, as The Trantham Family. He was an exceptional luthier. For many years, he led the Village of Yesteryear Heritage Craft Demonstration Program at the North Carolina State Fair in Raleigh. Jim also received a North Carolina Folk Heritage Award. He died in December 2019.

Roy French Kirkpatrick. (Photo courtesy of French Kirkpatrick)

ROY FRENCH KIRKPATRICK

French Kirkpatrick has been a major influence in the lives and careers of a number of the banjo players in this book. He is a remarkable banjo player. He has also been an indispensable resource for me in the writing of this book. He has, since the early 1990s, performed with Harry Robbins (vocal, guitar). Their duo is The Unexpected.

RAYMOND FAIRCHILD

Raymond Fairchild, a legendary figure and an extraordinary banjo player, moved to Haywood County when he was nine years old. Raymond worked for and was mentored by Ted Sutton, who owned the Hillbilly Fun House in Maggie Valley. He played many times on the Grand Ole Opry and also played nationally and internationally. He has received many accolades over the years and, in 2015, was inducted into Bill Monroe's Bluegrass Hall of Fame in Bean Blossom, Indiana.

He and his wife owned the Maggie Valley Opry House, where he performed during the spring and throughout the summer.[3] He died in October 2019.

JOE MEDFORD

Joe Medford (1932–1993), known locally as "Little Joe," was an exceptionally talented Haywood County banjo player. His father was the mayor of Clyde, near Waynesville. Carroll Best taught him to play the banjo. He played Scruggs style and performed with several bluegrass groups, including, among others, those of Mac Wiseman and Charlie Monroe.[4]

THE REDEEMED QUARTET

Gospel music was, and continues to be, an important aspect of the culture of the Southern Appalachian Mountains. Some of the banjo players in this book enjoy(ed) singing, including singing southern gospel music. There are a number of gospel quartets in Haywood County, some known only in their home churches. The Redeemed Quartet was organized around 1970 at Victory Baptist Church in Maggie Valley. Its initial members were Leon Bolden, Luther Sutton, Bill McMahan, and Jackie Hughes. Jeremy Bolden, one of the banjo players in this book, joined his grandfather in this quartet in 2004 and sang with them until 2016, when, due to the health issues of the older members, the quartet was disbanded.

CARROLL BEST

Carroll Best was born in 1931 in Haywood County, where he lived until his untimely death in 1994. He was an extraordinary musician and one of the pioneers, quite possibly the major pioneer, of the so-called "melodic" banjo, a three-finger technique that began by playing old-time fiddle tunes, note-for-note, on the banjo. He subsequently extended this technique to any tune. Tony Trischka has said, "Carroll definitely played a role in the evolution of the melodic three-finger banjo style . . . no one ever developed a full-blown melodic style on the banjo until Carroll came along."[5] Joe Wilson has said, "His contributions were in fact major ones, and if melodic banjo needs a father figure, he has first claim."[6]

He began playing the banjo when he was five years old and gave his first public performance when he was ten. Over the years, he played locally in Haywood County and in regional folk festivals, as well as nationally and internationally. He freely shared his melodic technique with others, particularly young people. In addition to being an extraordinary banjo

Carroll Best. (Photo courtesy of Hugh Carroll Best)

player, he was an excellent and universally respected gentleman. He was posthumously awarded a coveted North Carolina Heritage Award in 1994.

French Kirkpatrick (b. 1934/74) Carroll Best was a close friend and mentor, a good mentor. He was probably the most respected banjo player in our county. He was so creative. He was the first person I ever heard do the chromatic music—he was doing this in the sixties! Bobby Thompson picked up a lot of stuff from Carroll. Even though he has been dead almost a quarter of a century, Carroll is influential in banjo circles to this day.

Some guys had asked Carroll Best if he would come up there and play some music one Saturday afternoon. He said, "Yeah, I'll get some guys to come." So he got me and my brother, Bill, to go with him, and we went up there and played—and this was way back in the early to mid-fifties. I was in my early twenties. When we left, Carroll gave me eleven dollars. I said, "You don't owe me nothing," and he said, "Yeah, I'll give you part of it. You're one of us." And I never will forget that. That was so sweet of him. That was a lot of money back then, too.

You'll never meet another Carroll Best, there's only one of them.

"My dad took me to see Carroll Best play when I first started playing banjo, and I was real impressed with the way he played. I've heard it described as 'fiddle style,' 'melodic.' It was very much more of a melodic sensibility than rhythmic and driving like the Scruggs style and certainly, seemingly, very difficult to play that way on the banjo. It wasn't until I was much older that I began to aspire to play more melodically." (**Doug Trantham b. 1963/50**) "When I met Carroll Best and learned to respect what he did [melodic banjo], I realized that he was an unbelievably gifted player—words can't describe what Carroll Best could do. He was decades ahead of his time." (**Marc Pruett b. 1951/61**) "And he actually—if everybody will be honest and trace back from Nashville, the Bobby Thompsons and everybody, they came here to learn from Carroll Best—he figured out the fiddle tunes note-for-note on the banjo. I absolutely agree with French Kirkpatrick that Carroll was doing things in the fifties that guys are just now beginning to do today. What he played was just so sparkling. It was good." (**Steve Sutton b. 1956/60**)

• • •

Tracy Best (b. 1963/52) I had lots of influences from other older banjo players. Carroll Best would just kind of brag on you and make you feel good and help you along. He was just a great man, yeah. I'm sure I despaired of ever playing like him. I can remember being in some of the competitions around, and he would be playing. He and I would be playing outside somewhere, you know, and he'd say, "Man, I wish I could play that like you could," and me knowing all the time he was way better than I ever could be. He actually found the banjo I still have today that I play. He found it for me, and he told me that he couldn't afford it; he wanted me to have it. He could have bought it a dozen times over, but he just wanted me to have that banjo. And it has suited my style of music so much, and I still play it every day today.

Carroll would always, always win the old-time competition at the Smoky Mountain Folk Festival. But sometimes, I would place second right behind him—even though I'm nowhere near as talented as he was—and nobody else was. But that was an early memory that kind of kept me going.

"Carroll said, 'Phil, all you need to do is pick.' He said, 'Forget about all this other.' He said, 'Pick.' And from then on—I mean, for years, right on up until I quit fooling with it, that's what I did. And I picked and played what I wanted to play." (**Phil Hunter b. 1943/72**). "He was such a big man—had hands that long—he'd just play that banjo—it was unbelievable." (**Scott Evans b. 1964/50**)

BALSAM RANGE

Balsam Range has, since its inception in 2007, become a spectacularly successful bluegrass band. Its members include Marc Pruett (banjo), Darren Nicholson (mandolin, octave mandolin, vocals), Caleb Smith (guitar, vocals), Buddy Melton (fiddle, vocals), and Tim Surrett (bass, dobro, vocals). Four are from Haywood County, and all live in Haywood County. They are accomplished musicians and perform regionally, nationally, and internationally. Notable recent recognition includes the 2018 International Bluegrass Music Association's Entertainer of the Year. In addition, Buddy Melton was the 2018 IBMA Male Vocalist of the Year, and Tim Surrett was the 2018 IBMA Bass Player of the Year. They were recently the subject of a music review article in the *Wall Street Journal*.[7] Other awards have followed. The band has never lost sight of its origins and, from time to time, has played locally for a number of charitable causes. They are loved and respected by the people of Haywood County.[8]

PLAYING FOR DANCING

One cannot talk about music in the mountains without mentioning the major importance of the dance. Dancing was widespread. Some of the bands played for dancing, primarily clog dancing and square dancing, including competitions.

Lewin Burrell (b. 1943/72) Let me tell you—I'll tell you one place that's the most I've ever played in my life, and I don't know of anybody that's ever played that much. They had a dance festival at Toccoa, Georgia. And I can't think of the year it was, but it was when there was so many dance teams—at one time, there were forty-two dance teams in this area. They went from Jackson County northeastward plumb into Boone.

But anyway, they had this festival at Toccoa, Georgia—we played for eighty-five dance teams in one set. We started one morning at 10:30, and the next morning at 2:30, we quit. And we took a thirty-minute supper break. Each one of these dance teams danced eight minutes a set. So, if you're talking about making work out of it, now that's work. Along about 6:30, I thought, "I'm not going to make it." But we took a supper break, and you've heard of getting your second wind. We did. We went right on through from that point to 2:30 the next morning. And the funny part about it, there was a three-way tie, and they wouldn't play a record for them to dance to. They said it wouldn't be fair. And we had to play the three-way tie again. [laughs]

Yeah, we was wore out, I tell you that. I was probably twenty-eight. You had to be—you was in shape. You know, when you're playing for dance teams, the roughest position is if you're playing a doghouse bass. That's the roughest. Now, if you're playing electric, it ain't. The guitar players are having it the roughest, you know. And you heard the tempo on this record, and it's all—they wanted it that fast.

And when you're playing for square dances, you're practicing all the time. I told you the other night, part of the time they don't know what you're playing. If you keep them good time, some of them can't tell you what you're playing. If it was Christmastime, we'd play all kind of songs in there. One of them was "Jingle Bells." We'd throw "Jingle Bells" in there and play several versions of it. Half the time, there wasn't one of them noticed it. We'd just do it to see if they noticed it.

Roger Frady (b. 1960/55) My first professional gig was—I guess I was playing with Jim Sisk and the Carolina Country Boys, playing for square dances. For whatever reason, Lewin Burrell would be working or whatever, and I was kind of like a fill-in. I was a young guy, and I didn't really have any commitments, so I was ready, you know, when he called. And to me, that was like being on the Grand Ole Opry. I loved it. I'd start a lot of times at 5:00 or 6:00 in the evening and play for a competition till 1:00 or 2:00 in the morning—for the dancers. And they wanted it wide open [very fast]. And you didn't really do a lot of finesse playing—and that's where I learned to play fast because that's what you had to do. It was tough work.

June Smathers-Jolley (b. 1957/57) Our band, The Dutch Cove Old Time String Band, became the band for the Southern Appalachian Cloggers. We went everywhere with them. And the year we won the Smoky Mountain Folk Festival in Waynesville, we became the house band the next year, so we played for all the dance teams. We played for the opening and the closing and all the dance teams. All that time I was wishing I was on a dance team instead of there playing. I always wanted to be on a square dance team. And if you have one thing you've ever regretted in your life you didn't get to do, that's something I regret I never got to do—being on a square dance team.

JOE SAM QUEEN

Joe Sam Queen has been immersed in mountain music and dancing all his life. His grandfather, Sam Queen, was a lifelong enthusiastic supporter of, and participant in, mountain music and dancing. He formed, roughly ninety years ago, the Soco Gap Dance Team, which performed and competed successfully at dance festivals throughout the region. In 1939, they were invited to the White House to perform for King George VI and Queen Elizabeth during their state visit.

> I grew up going to square dances with my father and grandfather, especially in the summers at the Maggie Valley Playhouse. . . . Of course the banjo is a key instrument for those dances. . . . From a very early age, I was fascinated by my grandfather's calling the dance and his buck dancing as a highlight of those dances. . . . My grandfather often "rode me around" as a sidekick when I was younger, and one of our regular stops was his buddy, Ted Sutton's in Maggie Valley, where I was first introduced to Raymond Fairchild, who was playing the banjo on the porch at Ted's place to draw in the tourists.[9]

Joe Sam followed in his grandfather's footsteps and has been a major figure in the promotion of Appalachian music and dance. He was involved in the founding of the annual Smoky Mountain Folk Festival, an excellent two-day celebration of mountain music and dance. He is the recognized leader and MC of this event, recently celebrating its fiftieth anniversary. He notes that all the musicians and dancers come as volunteers. "They perform for free. It's the festival." He has also led and called summer street dances in Waynesville for over fifty years.

Finally, he has been a strong supporter of Western North Carolina, serving in the North Carolina House of Representatives as well as in the North Carolina Senate.

STRAINS OF MUSIC

Strains of Music, an iconic music store in Waynesville, was opened in 1958, in an old two-story frame home, by Hal Strain, the father of the current owner, Angie Messer.

Hal Strain was an extraordinary musician with a master's degree from Northwestern University. He had a well-known big band dance band that traveled extensively and played from the late 1940s until his death in the early 1970s. His sister, Madeline, also an extraordinary musician, was a member of the band and played piano.

Strains of Music. Angie and Alisha Messer.

Initially, the store sold mostly pianos. Subsequently, the store began to sell more guitars and banjos. The business grew and gradually expanded into the entire original building. Angie Messer became the owner in the mid-eighties. She and her daughter-in-law, Alisha, now operate the business.

Angie, a delightful woman with striking blue eyes and a great sense of humor, is knowledgeable, honest, and frank. She is respected and revered by all her customers, some of whom have known her since her family arrived here shortly after she graduated from high school.

The store no longer sells pianos but mostly guitars, banjos, and other instruments, including electric keyboards and sheet or instructional music. Alisha has played a major role in further expanding the business into PA systems sales and installation. Strains of Music is a place where musicians of any skill level are welcome to come in, pick up an instrument, and "try it out." It is a common occurrence.

JUNIOR APPALACHIAN MUSIC PROGRAM (JAM)

JAM is a weekly after-school program that teaches children, fourth through eighth grade, to learn about and play Appalachian music, predominantly folk and bluegrass. Lessons are available in guitar, banjo, fiddle, and string band. The music, following mountain traditions, is learned "by ear." There are roughly twenty-five to thirty students per year. Travis Stuart (also in this book) has been a major component of the JAM program

This Haywood County Arts Council Program also receives tuition and financial support from the North Carolina Arts Council.

A number of JAM alumni have gone on to continue their music, including at the college level. The most recent band, Possum on a Whale, all composed of JAM alumni, performs locally.

STORYTELLING

Tim Bradley (b. 1960/54) [Tim Bradley sometimes combines banjo playing, singing, and storytelling.] So basically, I just remembered the things I saw and heard. Well, a lot of it is things that I heard other people tell—that I thought was humorous, you know. Some of them are, I guess, what you'd call "tall tales." Because there's no way that they could be true, but that's what makes 'em funny. There's a lot of storytelling in the mountains. Yeah. Pretty much. It's about as widespread as the music. Anytime you had people gathered together, they'd play a little music, tell a few stories. And some of the songs that they had, they would make up, in a way, to remember a story, or news, to take it from one place to another. It was a way of remembering events and things—a lot of 'em back then couldn't read and write. So, even if they did have a newspaper or something, they couldn't read it. But they could remember a song most of the time—about somebody gettin' killed, or a train wreck, or whatever, you know. I wish I had recorded my great granddaddy a'playin'—and some of the singers and things that I've heard that have went on.

FIDDLERS' CONVENTIONS AND FESTIVALS

Several fiddlers' conventions and festivals featuring bluegrass and old-time music are held in the North Carolina mountains, foothills, and other locations each year. Historically, "fiddlers' conventions" preceded the development of "festivals." The conventions were largely competitions, although competitions are also present at festivals. In both instances, there is much social interchange as well ad hoc "makin' music."

Haywood County's Smoky Mountain Folk Festival has already been mentioned.

The Union Grove Fiddlers' Convention began in 1924 in Union Grove, North Carolina, located west of Winston-Salem. In 1969, its name was changed to the Ole Time Fiddler's and Bluegrass Festival. Its purpose, for nearly one hundred years, has been "the preservation of traditional old-time and bluegrass music in a family atmosphere." Many people camp out at this festival, and there are many spontaneous, often all-night, "jam sessions."[10] Some of the banjo players in this book attended this festival, including participating in jam sessions that included all-night jam sessions, competitions, and performing.

The Bascom Lamar Lunsford "Minstrel of Appalachia" Folk Festival, now almost fifty years old, had its beginning in 1927 in Asheville, North Carolina, as the Rhododendron Festival. It is a celebration, and preservation, of mountain music, dance, and crafts. An article about the Folk Festival appeared in 1948 in the *Saturday Evening Post*. It states that "then he thinks of the mountain music still alive in the hills, and of the schools that have dance teams now . . . and of the many youngsters playing the fiddle and picking the banjo like their grandfathers did. . . ." (Martin, Harold H., "Minstrel Man of the Appalachians," *Saturday Evening Post*, May 25, 1948) It is currently held each fall at Mars Hill University, Mars Hill, North Carolina.[11]

"Merlefest," a major four-day springtime folk festival honoring the memory of Eddy Merle Watson and son of Doc Watson, was "founded in 1988 to celebrate 'traditional plus' music. We are about the MUSIC, MOMENTS, and MEMORIES." It is held on the campus of Wilkes Community College, Wilkesboro, North Carolina.[12]

The International Bluegrass Music Association (IBMA) five-day World of Bluegrass celebration has, since 2013, been held in the fall in Raleigh, North Carolina.[13] It consists of multiple events and is the largest urban bluegrass festival in the world. Attendance in 2018, underscoring its popularity, was roughly 220,000 people.[14]

"MOLASSEE" (MOLASSES) MAKING

Making sorghum molasses at David Burnette's farm is a remarkable event. Until 2018, it was held on each of the first three Saturdays of September. This year, and in the future, it will be held on the first Saturday in September.

Jimmy Burnette (b. 1989/25) My father started making molasses—they've been making it longer than I've been around—for a year or two before I was born, anyway. It used to be they didn't have enough people to help carry the vat of molasses off. And then it kind of turned into—there'll be a couple of hundred people there on a Saturday. Three Saturdays in a row in September. Yeah. People bring food—now, since there are so many people that come, we've got one of Dad's friends who comes and cooks barbecue. Sometimes, usually one of the weeks, Sunburst Trout Farms will bring some trout and fry up. And then Dad, he'll fry a big bunch of taters, or we'll make a bunch of soup or something. And then everybody usually brings something to eat, so there's usually plenty to eat. Some people get there

Makin' Music at "Molassee."

a little earlier—most of the time, about four or five o'clock, people start showing up. Then everybody eats, and then, about before dark, or one or two hours before dark, some start playing music—and play music all the way until, sometimes, two or three o'clock in the morning. There's usually a lot of people with instruments. There'll usually be quite a few getting started playing some music. And then, different people will get up and take a break, and then there'll be a different—almost a whole new crowd play music, and then that crowd may kind of dwindle down, and then a few more people come in and start playing music. So there could be ten or fifteen musicians there, not playing, but they'd be there anyway. We just sit in a circle and sit there and play. There are no microphones. Most of the time it's the same people each week or somebody—usually, it's about the same people. Some people just come one week, some people all three weeks. All that day and early night, we're also cooking the molasses. We pour the molasses off, usually around nine or ten. And then the people start disappearing and—but the music's still going. [laughs] My daddy'll sit up until two or three, and he'll play a few songs now, but he don't play as much as he should. I usually play a good bit 'cause it's the only time of year I get to play music like I like—with different people. I usually play the whole time. Yeah. Or, I at least try to. I'll take, you've got to, take a break at some point!

Molasses making is similar to old-time corn shucking in that it is often followed by music and dancing.

WADE MEHAFFEY

Wade Mehaffey was an excellent banjo player, and his band, The Blue-grass Mountaineers, was very well known. His son, Scott, is one of the banjo players in this book. He is included here because he was specifically mentioned by three different banjo players as a major influence in their lives. This influence transcended simply teaching mere technical aspects of playing the banjo.

Gary Wiley (b. 1961/54) But the man that really did it for me in banjo is Wade Mehaffey. He was one heck of a gentleman. When I first started learning to play, my father found out where some musicians, including Wade Mehaffey, would get together. I would just sort of stand over to the side and play along behind them. I would watch everything that Wade's fingers were doing. They would be in the middle of a song, and he would see me trying to figure something out, and he'd go, "Hold on just a minute, guys." And he would pull me over to the side, and he would say, "Like this right here." And he would show me very slowly how to do it. And the next time they played it, he would pull me up there and let me play it with them

Wade Mehaffey used to live here in Haywood County, played banjo—they had a group. Wade was a good picker, excellent picker, and he would say, "Well, I'll be glad to show you what I know. I don't know if it's right or not." Then French Kirkpatrick—there's no telling how many hours upon hours upon hours French helped people. French was interested in us. And French is just that type of person, a giving person.

Jeremy Bolden (b. 1982/33) There was a guy here in the county, his name was Wade Mehaffey. He had a great influence on me. He was not family, but he actually taught me a few runs. He was a great banjo player. He sure was also a fine man. Anytime I wanted, he would give it to me, as far as teaching me anything I wanted to know. He cared about me. He really did. He cared about me, that's right.

Chapter 13

THREE JOURNEYS

Biographies of all the banjo players were presented earlier. In this chapter, the biographies of three of the banjo players will be presented in more detail, giving deeper insights into various facets of their makin' music careers.

DOUG TRANTHAM

Doug Trantham was born in 1963 and was interviewed when he was fifty years old.

I grew up in Bethel and graduated from Pisgah High School. After I got my MSW graduate degree, I went further down East to get a job—but got back to the mountains as soon as I could get a job here.

I think probably my earliest memories of music are of either my dad playing and singing or of recordings that he had in the house. My dad is an oral music historian. His thing was singing. He had, and still has, an awesome ballad-singing voice. He also built instruments. He would go to different festivals and listen, learn, and collect songs from some of the old ballad singers. Some of them he recorded. Of course, we had LPs and he had some vintage recordings of various folk musicians, mountain musicians, so those are probably my earliest memories of music around the house.

My dad got into performing in a more serious way when I was real small. I started going out with him when I was probably six, seven, or eight years old, actually going and listening and later started playing with him a little bit on stage at festivals.

I'm trying to think of the first time I actually saw somebody play a banjo. One of my earliest memories—I used to go down to the North Carolina

Doug Trantham. (Photo courtesy of Doug Trantham)

State Fair in Raleigh with my dad, and there was a man down there that was pretty famous, Willard Watson—he's Doc Watson's cousin. He played clawhammer style, and I remember being very much intrigued by his clawhammer playing. That was pretty early on.

I got a couple of lessons, maybe two, from David Holt and, otherwise, really, it was going to shows and watching people play and just trying to do it myself. I would record it, go home, and listen to it over and over again. And also, I learned by jamming with people at festivals. I can remember quite a few times that people would be pretty interested to see such a little kid playing the banjo. And some guy would come over and say, "Well, you know, kid, you could add this lick to it. Watch this." They would show me things. That happened quite a few times.

The sound of the banjo appealed to me. I think that part of that was being from this area—I just had a sense that the banjo was just the ultimate instrument. You know, people loved the banjo. I don't know how else to describe it, but it has a sound that's really—there's just not another instrument that sounds like it with the kind of short sustain that you get from it. I like the fact that it's very rhythmic as well as potentially melodic—it's not really one or the other.

I like to practice. When I'm doing it, I'm enjoying it, and so it's never been something that I was forced to do. I know a lot of times when kids have an instrument and taking lessons, there's kind of a lot of pressure. I never really felt that. I was always motivated, I think, intrinsically, to do it for the enjoyment of doing it. Certainly, there's the pressure of wanting to make good music and achieve something, so I do feel pressure when I'm not, you know, when I haven't got it right—and so I don't feel that as an external pressure. All the great players that I know, they all have this—they were attracted to music early on, and they were intrinsically motivated—they had that internal drive to do it. And that seems to be the key ingredient. People have different things that they love, that they feel drawn to do, and that's the key for sure.

When I was learning, I was probably getting in ten or more hours a week practicing. And if I was learning a new song or trying to get ready for a show or something, it might be quite a lot more than that. It's varied dramatically from period to period in my life—there's periods when I'm playing a few hours a day and, you know, really working on things, learning new material and stuff; and there's times when I'm really kind of on a break from it. So, it varies dramatically. But I've never practiced at the level that you've got to [in order] to get to where the big guys are.

The combination of the banjo and the fiddle, to me, is the ultimate combo, with the fiddle, in some ways, emulating the human voice and being very melodic by nature and the banjo being percussive and rhythmic. I love that drive. And to me—part of the reason that I like the banjo so much is that, to me, first and foremost, music is rhythm. And the rhythm, the energy from the rhythm, is like the foundation of it, and the banjo conveys that so powerfully when it's played well.

The festivals, or "conventions," in the Southeast were a huge influence on music in terms of connecting the past to the present. In those days, you had people like Bascom Lamar Lunsford as well as other very traditional musicians from all throughout the Southeast who would come and play, and there'd also be a lot of jamming. So, I have very fond memories of going to these festivals and jamming with the different performers, some of whom were famous. Some of them—I don't even know their names—were always willing to teach a young person and help you along. I used to bring one of those early portable tape cassette recorders and take it around the festival grounds at places like Fiddler's Grove. I would hear a banjo player and I would ask them if I could record 'em and I would take the tapes home and try to, you know, reconstruct what they were doing.

Clawhammer is the only style I've ever played. So, I've loved the banjo for basically as long as I remember. In the last fifteen years, I've played a lot of hammer dulcimer—that's a whole other dimension. But banjo is my heart instrument. I am just most comfortable with it and the thing that I most like is to just sit around and play and listen—it's my favorite.

If the melody of a song really strikes me especially, I can go home that night and play it. I commit the melodies to memory, and the process for doing that is repeating it, either humming it or, ideally, playing it really simply, phrase by phrase, and then I have it memorized. It's hard for me to memorize a melody completely without playing it some. A lot of folk melodies are not complicated, and so they are not often that hard to memorize.

I got more serious about my music when I got out of graduate school. I had a student loan. I barely got a little bit of a raise as a social worker, and I had a wife and three kids. My wife was taking care of the kids, so I was either going to have to get a second job and have no time for music, or music was going to have to make a little money. So when I was about thirty, I started music as a part-time vocation, made my first recording and started doing more shows and selling recordings. Then, the kids started playing with me. They started young, just as I had. Our youngest daughter had a beautiful voice, and that brought more attention to our band. We became "The Trantham Family," and that helped, very much helped, as a second income for the family for about fifteen years. It worked out good because we could do it as a family as opposed to me having some type of other job on top of forty hours a week. My wife has been very supportive. She's been kind of the manager of The Trantham Family operation in some ways—helping everybody get ready and be there.

I've made a lot of CDs over the years. They helped support my family. I used to do a lot more shows like weddings, etc., to earn a little extra money, and I don't do those anymore because I don't have to—so I pretty much just do the stuff I like to do now. We've won a lot of awards.

We've had plenty of support from the community. People enjoy it. That's probably the biggest motivator that I have—that's the way I connect with the community—do things like the street dances and the folk festivals and people that come year after year and enjoy the music. Then, I also really like sitting and listening to it—the festivals that I go to, I get out in the audience and listen to my good friends that come through and play. I like to hear what they're doing.

I love where I live and am very proud to be here. The way I think about it is the music is the one way that I connect with my ancestors. I don't live the same way that my grandfather or great-grandfather did. Life is very different now. But I'm still playing the music, my own version of it, that they were playing one hundred and fifty years ago. I really like that connectedness to the past.

Dance is a big part of our tradition here, and I learned to clog dance—which I love—when I was pretty young, too. I don't do it very often anymore, just at the street dances every year. When I was young, I got on a dance team, the Soco Mountain Cloggers. We traveled and danced at competitions and, one time, danced on the Grand Ole Opry—great experiences.

I remember that Larry Watson played banjo for The Southern Lawmen. He traveled a lot. He's talked to me about that and what a difficult time in his life that was. He obviously developed as a musician during that time, but it's not good for family life. I think that it would be really hard to maintain a marriage and a family when you had to travel that much. But you know, folks are wired differently. What I know as a mental health professional, some people are extroverts and they feed on that energy and so it's not draining to them. I'm someone who likes to do it but preparing and performing takes a lot of energy out of me. And so I need to rest up for a day or two. But some people, I've observed, are really quite the opposite and they really just thrive in that environment and those are folks that really succeed, especially as live musicians.

Other than my family, the only band that I really played with was when I was in my early to mid-twenties, living in Hickory. It was called "Possum Holler," a string band. We had sort of a classical old-time string band, and I played with them for several years and had a good time. I played with them until I moved back here.

I got more approval from adults or young people that were older than me. My peers, I think as I got older, appreciated it more and more. But a lot of the things that we were doing as kids, they generally weren't playing music with me. So, peer approval was probably not that significant. But it was something that I was good at, and people could recognize that—my peers could recognize it.

It is a delightful experience to see people enjoying the music that you are playing—with you. I will say that there is a mysterious aspect to it that I can't profess to really understand when it happens. But sometimes, you get that "flow state," and you're really—everything's really coming together, and you have an audience that's in a place to receive it. It's just really awesome. You look out and see their faces and—they're smiling and maybe singing along and that's a really awesome thing. When everything's perfect, it's just kind of a sparkle, I guess. It's just a beautiful, complete gestalt, where the rhythm is just right, the tempo is just right, the feeling is there—whatever the feeling of that song you're playing. And of course, it—you realize what a gift it is when you do that because it doesn't always come that way and sometimes it sort of hits you. "Mindfulness" is another term, a clinical term, that we would use. And I think it's very similar, if not identical, to what happens in meditation—I understand all of the great athletes, performers, in whatever field, they have a way of achieving this "flow state."

And I've watched it as a spectator—I've seen it with performers. I've seen it happen with some of these really great performers, and the ones that really impress me—they get up all by themselves, maybe just a guitar, one instrument—guitar, banjo, or whatever—and just absolutely captivate an audience, and it's magical. If I could capture that in a bottle and open it whenever I needed to, I would certainly do it.

There's something about the reciprocal interaction between the performer and the audience that really goes beyond either one. I think it's very much that the audience is part of, in a way, the performance. It's a neat thing. I don't profess to be real accomplished in that way because I am a pretty introverted person—I'm not as gifted in that arena as some folks—I have noticed that there are really good musicians that are not that great a performer, and there are really great performers that, from a technical standpoint, aren't that good a musician. And there are some performers that are better live, and you have to hear them live to really appreciate them

I think that there is a real primal sense of rhythm that some people have—most people have it to one degree or another. It's such an important part of music, and I think that really good players have a sense of it and they play with it. Some of these great old-time banjo players may be playing something that you could even play, but there is such "attitude" in it. There's a technical rhythm that's more or less a metronome that's clicking along, and that's what you would strive for, as a classically trained musician—to really make music. But for it to be really musical or beautiful, you don't want to be the metronome, you want to play around the metronome, and you're literally attacking notes a little quick or you're coming a little behind to achieve that sort of sparkle and snap—and I think that's what it is. I don't know that musicians are necessarily thinking analytically about it in that way, but I think that's one of the things they're doing that makes it so musical—that playing "around." I think that we unconsciously do these things that are very sophisticated. It's like you and I are doing right now—we're not having to think about how we're doing it—we're just communicating.

Music is that way, too. It's hard for musicians to find words to describe, probably, how they are doing it.

Showmanship is a really important part of a good performer, and I can't profess to have any proficiency. You know, part of that is connecting with the audience, not just on a music level, but you're also engaging them verbally, and you're bringing them into what you are doing.

We'd always practice and warm up before doing a show. I never like to go into a show cold. So, if it's for me to enjoy doing a show and I always like to have fun, I need to be prepared. I want to run through every song that we are gonna do—I want to run through any of the parts that are troublesome or that can hang us up and make sure that everybody I'm playing with (usually my girls, now) know and are comfortable with their parts and then when we get up and do it, it's fun, and I'm just having a good time doing it. And I like to warm up in close proximity to playing—like, you know, within a couple of hours of doing it, I like to have run through it.

Learning to play the banjo was my most proud accomplishment as a child. The instrument's capacity for rollicking rhythm and intricate melody touches my soul. When I play, I feel an intimate connection, not only to my Southern Appalachian ancestors, but to the African slaves who, in spite of unimaginable hardship, developed the banjo and laid the groundwork for the clawhammer style. The banjo is a fine example of American ingenuity.

STEVE SUTTON

Steve Sutton was born in 1956 and was sixty years old when he was interviewed.

I grew up in Waynesville. I lived in adjacent Buncombe County for about twenty years but then came back home.

You know, I would agree that this area does seem to have more banjo players than anyplace that I really have been before—I mean really, really great banjo players, too. I'm not sure why. It's always been said since I started going to Nashville, if you wanted a musician with a certain feel, you came to Western North Carolina to get it.

My earliest memories of music when I was growing up were on a black and white TV—any music program—I just seemed to be drawn to it. Of all things, *The Lawrence Welk Show* was popular when I was young, and I would just watch it, not so much for the music or dancing, it just was for the players. They all always seemed so happy when they played on that program. They loved what they were doing is how it came across to me.

And then, this being a tourism area, there were so many little roadside stands that had musicians. And my dad loved the music, and we would go up on a weekend afternoon or something to just watch some of these players beside the road.

I graduated from Tuscola High School here in Waynesville and then went to Western Carolina University. By the time I entered college, I was already playing the banjo on the Grand Ole Opry, so I wanted a university to go to that was close enough to where I could still go do the Grand Ole Opry on the weekends. I got a minor in music [trumpet] and majored in marketing.

My struggle in the WCU music department was the actual reading of music. I had always learned, from the time I was a child, to play by ear. So, if I could hear it, I could play it, but just to read it blind, I struggled with some of that.

I probably first saw and fell in love with the banjo with the old Flatt and Scruggs TV shows on Saturday. And then the first live banjo player that I remember seeing was Raymond Fairchild. Banjo was my first stringed instrument. I started playing the banjo when I was seven years old. I also play the guitar and a few other instruments

One day, I was over in Asheville with my parents, and we were crossing the street. I kicked a little silk purse, and it had some skeleton keys in it and thirty-five dollars. No one ever claimed it. So, I used that thirty-five dollars to help pay for my first banjo—a little Harmony banjo. The keys would open any cedar chest that's ever been made.

I don't know how to describe the banjo other than "bubbly, bouncy." It was fun. It felt good. The fast ones were really fun to watch and hear. You could play different styles on it—but it was just the rhythmic part of it that was great. There's no other instrument that I know that has that much rhythm from these three fingers.

I love the rhythmic drive of a clawhammer banjo, but I wanted the three-finger syncopated thing of Earl Scruggs, and also Ralph Stanley, along with a few others on TV. But I also loved String Bean, who played clawhammer. It was just so much fun, and everybody around him was laughing at him, and he was laughing at himself and just playing the time out of that banjo. I can also remember that my dad and I would go out in the car and listen to the Opry because that was the best radio we had. When String Bean would come on, you could just hear over the radio the whole audience just light up. So, the banjo was a really fun instrument.

I loved Carroll Best's melodic banjo playing and tried to do some of that. And then about that time, there was the style they called chromatic. Chromatic had a lot of dissonance notes, a lot of scale notes where you just go a half-step, a fret away from each other. I started learning a lot of that. There was a banjo player with Bill Monroe when I was in high school named Jack Hicks, and he was one of the first chromatic innovators. I learned all of his breaks that he played on Bill's records. When I heard that he was going to leave Bill, that's when I went and auditioned for his job. I knew all of his breaks! So, I did get into the chromatic thing with Bill.

I'm pretty close to having perfect pitch. When I was on the road with Rhonda Vincent, Michael Cleveland played fiddle. We would play this game going up and down the road of basically "name that note." And if we heard a light fixture humming or if there was a truck with a note on the exhaust, we would try to name what that note was and find it on an instrument. Being a music major helped also.

Tablature has been a big help to learn or try to teach. It was a lot easier for me to read tablature than the actual music notes. I can look at both music and tablature and hear the tune pretty well. I can hear it in my head.

Well, "improvisation," of course, depends on what I'm doing. Actually, what's kept me working throughout the years is my ability not just to flash you with a banjo instrumental or something like that. What's kept me working out of Nashville is backing up the singer. And that was really taught to me by Jimmy Martin. He said, "Don't just listen to bluegrass and do what they do." He said, "Listen to a country record and see when the steel comes in or the fiddle comes in behind the singer." And they're not just taking a break behind the singer. They're playing—filling the holes. Backup is probably the greatest strength that I have—to be able to actually put a banjo in a country song where it adds to the song. I call it "the prettiness" of the song. You can get overwhelmed with banjo—because everybody likes to talk about the drive and all that, but I really like to be able to take it and put it in a country setting to make it pretty. I love doing that. So some of it is "this is what we're going to do." But other times, it's spontaneous, just—it's there. That's a good way to look at it.

I learn new songs easily. You know, if I'm going to record, they will send me a chart of the song that's charted out roughly with the Nashville Number System.

Probably the most influential teacher I had was my high school band teacher and mentor, Jim Crocker. I fulfilled all my requirements in high school early to where my senior year, I only had to take one English course and five periods of band. So, I hung out in the band room with Mr. Crocker

Steve Sutton, Tuscola High School Marching Band. (Photo courtesy of Juanita Sutton Hendricks)

all the time. I was still a senior in high school when I went to ask Bill Monroe for a job, and I got hired before I graduated. And when, shortly after that, I went to Nashville and started playing with Jimmy Martin, I got my first union card—they just didn't give you a union card if you paid dues. You had to be a legitimate player. On the way home from Tennessee, with my first union card, I stopped at Mr. Crocker's house to show it to him. He was the first person I wanted to show it to. I remember it was little and red, and I told him, "I got it."

Also, Jim Crocker, and one of my professors at Western, Mr. Trevarthen, scored some music for the high school band that involved the banjo and wrote charts for the band to play featuring a banjo. And we took that to Florida and won. I was playing Scruggs style. I was playing with a full band. I still have the old newspaper clippings of "Hillbillies Invade St. Petersburg." But we went down there and took the trophy. My mom's got some pictures of me in a Tuscola High band uniform with a banjo slung around my neck, marching with it.

I never had any banjo teachers. When I was first learning banjo and as I've learned banjo over the years, it hasn't been by reading music; it's just listening and doing. If I could hear it, I could figure it out and play it. It was just me. I'd take an album, of course; that was the format then. I could slow it down from 33 1/3 to 16—you're basically in tune with that, just an octave lower. I would take that and figure it out—set the needle over and play it again, set the needle and play it again. I never had anybody show me anything. I stole a lot now! That's a different thing, you know. There's no substitute for learning to play the banjo than to see it done. It was so much, "Oh, that's how they're doing it," you know.

From the time I got a banjo, I practiced religiously. I didn't have to have any prodding to practice. I just couldn't wait to get ahold of my banjo because every time I got it in my hands in those days, I learned something, something new. So, I couldn't wait to practice. God bless my parents, but I would get up and play it before breakfast, before I went to school, get home from school and play it till supper, till dinnertime, eat, do my homework, and then go back in the bedroom and shut the door. And I don't know how many times my parents have come in and taken it off of me where I had fallen asleep with it and right back the next day. And I know maybe people don't believe this, but I know it's happened to me. Maybe if I was trying to learn something or thinking about something and whatever I was working on, I—or maybe it just came out of nowhere, but I've actually had dreams of how to do something, of how to play a certain lick. I'd get up and play it. I mean, that's happened a lot.

I would damp my strings to practice so my mom and daddy couldn't hear me practicing. I would take two wooden clothespins and when you put them on each side of the bridge, it completely changes it. You could also put small electrical alligator clips on the bridge. And the volume is like cut by 80 percent. I once showed a former student that trick. Years later, he gave me his banjo and inside the case were the old clothespins that I had given him thirty years ago.

The country music of the time was the thing that we listened to when I was growing up. The radio we had was in the kitchen, and that station would be on country radio. Daddy listened to a little bit of big band. There was no jazz, no classical music.

My parents were very nurturing in my banjo—very supportive, yeah. Absolutely. Because if it was someplace I could go and had a chance to play in public, they would sacrifice time—never miss a day's work, but they would make sure that I'd get there and back.

Playing a banjo wasn't a popular thing to do when I was growing up. My friends had Elvis and the Beatles, and they were not supportive. No, I was made so much fun of because it wasn't popular with kids my age. And then what made it worse would be to go up and play, say, beside the road in Maggie Valley and dress up like a little hillbilly for the tourists and then have to go to school and hear, "Hey, we saw you with the overalls and, you know, like the clown suit and playing by the road." And then, about that time, *The Beverly Hillbillies* came out, then *Hee-Haw* and *Deliverance*. That just gave them a little bit more ammunition to make fun of me. When it really kicked in for my friends was when I was eighteen, I started doing the Opry.

I had excellent community support. Excellent. This county has really, really been good to me, good for me. It feels like home. It is home. I don't know how I could have gotten any more support from a community for what I do. There was a period of time when I thought, "Well, I've done this. I'm ready for a career change." And so, I got into landscaping and put all my instruments up, and actually put them up for sale. And my wife at the time said, "No, just play around the house?" I said, "No, if I do that and the phone rings, I'm going to be gone again, I know." So, I put them up for a couple of years, and one day I ran into a lady here, and she just said, "How selfish of you." And I said, "Excuse me?" She said, "How selfish of you to put away something that makes so many people happy." And, wow—I didn't know what to say. "How selfish of you to take that away." And I'd never thought it meant that much. Evidently, it did. And so, I got it back out.

I have said in the past that banjo players are, in general, either performers or competitors. They're two different animals, really. Competition players are totally different than performance players. The competition players generally would make good studio players. Because they think, "This is what I'm going to do, and I'm going to play the strings off it." And their material shows off everything they can do on the instrument, you know. A lot of competition players only have two or three instruments backing them up. But when you put them in a band situation, sometimes they don't know when to stop—and vice versa. And that's not saying one is better or worse than the other. They're just two different animals. And then you could also add into that mix studio players. People that are locked into that way of playing, the structure of it, and can just sit there and are so comfortable in the studio generally don't make band players at all. And as great as they are in the studio, they just—it doesn't work on stage, it doesn't come across, and vice versa. That's just an environment thing, I guess. If they're in the studio, they're locked in their zone, and it's all controlled. But to me, stage

Hillbilly Campground, Maggie Valley. Left to right, Ted Sutton (owner), Tommy Malbouf, Steve Sutton, Lloyd Sutton. Hardy Brendle (right). (Photo courtesy of Juanita Sutton Hendricks)

players, like myself, are on the edge, a little raw, you know. And there again, when I'd go in the studio, it takes me a little while to get back in the groove of that. The "touch" of the instrument is another thing. On a competition player, your instrument is set up with a very low action. If I were to take that same instrument on a stage, as hard as I play, I would play through it. I would just claw the face off of it. They set it up for finesse playing, but if you're live, you've got to have that little bit of edge, I think, a little more power. Competition players struggle with that.

I realized that I was pretty good not too long after I started playing. Well, from the time that I got my banjo, it was like six months that I was playing beside the road in Maggie. And as I got up, you know, toward ten, eleven, twelve, then I started realizing that for a summer job, I'm making money, you know—I'm bringing in pretty good money. I played at the Hillbilly Campground, which was owned by my second cousin, Ted Sutton.

He gave Raymond Fairchild his first opportunity. So, I was Little Stevie Sutton on the banjo. And, of course, they'd come and get me—I'd play alone sometimes when Raymond wasn't there and had gone off to play at another place or whatever. But I can remember my dad trusting Raymond. He would take me up there at noon, and he'd come and get me at midnight, and I'd play all day long. And we couldn't start playing on Sunday until the church bells rang. And the minute that last bell rang, I fired it up.

Playing beside the road would be like at a gift shop, a craft shop, a dish barn. You just set up wherever you were. And you would have a covered porch or maybe even a small stage, but at Ted's place, it was on the porch. And at that time, it was a two-lane road, so all the traffic had to go through Maggie Valley. And the tourists would see us and say, "Hey, let's stop here." Well, traffic would back up. There was enough room to the left or right of the two-lane where they could pull a car in and basically just sit there and watch a show like you're watching a drive-in movie. They'd stay in the car—and we'd pass the hat, go around the cars. And we'd go ask for donations. My dad taught me, "Son, if you have a crowd, you'll draw a crowd."

So, if you can ever get the first group in, everybody is going to stop to see what's going on over there, you know. So, once we drew a crowd, we had a crowd, and that's how that worked. And literally, we were out almost parking cars to get as many in there as we could, and they would just pull in up to the front porch of this business that sold crafts and drinks and stuff, snacks. And we were on the front porch with one microphone, some speakers, and play all day long. And we had—our tip jars—back in the sixties, there used to be things called Jack's Cookies. They came in great big jars. And I can remember going up there and filling one of those empty cookie jars two and a half times in a day, and then they gave me the same cut and pay that all the adults made. So when they counted the money at night, I got my share.

Earl Scruggs was an excellent positive influence on me. And knowing Earl, he couldn't have been a more gracious, calming-type personality and yet be so inventive. He was a "silent genius," in a way. He seemed so level-headed, but he was inventing styles and everything. And as I got older, I got to be around him more—I loved being around him. He was always so much fun. He was a gentle man and a gentleman. And in the business, he couldn't have been more respected. Playing with Earl was kind of a "feather in my cap."

Marc Pruett is another significant person in my career. We've been friends ever since we were kids. The first show that Marc and I ever did together was at a restaurant in Gatlinburg. My dad drove us down—I was eleven, and Marc was fifteen. And as I mentioned before, I had the Earl Scruggs book. Well, Marc didn't, and it was really difficult to get. And so, Marc would call me on the phone, and we'd be playing notes over the phone to each other, and then he would borrow my book and give it back. So, we basically grew up together playing in this county. And I guess people would think there was a lot of competition between us, but we're two totally different animals, you know. So, he would have been one of my best friends growing up and playing.

Marc Pruett (foreground) and Steve Sutton. Marc Pruett is fretting the left hand for Steve Sutton's banjo and Steve is fretting the left hand for Marc's banjo. The song was usually "Cripple Creek" or "Foggy Mountain Breakdown." (Photo courtesy of Juanita Sutton Hendricks)

I was fortunate that I never had to play in bad bands or in bands really with anybody my age growing up. I was always with older people, and one being Ralph Lewis, along with Arvil Freeman and Don Humphries and Larry Holcomb, from over here in Asheville.

I played the Grand Ole Opry the first time in 1974. I was seventeen or eighteen years old, and 1974 was the year that they moved to the Opry House from the Ryman. I remember just being backstage. When you're eighteen, you're just bulletproof, you know. I had no fear. "Let me out there." Now, probably, I would get more stage fright. I remember that once I stepped into that twelve-foot circle of wood, you were just like, "Here's for all my heroes, you know." And that was really—it was awesome.

Well, after Earl, I kind of had that feather in my cap that certainly was something. I wasn't really in a bluegrass band at that time. I was still playing beside the road in Maggie. Then, I got involved with Ralph Lewis over in Asheville, and he had been friends with Bill Monroe. So therefore, if I went to any festivals with them when I was young, you know, fifteen—I grew up around the Osborne Brothers and Bill Monroe and Jimmy Martin, and they all knew me. By the time I asked them for a job, they had seen me grow up at these festivals playing.

Bill Monroe and Jimmy Martin were important for me. And then the Osborne Brothers kind of took me under their wing. They knew what it was like out there on the road in the seventies, you know. There's a lot of it that's pretty rough. And so, they kind of made sure that I was doing okay at these festivals and trying to keep my head in the right place. I was pretty lucky to be around that. So, I was doing the college in the winter and those festivals in the summer.

When I got out of college the next fall, 1978, there was a restaurant that opened in Asheville, a barbecue place called Bill Stanley's Barbecue and Bluegrass. The band there was composed of Marc Pruett, banjo, Mike Hunter, mandolin, and Randy Davis, bass. They lost their guitar player early on and came to me and asked if I would play guitar. The band was called the Marc Pruett Band. And the reason we named it that is because Marc was more in debt than anybody else and he'd be the last one to quit, and so we figured the name would stay! [Marc Pruett has described the band's playing schedule in his biography below.] We held onto that for ten years and finally, mutually just decided to disband on Labor Day in 1988.

After I left Bill Stanley's, I played some with Ronnie Milsap. Then I was kind of out of a job. While I was in college, I played with a Southern Railroad band, the Southern Lawmen, and when they merged railroads, it was the Norfolk Southern Lawmen. And you lived on a train five months out of the year. I remember counting up the nights that I was out of my own bed that year—it was 282 days. After that, I stayed around here just playing, doing a lot of local things.

And then, probably '98 or '99, a call from Rhonda Vincent got it all kick-started again. I wound up playing with her about two and a half seasons, I think. I wanted to get married, and plus, there was "the road"—the last year that I was on the road with her, I was out of my bed 330 days. And she said, "We'll take the month of December off to be with our families." Well, she put in for the Opry every weekend. That's not taking the month off, you know. That meant I might have to drive down to Nashville and play two songs and drive back. I don't know how many times I've done that. Or if you had the show on the Saturday Opry, you did two segments, which was four songs, and drive back home. After that, I decided, well, I'm going to get off the road for a while and get into landscaping.

Then, around 2003–2004, Alicia Nugent called and I played with her band about three years. She said, "I know that you're kind of out of the business, but I've got the Grand Ole Opry this weekend." This was on Wednesday she called. That's when the Opry always makes their schedule out. So, I called her back and I said, "Yeah, I'll come down." And then she said, "Do you know a mandolin player?" I knew Darren Nicholson. He and I had played together in some gospel bands. And so, we went down, and I got Darren on the Opry the first time—she put together a great band. Well, the next Wednesday, the phone rings again. Alicia said, "I've got the Opry again—and bring that guy that played the mandolin." So, we went back the next weekend and then is when she asked me to be her band manager and put together a band. And that's what we did, and then stayed with that about three seasons.

Well, it's like the playing is the reward for all the travel. I remember—it was Woody Guthrie or Arlo. I remember him introducing himself one time on stage, "Hi, I'm Arlo Guthrie, and I travel for a living, and every now and then, I stop and play some music." But that's really, truly what it was. The hardest thing to me, you've got to work, as any family would, to travel in a bus. I don't care if it's a forty-, forty-eight-footer. You're basically in a tube going up and down the highway with four other people, or five, that you have to get along with. And you sleep with them. You eat with them. You perform with them. You shower with them. You've got to have that right combination to stay on the road because it's not, by any means, all glitz and glamour.

I've played in Germany and Switzerland and Italy. Been over there a couple times. Believe it or not, bluegrass is really big there.

Getting up for the show, that—that's usually not that difficult, truthfully, because once you get there, you start feeling a little adrenaline and all. You know, to me, the hardest thing, the older I got, was the format they use at bluegrass festivals where you do two performances a day. Those I don't like. But say if you play at three in the afternoon and then nine o'clock at night, what do you do for six hours? And, you know, there again, you're kind of like in competition with yourself. If you're doing two a day at a festival, almost always one show would be better than the other, and it might be the first one. It may be the second one. And those to me when you do two sets there that day, then you drive all night, get to another place and you do two sets there, and then another place. I would rather just stay on stage for an hour and a half. And, you know, to me the most important thing about having a bus was not the travel from one city to another as it was a place to go to between shows. To go and eat and get away from the people, sleep, you know, something, watch TV, you know, anything.

When Darren and I left Alicia Nugent and came home, Balsam Range started forming, and I went to work with Whitewater Bluegrass over here in Asheville. So it's been quite a ride, yeah.

Sometimes, it's perfect. There are times when I walk off stage and just— and I'll say to whoever is with me, "What did we just do? God, that felt so good. How did that happen?" It doesn't happen often. No, those—you know, and I wish in a way there were more, but probably it's a good thing there aren't more because it might become old then. It's like I like ice cream, but after three gallons, I wouldn't. Sometimes they come from, for me, anyway, they come from some of the strangest combinations.

Now, I try to play every night. I'll take it back and sit on the edge of the bed and play along—even with the TV on, but I'll put in a good hour or so every night. When you've got a challenge or a new band or a session and stuff, of course, you've got to work on that. But the older I get, I go back to the basics lots of times. I mean, I'll go back to that old Earl Scruggs book. I'll drift too far from shore maybe, you know, and I'll go back to the basics sitting up there practicing.

"Makin' music" was always associated with a good time. It was generally associated, to me, with something else going on—"Come over to the house, we'll make some music while we do something else. Yeah, let's go make some music." All my life. It just happened. It was everywhere in the county. But making music is just a great big good time, you know.

I consider myself more of a showman than just a banjo player. And, you know, sometimes I might sacrifice technique or different things to actually portray it as being better than it is. All the years when I was growing up, if I ever went to a festival, everybody dropped what they were doing to go catch Jimmy Martin's show. You know, he didn't just get up there and play technically all the time—he was also a showman, and I just learned that from him. I'd call it "eyewash"—stealing the crowd. And that is just to—just absolutely make it look like I'm doing ten times more than I am. I can almost do this just playing one note, you know—that's showmanship. Roy Clark was another showman, and he could sell it. My stage persona is happy-go-lucky. I don't want people to look at me, as I see some other players, where it looks like it's a chore for them to play, where they're just so concentrated, like they're at work, like they're not having any fun playing, like it's a chore. That's the last thing I want anybody to think when they see me playing. I want them to think, "I'm not going to have fun unless he's having fun." So if I'm having fun, they'll have fun.

I wouldn't have had a career had it not been for Earl Scruggs. I owe everything I am and have and own or lost to Earl Scruggs. I would not have been around the world. I've been in forty-nine states. I've traveled. I've been blessed to make a living with it. I've made some of the best friends that I'll ever have with musicians and fans. I love it as much today as I ever did. It's just become so much a part of me. It's given me a lot of fun, joy, hard times, and struggles. It's been everything to me. Can't imagine anything else. I hope that when people think of me, they will think of a good time. I want to be remembered with, "We're going to have fun now."

And I don't know what I would have turned out as had it not been for the banjo. I just can't imagine—I can't imagine putting it away, why I would want to ever put it away. It's just become so much a part of me. What I'm associated with is a banjo. And at the same time, I'm hoping that when people think of it and me, I want it to be associated with, "We're going to have fun now."

And I just think it's made me who and what I am by giving me all those experiences to travel and go and do and be blessed to be able to make a living with it. Can't imagine anything else.

Steve died unexpectedly in May 2017.

MARC PRUETT

Marc Pruett was born in 1951 and was sixty-one years old when interviewed.

Well, define a "great" or "gifted" banjo player? I don't know if I know a definitive answer. That would certainly be subjective in many ways. But I think that if a person makes the best of the aptitude that they have, if they have a passion for what they're doing music-wise, certainly, that's a gift. I think passion and direction would be considered as much of a gift as aptitude would be. Gosh, all the other folks that I have named are about that way, too. They love it, and they keep moving into it. That would have to be one component of whatever greatness is. A lot of people, like myself, who were born into the rural Appalachian South, were in an environment where we heard Earl Scruggs. I was not in a place, for example, to hear jazz musicians like Charlie Parker or some of the other greats in New York. But you bloom where you're planted, I guess.

My earliest remembrance of music would probably be songs that my mother sang. I would sit by her in church, and she would sing hymns from the old red book that a lot of people remember. I listened to a lot of different music as a boy. It was constantly on radio and TV. I was immersed in it but pretty well stayed with bluegrass music all the way through up until now. But I made little side treks to a lot of different types of music; mostly it would be under the heading of country music. I loved old-style country music. I was just a huge fan.

My brother was a big rock and roll fan, so I heard all his records. When the Beatles came out in 1964, I was thirteen. That same year there was a rock and roll star named Conway Twitty who had metamorphosed from rock and roll into country music. My mother took me to see him that year at the old Asheville City Auditorium. We used to go listen to other performances at the City Auditorium. My mother took me to the shows because she knew how much I loved and cared about it. My mother also listened to classical music. My dad loved jazz and a lot of old swing band music. I remember going once with Hal Strain [then-owner of the Strains of Music store in Waynesville; see chapter 12] to hear Count Basie at Western Carolina University. Ours was a home full of music.

The first banjo stuff that I ever remember hearing, I was probably nine or ten. I would get home from school, and my mother would let us hear the radio and have a snack for thirty minutes or so before we did our homework. There was a little radio station in Waynesville, and there was an afternoon program on there called "The Cornbread Matinee." [A few of the other banjo players in this book recalled listening to the program.] I used to love to listen to it. It was country music, bluegrass—all of it. Back then, bluegrass was a component of country music.

One day, I heard the music of Lester Flatt and Earl Scruggs, and I heard that banjo. It was just like magic. It just jumped into my heart, you know. And I could feel it saying, "That's part of who you are too, Bud." I felt it, you know. There was a perfection in it that, frankly, I have never heard equaled. I will be sixty-two years old this year, and I can say very clearly that I still haven't heard it equaled. It was pure. It was perfect. It gave my life a quality that few things have. I had never seen a banjo or recall hearing one prior to that. I got a little banjo for Christmas in 1962 when I was eleven years old.

With all these years of retrospection, there were several components of the banjo that, from a human nature standpoint, spoke to me. Scruggs's banjo playing had a timing—I could just hear that "tic-ah-tic-ah-tic-ah-tic." It was magic. And it was syncopated in the way that he did it. But also, he had a unique instrument—the tone of Scruggs's banjo was remarkable. It was unique, and it allowed him to play every little nuance. I have tapes of me playing Scruggs's banjo in 1982. You could touch it with your right hand and do a hammer-on or a slide [demonstrates]—beautiful sustained, the notes didn't die, and I get chills thinking about it. The banjo worked, his hands worked, he had wonderful timing, he knew how to bring the volume out right, and it was just a beautiful thing, the real thing.

I was out in the country and had a bicycle and a newspaper route like a lot of kids in those days—*The Grit* newspaper. They would ship them to me once a week. I would buy them for a dime and sell them for fifteen cents, so I made a nickel a paper. That's how I saved up my money to buy Flatt and Scruggs records and Bill Monroe.

My little banjo, which I had gotten when I was eleven years old, sat in the corner basically and gathered dust for two years. It absolutely frustrated me to no end. I felt like I had something in my heart. I listened to it. I listened to those records. I remember sitting on my bed with tears in my eyes, feeling that it was in my hands, but I didn't know what to do. And my mother would show me a few little things—she knew some of the Stephen Foster songs and I knew how to tune my banjo to a C and I would play the C, F, and G7 on "There is a Tavern in the Town" and some of the old gospel tunes, maybe.

The first song that I learned to play on the banjo was the old Stephen Foster song, "Way Down upon the Swanee River." My mother would sit at the kitchen table and hum it and I would pick it out with one finger, one note at a time, till I could get the notes of it. I didn't know the names of the notes. I played it until it sounded like the notes that she was singing. That's the way I did it. But I didn't know how to put the three fingers [right-hand roll] with it. Then later, I learned a few chords from a little book. Up to that time, I never took any lessons.

It seems as if my parents took me to a square dance in Maggie Valley, where I was able to meet French Kirkpatrick [also in this book]. He was, early on, particularly helpful to me. My mother begged him, "You just don't know how this boy wants to learn to play. Will you help him?" So, I developed a friendship with him, and he taught me. Sometimes we would just sit and listen to records. He and my daddy would drink coffee, and we would laugh and talk. Sometimes, he would show me how to play a little tune or passage. Or he would say, "You need to listen to such and such record." Or he would play, and I would just watch him. Sometimes, it was more of a social visit than what you would call a lesson. I would sit in our car on the way home after a lesson trying so hard not to forget what I had learned before I got home. I didn't know how to write it down in tablature. I would try to keep it in my head. I would get home and try to play it again. Sometimes, I would get part of it and another part of it. Sometimes, I would go back the next week and say, "How did you say to do this?" I learned from watching his hand positions and him telling me what to do. I had no idea what some of those little chords were that he was playing. I wanted to follow more of the Scruggs style of playing. French, in retrospect, had

knowledge, not only of Scruggs style but of other styles as well. He knows
a lot of music. I wanted to develop more into the Scruggs and J. D. Crowe
"power picking" style. I was with French for about a year, and he taught
me power picking.

In addition to my friendship with French, I developed a friendship
with the Conard boys. About late '63 or '64, when I was really searching,
I had met them in Stamey Cove, Larry and Jim Conard. I would go listen
to them, and they would let me kind of struggle on and, in retrospect, I
am sure that they were frustrated with my novice efforts. They knew Mike
Pressley [also in this book] and they introduced me to him. Mike was a
couple of years older than me. Well, Mike was easier for me to get to. It
was a long way, but I could walk there. I could go over there and spend
half a day and hang out.

Then there was another banjo player, Shorty Eager. I have found in certain people things that I love that they do, and I seek it to the depth that
I can achieve while still looking in all directions to try to hear something
different that is maybe more. French, Mike, and Shorty were the Haywood
County boys who helped me most. They were really important in my development as a banjo player.

Earl Scruggs published his book, *Earl Scruggs and the 5-String Banjo*,
in 1967, and that was a "eureka" moment for all of us. It was like handing
a kid a bag of candy. It was great, but it was frustrating at the same time
because there were also a lot of mistakes in that book. The second edition
of the book corrected a lot of stuff.

I listened to records over and over and over and over and, back then,
it took some imagination. But with the old records, you could slow a 33
record down half to 16 or a 45 down to 33—the slower, the lower the tone,
especially 33 to 16, which was much lower [demonstrates]. You had to use
some imagination as to what the notes were at the slower rpms. Going from
45 to 33 was a little less demanding. [Current technology makes it possible
to slow the tempo of a song yet maintain the tone.]

My family first had to learn to put up with my banjo because they loved
me, I guess. I beat my family to death with bluegrass. I beat them to death
with it. Then they learned to enjoy it, recognized my ability, and learned
to support it. Although he was more accepting, early on, of more styles of
music, my brother loved it too. I had friends make fun of me because I liked
Flatt and Scruggs. But never did I waver from my dedication to the music
I loved. A lot of my friends thought that what I was doing was really great.
A lot of them did. That's who you gravitate to. My community recognized
me as well.

A buzzword that we would use today is "networking." And, oh my good-
ness, I was a networker. If I could, I'd be the first one to get there and the last
one to leave. I wanted to know everything that went on with bluegrass music.

Oh gosh, I practiced as much as I could—a couple of hours a night on
school nights. And on weekends, I'd play all day long on Saturdays up into
the night. Played on Sundays. Nobody ever told me to practice or made me
practice. I chose it as my own and made it happen. I'm that guy that made
it happen. I would play for hours on end.

Steve Sorrells was a school bus driver when Marc was in the ninth grade.
He relates:

> When I stopped in the morning to pick up Marc, he'd be standing
> there at the school bus stop, waiting on the school bus, playing his
> banjo and practicing, and then he would take the banjo to school
> with him and in the afternoon, he could play it on the school bus—I
> let him play it on the school bus. I told the kids on the bus that if
> they would be quiet, I would let Marc play his banjo—they would get
> just as quiet! In the evening, I can clearly remember him getting off
> the school bus, putting the banjo strap around his neck and walking
> to his house practicing on the banjo. So he played it a lot, I know."[1]

I knew how important my family unit was—my mom and dad and
my brother. I had good parents. They gave me good structure, good tight
parameters. I'm lucky. I was given opportunities that a lot of kids weren't.
My parents didn't have a lot, money-wise, but I learned what a positive
attitude was. Music was very high in my priorities. Church was, too. You
know, I didn't play ball. Once I felt the intense gratification that the act of
playing music can give you, I wanted more. But once that banjo hit me, it
was the demanding thing in my life. I served it.

In 1967, I was hired to play at Ghost Town [at the time, a large, popular
Wild West theme park in Maggie Valley, near Waynesville; see chapter 2],
a crucible for mountain musicians to come to. I was fifteen years old, so
I couldn't even drive up there. My parents took me there or some friends
did. That experience seasoned me pretty good.

August 1967, three months after starting playing at Ghost Town, was
another turning point for me because I met a guy named Tom McKinney
at the Bascom Lamar Lunsford Folk Festival [now the Bascom Lamar
Lunsford "Minstrel of Appalachia" Folk Festival, which continues annu-
ally in Mars Hill, North Carolina; see chapter 12] who changed my life. He
was one of the first people that I ever saw who had that hunger all the way

through. And he knew the Scruggs-style picking, he knew bluegrass music. I thought, "There is what I'm after." Once I found Tom McKinney, I had come to the top, definitive power picker. He had it. I spent many a Saturday at Tom McKinney's house. I get chills thinking about my exposure to him. He was quite a volatile person and can be hard to get along with. But for some reason, he liked me. He became my friend, and I would just hang out with him. He would take me to shows. The first time I ever played on the Jimmy Martin show, Tom McKinney had taken me to the old Lake Norman Music Hall, maybe '68 or '69. Jimmy got me up on the stage with them to play "Train 45." And I recall that I really laid into it good. In summary, Tom McKinney put his arm around me in a symbolic way, and I learned—I took fledgling banjo music to a whole different dimension once I met him. That was when it all began to come together for me.

My mother had made me a little business card that she had printed up at the Canton paper. I remember thinking that they were so special because they were two-color and they had rounded corners, and they just said "Marc Pruett, 5 String Banjo," along with my home address and a telephone number. I gave Jimmy Martin one of those. When I was in college, he called me—I was one of the banjo players he kept in his shirt pocket. [laughs]

Well, in many ways, when I was fifteen, the exposure at Ghost Town really put me out there, at least regionally, because they had people from all over the world coming there. There was a banjo player from Monroe, North Carolina, named L. W. Lambert. He would come to Ghost Town. He was a wonderful three-finger bluegrass Scruggs-style banjo player. He was a contest player, had a fine bluegrass band, and won a lot of contests playing his version of "Beer Barrel Poker." I could say, "L. W., how do you play that?" He'd sit right down and show me. He's my friend still today. I don't see him much, but L. W. Lambert was an inspiration to me when I was fifteen.

I played three full summers at Ghost Town—'67, '68, and '69. And then I started in the summer of 1970, but there was not a place for me in the band that year. I had played in a little college band, The Tilley Creek Ramblers, in the winter of '69 and '70. One of the band members, Buddy Davis, subsequently became the entertainment director at Gold City [a Ghost Town mimic in Franklin, North Carolina]. I passed him on the interstate one day. I was going one way, and he was going the other. I felt that I needed to catch up with him—they might need a banjo player at Gold City. I cut across the four-lane as fast as I could go, and I caught him, stopped him, and asked if there was a place for me at Gold City. The Gold City manager, Andy Smalls, was a big Type A personality—he liked me, he befriended me, he liked what I did. Andy Smalls took me places and got me some TV appearances. I was his banjo guy. I went from making seventy dollars a week to making ninety dollars a week—and playing fewer shows. I lived in an apartment on top of the Gold City Saloon in a beautiful mountain setting—it was fabulous, it was absolutely—you talk about "golden years" of a kid's life. It was golden.

Well, I knew that I had my own little thing—and I made it work for me. I paid for a quarter of my college, my music paid for a half, and my dad paid for the other quarter. I never paid anybody that I ever learned from for a lesson. My mother may have sent them some strawberries, a pound of coffee. I just learned it the old-time way—through osmosis.

I was a regional player until I was in college. In the summer of 1973, James Monroe, at the suggestion of Tom McKinney, called me and offered me a job. It opened the world up to me, and I accepted it. I had played on stage some with Jimmy Martin at that time, and I knew other people and things would bubble up and spike for me over the years—great little things. But James Monroe came along and held me there. I got to be with Bill Monroe, I got to be with Lester Flatt, I got to be with Ralph Stanley, Jim and Jesse, all the greats, all the first-generation greats. I was a young peer. I was accepted in that circle at that time because, technically I was a professional banjo player. I was still in college.

When "Will the Circle Be Unbroken?" became such an astounding success, Bill Monroe approached MCA records about doing his own compilation album and in the summer of 1973, in June, I think it was, at his festival in Brown County, Indiana, Bean Blossom Bluegrass Festival, they recorded a live album. Lester Flatt, Jimmy Martin, Jim and Jesse, Carl Jackson, James Monroe were on that album. I was with James Monroe on all four of the songs that James did. James Monroe introduced me personally on that album. I don't know how many people I've had say, "I first heard about you from on the *Bean Blossom* album." You know, bluegrass fans being the total fans, that was my subculture introduction to all those people.

I was first on the Grand Ole Opry in October 1973 or ['7]4. It was maybe the last year that they had it at the Ryman. I played with Jimmy Martin down there—I think it was '73. It was exciting.

Back then, they had what they called the DJ Convention in Nashville. It was two weekends with a week-long in between. All the country DJs would converge on Nashville and showcase all the country music artists at the old Noel Hotel. All of the bluegrass stars had a wing—The Country Gentlemen, Don Reno, Bill Monroe—they were all there. You could just take your banjo, walk up and down the hall, and jam with different people. I can remember sitting with Don Reno on a couch—the great Don Reno! I was just a kid.

The Grammy Award has been a blessing. I played on five albums with Ricky Skaggs, including his first album in 1974. The Grammy was with Ricky Skaggs in *Bluegrass Rules!* in 1997–98. You know, that's top of the top in the music world. I played all the banjo on that album. When I was playing with Ricky Skaggs, he would sometimes practice all day long with the band. I can remember a lot of times practicing with him five or six hours, then go do the show. You'd wear out a brand-new set of strings in a day and would have to restring before you did the show.

I played at Bill Stanley's Barbecue [a barbecue and bluegrass restaurant in Asheville, North Carolina] from October 1, 1979, to September 1988. I did three to four shows a night, six nights a week. Then I would practice some during the day. For ten years, I probably easily played four to five hours a day. Trying to work up new material, we practiced a lot, and there were many days, many days, especially Saturdays, when Bill Stanley would do catering jobs, and we would play two catering jobs, two to three sets the first and two to three sets the second in the afternoon and then three to four sets that night—many times we would do ten to eleven sets a day. It was unbelievably intense.

In 2007, Buddy Melton, Darren Nicholson, Caleb Smith, Tim Surrett, and myself formed a band, Balsam Range. All of the band members live in Haywood County. We have been remarkably successful to the present time. [See chapter 12.]

Finally, I had the honorary Doctor of Arts degree bestowed by Western Carolina University in May 2010. I had some really good people pulling for me. Rhonda Vincent actually wrote a recommendation for me. I played on her first number one album in bluegrass music.

I play three-finger Scruggs style. I can play clawhammer, but it has always been tough for me. I can play melodic. Band music, with the dynamics of the whole band, rising and falling at the right place, and with great vocals, is something. It will change your life—it's truly—words can't describe how that affects you.

I read tablature, but I never learned to read music. I'll tell you this, I can take you to the place, right now, where in the seventh grade, I knew that I was walking away from formal music training. I had a cousin, Bill Holtzclaw, who was the band director at Bethel School. He wanted me to learn to play the clarinet and the time kept going on in the school year and it came down, one day, to saying "yes" or "no." And I stood right there on that bank, and I knew that the banjo called me deeper. But I remember telling him, kind of hanging my head and saying, "Well, Mr. Holtzclaw, I think I am just going to try to stay with my banjo and learn how to play that." And at that point, it cut me from formally learning music, and that still hurts me today. I knew. It happened to me early. I don't know why but I knew what I was giving up.

I can sit down and probably play hundreds of songs from memory. I could tap back into them. I'm not going to say that I could play it flawlessly, but I'm familiar with a lot of songs. When you play for a lifetime, when you love it for a lifetime—you grow up in lots of jam sessions, lots of Fridays and Saturdays, lots of weeknights.

I learned more hand positions than notes. Now, they all have—each fret, each string has a musical note, as you know, but since I'm playing so fast, I don't equate it to individual notes. I can't think that fast. It's just a position. If you know where you are starting, you can then go to the next positions. You don't always have to know the notes, although I know most of the notes. I'm not sure that I can "see" notes as well as others. I am open-minded enough to know that some banjo players, French Kirkpatrick, for instance, can "see" real melodic fiddle songs—they can hear it, see it, visualize it, but my mind doesn't really think that way—too much depth.

If you play what you know and you play it with power, you are always going to appear credible. If, for example, I tried now to play "Red Haired Boy," someone who heard it would ask why you are interviewing me. You have to know your limits in order to present well. Plus, not all banjo playing is achievable for me. I've thought about that. It may be that I am just not that interested in certain aspects of it. Some of it doesn't captivate me.

I have never drooled on my banjo [laughs]—not that I can remember. But I can tell you what I have done on it—I have sweated on it. That speaks to the depth of concentration that you can go to, that you totally lose feeling of your physical consciousness. You don't really pay attention to yourself. Just what you hear, what your feel—there's a wonderful flow of creativity—I guess I can say that—something's happening. I don't know what it is. I can see that happening.

It's hard to say what it feels like when I am playing the banjo. There are so many things to think about. Sometimes, my banjo playing goes on automatic pilot—too much of the time it goes on automatic pilot—and I perform to a level that is adequate and probably 999 people out of a thousand would not know the difference. I try to work on the entertainment facets—smiling around a little bit, interacting with the other band members, acknowledging somebody in the audience—trying to make a total connection. I need to work more on that fluid musicality that really comes when you play your break, and it's just total heart and total feeling—I'm trying to reach that more now.

There are times when knowledge and practice come together perfectly. It rolls up in you, and you know that you know. That is "priceless" and "a purifying experience," a very purifying experience. I don't have that as much anymore as I did when I was younger. When I was young and I would play seven to eight hours a day, especially with the Conard boys, I could come home and it would feel like a religious experience had just happened. It was like being "saved" in the church or just like really being washed completely clean—it was wonderful. Sometimes when I play at home now, I come close to that old feeling.

A fitting summary of Marc's career comes from his Western Carolina University Honorary D. Arts proclamation. A portion reads:

> Marc Reagan Pruett, your musical accomplishments alone are exemplary and worthy of great acclaim, but let it be noted that during your musical career you truly have been an ambassador with a banjo as you have traveled the world, representing your university, your mountains and your people with outstanding humor, warmth and personality. You have carved your own niche as one of Western North Carolina's great cultural icons and as a beloved son of the mountains. . . .[2]

Chapter 14

THE FUTURE

It is clear that "makin' music" is a major cultural phenomenon in Haywood County. There have been changes over the lifetimes of the banjo players in this book that have diluted its in-home folkway roots, but significant remnants remain. This chapter will explore some of these changes and look to the future.

POPULATION DYNAMICS

The population of an area is determined by "natural increase" (births minus deaths) plus "in-" and "out-migration." The Haywood County estimated 2020 population is 63,813. The population in 1980 was 46,495 and had increased to only 46,942 in 1990. In each of the ensuing decades beginning in 1990, there have been major population increases,[1] all due to net in-migration. Similar trends are projected out to 2040. The 1980 >65-year-old age group represented roughly 13.5% of the population compared to the 2018 >65-year-old age group, which represents roughly 24% of the population, the population clearly aging.[2] Using current "urban-rural population density" criteria, the 2010 population of Haywood County is roughly 55.4% rural and 44.6% urban.[3] The county "feels" more rural than that.

    The large net in-migration change in Haywood County began in the 1970s and has continued to the present day. The advent of tourism in the 1950s and 1960s allowed Haywood County to be "discovered," contributing to the subsequent striking in-migration.[4] Haywood County migration estimates for 2012–2016 show an in-migration of roughly four thousand people. Florida is the major source of in-migration from outside of North Carolina. There was an out-migration of roughly three thousand people.[5]

SEASONAL HOUSING AND PROPERTY OWNERSHIP

Seasonal housing and property ownership is another measure of population dynamics. In 1980, there were roughly one thousand Haywood County seasonal housing units. In 2015, that number had increased to roughly 5,500.[6] The great preponderance of seasonal housing is used primarily as summer vacation or second homes but also includes rentals to people who come to Haywood County to escape the summer heat. Most of the people who rent these houses are from the Southeast, especially Florida, as are most of the seasonal housing owners.[7]

There were, in 2014, approximately fifty thousand Haywood County property owners, roughly 75% located in North Carolina and 50% in Haywood County. The remainder, not surprisingly, included 14% located in Florida and smaller percentages in neighboring states and elsewhere.[8]

Additional population details are presented below, in the Appendix: Additional Demographics, in the section on population dynamics (pages 218–20).

AGRICULTURE DATA

Recall that "makin' music" is a largely rural phenomenon. The total number of farms in Haywood County has decreased from 1,309 in 1969 to 541 in 2017, and farm acreage has decreased from 112,169 acres to 52,244 acres in the same time period. Slightly more than half of the farms over the years have totaled fewer than fifty acres. Only about one-third of farm producers (formerly "operators") have, over the years, listed farming as their primary occupation.[9] A large percentage of decreases in farm numbers and farm acreage has been due to the conversion of the agricultural land to private real estate and to real estate development.

SCHOOL CONSOLIDATION

A major Haywood County milestone occurred in 1966 with county school consolidation. It was a contentious issue. Seven County high schools were merged into two new high schools—Tuscola, in Waynesville and Pisgah, in Canton. A new elementary school was added, and junior high school districts were redefined. Over the ensuing years, elementary schools were consolidated and upgraded. Consolidation meant that "schools in rural communities would close, and at that time, community identity was tied to successful sporting teams, school plays and other activities at the school that pulled people together."[10] Although consolidation proved to be, overall, a success, the downsides for some of the rural communities were significant. Many of the students from the 1966 rural communities came from "a different kind of life,"[11] and adjustment to the new schools was not easy for many of them.[12] These rural areas, as shown in this book, are associated with a strong "makin' music" in-home folkway. Indeed, rural schools were specifically recognized by a couple of the banjo players as being places of significant exposure to the banjo. "You know, at the school when they would have those [musical programs]—I can remember French Kirkpatrick playing, Carroll Best, and they just—you know, they just made it so lively and that was—that was what I wanted. The sound and the rhythm." **(Tracy Best b. 1963/52)** Consolidation has probably had, overall, a less-than-positive impact on the county's in-home folkway, including the banjo.

CHURCHES

The importance of the church in the in-home folkway has been mentioned in part II. Yet, church attendance in Haywood County, particularly in rural churches, has, in general, significantly decreased over the years. It is, for a number of reasons, difficult to assess church attendance data and the data vary by the parameter analyzed. Haywood County Baptist Association data suggest that between 2004–2016, Baptist church attendance decreased by, very roughly, 25%.[13] Data from the Methodist churches in Haywood County, using a different method of computation but a similar time frame, shows overall worship attendance down roughly 19%, with a markedly greater decrease in the rural churches.[14] More of the young people, including rural young people, seem to be increasingly going to the larger urban and suburban churches in the county or not going to church at all.

MOUNTAIN DANCE

A couple of the banjo players have noted the striking decrease in the number of mountain "dance teams," which, as has been shown, have a striking positive relationship with mountain music, particularly the banjo. One of the banjo players noted that two of his elementary schoolchildren had, a couple of years ago, dropped out of "clog dancing" so that they could pursue volleyball and football.

DRUGS

The prescription drug/heroin problem is a major crisis in these mountains and elsewhere. It is obviously not good for the banjo or for anything else.

All these factors certainly raise concerns about the future of the banjo in Haywood County. With the advent of phonographs, radio, and the automobile in the early twentieth century, the "isolated" communities are essentially no longer isolated and cultural dilution of the in-home folkway of earlier generations has increased. There has been, over recent decades, significant population growth, with a marked relative increase in elderly citizens. The population in-migration is due, to a significant degree, to retirees, a large number of whom are from out of state, particularly Florida. While in-migration, as well as "seasonal" population changes, certainly bring outside strengths with them, they also bring challenges. The population has become increasingly less rural. Historical pillars of society, including rural life, communities, and churches, are continuing to undergo significant changes.

Despite the serious concerns about the banjo's future in Haywood County, there are also significant positive developments.

MAKIN' MUSIC

Makin' music, and the joy that it brings, persist in Haywood County, although it is not as widespread as in the past.

ELECTRONIC MEDIA

The explosion of media, from radio to television to the internet, has been astonishing. At times, it has had a negative impact on the banjo. On the other hand, it has also been helpful. A local FM radio station has daily offerings of mountain/bluegrass music, including several hours on Saturdays. Regarding the banjo, the internet has, in recent years, played a very positive role by increasing exposure to banjo music, not only in old-time and bluegrass but also melodic to avant-garde banjo music. It has also provided numerous sites and aids for learning to play the banjo. If one did not get to hear Earl Scruggs play in person, he and vast numbers of other banjo players could now be heard (and seen!) on YouTube. On the other hand, Travis Stuart and others have mentioned the importance of listening to and watching live music and having the opportunity for face-to-face interchanges with the musicians.

MUSIC VENUES

There are, in Haywood County, several venues for live banjo and other mountain/bluegrass music. The summertime Pickin' in the Park in Canton offers weekly opportunities to hear mountain/bluegrass music and also in scattered jam sessions to "make music." The annual Fines Creek Bluegrass Jam and the fall Smoky Mountain Folk Festival (now in its fiftieth year) offer two days of excellent mountain/bluegrass music. Waynesville also has, during the summer, a number of street dances on Friday evenings. Joe Sam Queen, following in the footsteps of his grandfather, has played a major role in the Smoky Mountain Folk Festival and also leads the Friday street dances.

UNIVERSITY PROGRAM

There is now a Bachelor of Arts program in Bluegrass, Old-Time, and Country Music Studies at East Tennessee State University. This is the first degree program of its kind in the world. One of the banjo players in this book, Travis Stuart, is a faculty member of this program.

SHAPED-NOTE SINGING

The annual shaped-note singing in Dutch Cove has already been discussed. It is a cultural treasure. Morning Star United Methodist Church, the home church of the late Quay Smathers, has recently been honored as a site on the Blue Ridge Music Trails and holds a shaped-note "sing" in spring, late summer, and fall. The annual shaped-note school hosted by June Smathers-Jolley, one of the banjo players in this book, and her sister has been mentioned in her biography.

FOLKMOOT

For over thirty years, Waynesville has hosted an international folk dance festival, Folkmoot. This three-week festival in early summer hosts a dozen or so folk dance teams from around the world. Over the years, more than two hundred groups from one hundred countries have participated. Local dance teams from Haywood County have also participated in the cultural and musical interchange. Future plans call for increased participation by Haywood County dancers. This, of course, also means increased participation of Haywood County musicians, including banjo players.

THE YOUNG PEOPLE

Then there are the young people.

The Junior Appalachian Music (JAM) after-school program has, for years, nurtured young musicians in mountain and bluegrass music and continues to do so. As noted above, a new bluegrass band, Possum on a Whale, composed of JAM alumni, is now performing locally and has released its first CD.

ANDREW MEDLIN

Andrew Medlin was sixteen years old when interviewed and had been in the JAM program for four or five years. He has an open back banjo and plays clawhammer style. He also likes to sing. He learned to play the banjo, like most of the others in this book, by ear. His teacher, Travis Stuart, played note by note and showed him where to put his left-hand fingers and how to play the strings with his right hand, "hearing the notes and playing them out." Over the next several months, he "got better at it" and can now play a song if he can "hear it." Andrew practices one to three hours a day. When asked what it feels like playing the banjo, he answered with one word, "heaven," and, from time to time, has experienced a "flow state" while playing. He had recently played on stage, at the local county fair, for the first time. He and his mentor, Travis Stuart, played for some dancers.

He says that he would probably not give up the banjo "for anything" and continues, at age eighteen, to love playing the banjo. He is "makin' music" with friends in Burnsville. He wants to be an electrician and is waiting to hear about an electrician "apprenticeship" application that he has submitted. He is engaged to be married in a year or so.

He also enjoys the outdoors, including hiking up in the mountains, as well as trout fishing and occasionally hunting.

RILEY BOLDEN

Riley Bolden is sixteen years old and is a son of the in-home folkway in Haywood County. He is probably a seventh consecutive generation banjo player in the Bolden Family. The first known family banjo player was probably William Bolden, who was born in Haywood County in 1824 and died in 1926.

Riley is quiet and soft-spoken and seems a little shy. He usually has a gentle smile on his face. He comes from a musical family. His grandfather is an excellent musician, as was his great-grandfather. His father plays guitar and sings. His uncle, Jeremy Bolden, is one of the banjo players in this book. His maternal and paternal cousins play guitar. He will be a senior in high school next year and is home-schooled. Riley also plays guitar or piano "every day or so." Riley is not in the JAM program.

Riley has been exposed to banjo music all his life and has always liked it. He "tried," with little success, to learn to play the banjo when he was a young boy. At age twelve, he began taking lessons from his Uncle Jeremy and watching videos of his Uncle Jeremy and others on YouTube. He currently has a private teacher and practices, on average, an hour a day. He says that he does not have perfect pitch but that if he hears a note, he can usually find it on the banjo rather quickly. He plays by ear.

Riley works with his brother in a lawn care business and was recently able to purchase, with a little help from his grandfather, an RB-350 Gibson Banjo, which he loves to play. He also currently works with his father, Cameron, who is a home builder.

He enjoys hunting and trout fishing.

JAYDEN BOLDEN

Jayden Bolden is eleven years old. He, like his cousin, Riley, is probably a seventh consecutive generation Bolden family banjo player. He is a stocky boy with bright eyes. He is alert and intelligent and converses with uncommon poise for an eleven-year-old.

Jayden began taking banjo lessons from his father, Jeremy, when he was ten years old and now has a private teacher. He says that he loves playing the banjo and enjoys practicing. He is currently working on "Cripple Creek." He plays a Raymond Fairchild-autographed banjo.

Jayden has many interests. He enjoys working in his family's garden and helping his grandfather, who is a painter. Hunting, fishing, and archery are his major hobbies. He has killed three deer and three wild turkeys. He also enjoys clog dancing.

BALSAM RANGE

Finally, the last decade has witnessed the emergence of the Bluegrass group Balsam Range (chapter 12). All five members live in Haywood County and are accomplished/award-winning musicians. Marc Pruett, who, from the outset, has collaborated on this book, plays banjo for the group. Balsam Range has won several International Bluegrass Music Association awards. They are held in high esteem by all the people in the county, including prospective, and budding, banjo players.

SUMMARY

In summary, the story of the banjo in Haywood County is remarkable. While "makin' music" is not as widespread as in the past, it still has a strong presence, buttressed by significant remnants of its historical in-home folkway. Over the years, it has evolved along with the music and will continue to be shaped by strongly challenging but also strong positive forces. Young people are still actively and joyfully playing and learning to play the banjo. The future will be shaped by how this remarkable mountain culture continues to adapt to these challenges.

IN CONCLUSION

Several years have now passed since my neighbor's pre-Christmas dinner, and a few years have passed since I decided to write this book. It has been enjoyable and fulfilling. I have learned much about the banjo and its history, and in the process, I have learned much about Haywood County and its people.

Over these years, I have met many people who were interested in what I was doing and who were encouraging and helpful. Some were already friends. Many have become friends.

The single greatest thing that has happened to me in the writing of this book is getting to know the banjo players. They were/are good musicians and excellent people with remarkable stories. They have been interested in and supportive of my efforts. I have learned much from them and am grateful.

My major regret, and I have thought of it often, is that Smiley Burnette, Larry Watson, Stan Nichols, Steve Sutton, Jared Best, and Thomas Smathers did not live to see the completed book. I hope and trust that this book will be a blessing for their families.

Makin' Music. Singing Bluegrass Gospel. Left to right, Jeremy Bolden, Dwayne Riddle (friend and former pastor), Cameron Bolden (brother), Terry Jones (friend).

EPILOGUE

A couple of years ago, I had an opportunity to attend a fish fry at Jeremy Bolden's home, built by Jeremy, his father, and his brothers. Jeremy's family, including his parents, his brothers and their families, and several friends, were present. After dinner, I sat with Jeremy's father in the great room. Most of the women and young people were in the large kitchen, separated from the great room by a counter. Several preteen and teenage people, including Riley Bolden and his brothers, were there. There were multiple quiet conversations going on simultaneously. As I sat talking with Jeremy's dad, I noticed that Jeremy, his brother, a cousin, and two friends had walked across the great room to an area beside a window and adjacent to the fireplace, where they began to casually unpack their instruments—Jeremy's banjo, three guitars, and a bass. As the conversations continued, chairs were placed in a loose circle, and they sat down and began to tune their instruments. And then, like the five consecutive Bolden family generations before them, they made music, mostly bluegrass and gospel, but often I could hear that banjo ringing. A few people came into the den to listen while others continued visiting. Between songs, the musicians talked softly with one another. Jeremy's dad and some of the younger people, including Jeremy's nephew Riley, a seventh consecutive generation Bolden banjo player, later joined in "makin' music." It was a memorable evening for me. I knew that I had witnessed something that was very precious.

REQUIESCAT IN PACE

LARRY DEAN WATSON 1952–2014
JARED BEST 1990–2016
HOWARD JEFFERSON "SMILEY" BURNETTE 1937–2016
STEVE SUTTON 1956–2017
WILLIAM "STAN" NICHOLS 1958–2018
THOMAS SMATHERS 1957–2022

APPENDIX: ADDITIONAL DEMOGRAPHICS

A. HAYWOOD COUNTY

Overview

Brief demographic data were presented in the introduction and in chapter 3. In review, the July 2018 NC Certified Population Estimate of Haywood County was 62,433, including 93.1% "white alone, not Spanish, Hispanic, or Latino," 3.74% Hispanic or Latino, and 1.03% African American. In addition, 55.4% of the 2010 census population was rural and 44.6% was urban. In 2017 estimates, the median family income was $47,538, a 5–6% growth over 2016. Roughly 16.6% were below the poverty level.[1] Roughly 81% of the population has a high school or equivalent degree or higher.[2] Haywood Community College, in addition to its robust continuing education program, also offers one- to two-year post-secondary certificates and, in 2017, conferred 692 associate degrees.[3]

In 2018, roughly two-thirds of workers residing in Haywood County worked in the county, and the remaining one-third worked outside. The largest employers were Retail Trade, Government, Manufacturing, Health Care and Social Assistance, Accommodation and Food Services, and Public Administration.[4]

Tourism has been a significant part of the Haywood County economy since the late 1800s, with a striking increase in the 1960s. Tourism has continued to thrive. The 2017–2018 county 4% occupancy tax rate revenue was roughly 1.5 million dollars, a 57% increase since 2009–2010.[5] The population of the county significantly increases in the summer with the arrival of seasonal visitors and tourists.

Population Dynamics

The population of an area is determined by "natural increase" (births minus deaths) plus "in-" and "out-migration." The Haywood County estimated 2020 population is 63,813. The population in 1980 was 46,495. It had

increased to only 46,942 in 1990. In each of the ensuing decades beginning in 1990, there have been major population increases,[6] all due to net
migration. Natural population increases (births minus deaths) in Haywood
County have been negative since the mid-1990s.[7] Similar trends are projected to 2040. The 1980 >65-year-old age group represented roughly 13.5%
of the population compared to the 2018 >65-year-old age group, which
represents roughly 24% of the population, the population clearly aging.[8]

Haywood County has historically been a decidedly "rural" county.
Determining rural/urban population ratios is difficult, and criteria have
changed over the years. "Place" populations and "urban-rural" populations
are defined very differently, the latter based strictly on population density.[9]
Using the current "urban-rural population density" criteria, the 2010 population of Haywood County is roughly 55.4% rural and 44.6% urban.[10] The
county "feels" more rural than that.

Rural counties dependent on agriculture have chronic out-migration
trends. On the other hand, rural counties, such as Haywood County, with
scenic beauty, excellent amenities, and adult children, have significant,
long-term migration gains in Family Age and Older Adult populations.[11]
From the 1950s–2000s, Haywood County, like other rural areas, historically experienced net out-migration among Emerging Adults and Young
Adults groups, the nadir in each decade in the 20–24 age group. However,
a large net in-migration rebound began with the 1970s Young Adults age
group, and marked in-migration continued into Family Age and Older
Adult groups. These trends were basically duplicated in the 1980s–2000s
as well. There had been only overall modest in-migration in the 1950s and
1960s. The advent of tourism in the 1950s and 1960s effectively "opened"
Haywood County, contributing to the subsequent striking in-migration in
subsequent decades.[12]

Haywood County migration estimates for 2012–2016 show in-migration
of roughly 4,000 people, half from counties in North Carolina and half
from counties outside North Carolina. Adjacent Buncombe County is the
major source of in-migration from North Carolina. Florida is the major
source of in-migration from outside North Carolina, and South Carolina
is second. There was an out-migration of roughly 3,000 people, half to
counties in North Carolina and half to counties outside of North Carolina. Here again, Buncombe County and Florida were the major destina-
tions of out-migration. The greatest numbers of Haywood County in- and
out-migrations occurred in 1995–2000. There were marked decreases in
both in 2006–2010, and both have remained at similar levels in 2012–2016
estimates.[13]

In 1980, Haywood County's seasonal housing units were roughly 4.4% of 20,363 total housing units, compared to 15.8% of 35,086 total housing units in 2015.[14] The great preponderance of these is used primarily as summer vacation or second homes but also includes rentals to people who come to Haywood County to escape the summer heat. Most of the people who rent these houses are from Florida, as are most of the owners.[15]

Finally, 2014 data compiled by the Haywood County Economic Development Council on the location of the almost 50,000 Haywood County property owners are instructive. Roughly 75% are located in North Carolina, 50% of them in Haywood County. The remainder includes 14% located in Florida, followed by neighboring states South Carolina (3%), Georgia (2%), Tennessee (1%), Virginia (1%), and elsewhere. Some of these represent people who own property in Haywood County and have moved out of the county.[16]

B. THE BANJO PLAYERS

Instruments Played/Singing

Most of these musicians played, in addition to the banjo, another instrument, usually (26/32 persons) the guitar. Eight could play three instruments, four could play four, and seven could play five or six instruments. It was said of one of them (Steve Sutton) that "he can play a chair!!" Eleven persons could play bass, eight mandolin, five fiddle, four dulcimer (including one who could also play hammer dulcimer), four dobro, four piano, three harmonica, one electric bass, one trumpet (majoring in trumpet in college), one bugle, one tuba, and one autoharp. Roughly half to two-thirds specifically noted that they sing. Roughly a third can do at least some shaped-note singing.

Music Listened To

Most of the banjo players, when growing up, listened primarily to old-time/mountain, country, gospel, and bluegrass music. Some also listened to contemporary, pop/rock, and big band. A small number also listened to jazz and classical music. Five or six, included above, said that they listened to all types of music—they represent the bulk of the big band, jazz, and classical listeners.

The contemporary listening patterns for the banjo players were roughly similar to those when growing up.

Festivals

The great majority of the banjo players attended festivals. In addition to impromptu "makin' music," roughly half have performed at festivals, and a third have competed at festivals.

Performances

All the banjo players have performed locally, and two-thirds have performed regionally. Six and five have performed nationally and internationally, respectively, one of them (Gary Wiley) primarily playing a bass.

Still Pickin'

Six of the banjo players are deceased. All of them were still actively playing the banjo around the time of their deaths. Seven now play very little for various reasons, including illness, aging, loss of a *pickin' buddy*, loss of a father, other interests, and familial and business obligations.

Family Histories: Banjo Players' First-, Second-, and Third-Degree Family Relatives

For analysis, family relatives were divided into first-, second-, and third-degree relatives. A first-degree relative is a close blood relative, including the individual's parents, full siblings, or children. A second-degree relative is a blood relative, including the individual's aunts, uncles, nieces, nephews, grandparents, grandchildren, or half-siblings. A third-degree relative is a blood relative, including the individual's first cousins, great-uncles/aunts, great-grandparents or great-grandchildren

First-degree relatives have the strongest association of a shared "gift" (in this case, musical ability), with second- and third-degree relatives having a decreasing association. A complication of this is the fact that, within each "degree," the greater the number of relatives, the greater the chance of having a particular inherited gift appear.

Banjo Players' Relatives' Musical Ability

It is difficult to quantify "musical ability." Each banjo player was asked to rate the overall musical ability of each relative as "below average," "average," "above average," and "way above average." This is, of course, subjective, and one person's evaluation of musical ability may be quite different from another's. Thirty-one of the banjo players had a total of 210 first-degree relatives (mean 6.8, median 6, range 2–14). Sixty-one (29%) of them had "above average" musical ability (mean 2, median 1, range 0–7), and 27 (13%) of them had "way above average" musical ability (mean 0.84, range 0–5). It was not possible, for a number of reasons, to obtain enough ancestral information to accurately define the numbers and musical ability of second- and third-degree relatives of the banjo players.

Banjo Players' Relatives Who Play(ed) the Banjo

All but five of thirty-two banjo players in this study had at least one first-, second-, or third-degree relative who, with varying ability, played the banjo. There was a total of thirty-two first-degree banjo players' relatives. Twenty one of the thirty-two banjo players had at least one first-degree relative who played the banjo and eleven had none. There was one mother, three sisters, and one daughter among first-degree relatives. There are, in this study, two father/son pairs: David Burnette/Jimmy Burnette, with five first-degree relatives, including themselves, combined; and Joey Massie/Patrick Massie, two first-degree relatives, including themselves, combined. Of the eleven banjo players who did not have a first-degree relative who played the banjo, six had at least one second- or third-degree relative who did. This should be recognized as a minimal number due to the incompleteness of second- and third-degree ancestral information.

Singing

Roughly a third of the banjo players came from families where singing was an important component of their music. Singing, in general, appeared to be a common occurrence and was often associated with church. Three of the families participated in shaped-note singing.

The Great-Grandparents

Roughly half to a third of the banjo players had no knowledge of their great-grandparents' musical ability. There were eight known great-grandparents (including two great-grandmothers) who played the banjo. I presumed, for the sake of this discussion, that they had all learned to play the banjo by the time they were twenty years old. Three of them were from outside

Haywood County. Sally Naillon Gates (1899–1990), maternal great-grand-mother of Mitchell Rathbone (in this book), lived just outside Haywood County in Tennessee. John Sherrill (late 1880s-1977/78), the maternal great-grandfather of Thomas Smathers, lived in neighboring Jackson County, as did his son, who did not play the banjo. Ernest Samuel Young (1898–1940), maternal great-grandfather of Brandon Henson, lived in southern Pied-mont, North Carolina. It is likely, given the proximity to Haywood County of the first two of them, that there was intrafamily exposure to the banjo.

Mark Rich (1897–1986), an above-average banjo player, Tim Bradley's paternal great-grandfather, lived in rural Soco Gap and upper Maggie Valley. Dances were often held at his home. Joe Dallas ("Dibe") Duckett (1884–1974), paternal great-grandfather of Tracy Best, lived in the White Oak community of Haywood County. The family's story is that his bride repeatedly told him that he should stop playing the banjo and get a job. One day, he became angry, put his banjo under the bed, and never played again!

Three of the great-grandparents' families have retained much of the in-home folkway.

Hugh Carroll Best Sr. (1900–1955), patriarch of four consecutive gen-erations of banjo players, including his son, Carroll Best, was the great-grandfather of Jared Best. He lived in the rural Upper Crabtree section of Haywood County and played a two-finger style.

Martha Jane Rathbone (1864–1947) is the earliest white banjo player in Haywood County that I have been able to document unequivocally. It is probable that there were others before her. She was the great-grandmother of Charles Rathbone (in this book), was "above average," and played a two-finger style. She would have been twenty years old in 1884. Although her children did not play the banjo, her grandson (Charles Rathbone's father, now deceased, primarily a fiddle player, could play "anything") and her great-grandson Charles Rathbone is an exceptional banjo player.

James Austin Bolden (1894–1977) was born in Haywood County and lived in rural Saunook. He would have been twenty years old in 1914. It is clear that, over the years, family and friends would often come to his home and make music.[17] A banjo player has been in every subsequent generation of James Austin Bolden's family. James Austin Bolden's great-grandson, Jeremy Bolden, is a fourth consecutive generation Bolden banjo player and his son, Jayden, and nephew, Riley, are fifth consecutive generation banjo players.

It is probable, but not firmly documented, that James Austin Bolden's father, James William Bolden (1857–1900) and grandfather, William Jackson

Bolden (1824–1926), twenty years old in 1877 and 1844, respectively, and both born in Haywood County, also "made music" and played the banjo. Indeed, over the years, the Bolden family has believed that this was the case, but there are no longer elderly relatives to firmly document this.[18] It is probable that William Jackson Bolden was one of the first, if not the first, white banjo player in Haywood County, and both he and his son would have been part of the developing in-home folkway. In that case, Jeremy Bolden would be the sixth consecutive generation of Bolden family musicians who play(ed) the banjo and his son, Jayden Bolden, and nephew, Riley Bolden, would be the seventh.

Musical Aptitude

"Above average" to "way above average" musical achievement was a prerequisite for participation in this study. Musical aptitude is a measure of a person's potential to achieve in music.

"Musical aptitude may be thought of as relating to the "inner possibility," and musical achievement to the "outer reality." Audiation is the basis of musical aptitude. Thus, it becomes the basis of music achievement. To "audiate" is to hear and comprehend music for which the sound is not physically present. Audiation is to music what thinking is to language.[19]

Advanced Measures of Music Audiation

"Advanced Measures of Music Audiation," a musical aptitude test developed by Edwin Gordon, PhD, was used in this project. One of the original aims of Dr. Gordon was to identify students with high musical aptitude and encourage them to develop this aptitude. The test does not measure musical achievement. It measures aptitude.

The test lasts roughly twenty minutes and consists of thirty musical "statements," each followed four seconds later by a musical "answer." The four-second interval does not allow time for "replaying" the statement in one's mind. The subject is asked to decide whether or not the musical statement and answer are the same or different. If different, the subject is asked to define whether it is different by "tone" or by "rhythm." A "raw score" for Tonal, Rhythm, and Total for the thirty musical statements is compiled for each subject. The raw scores (Tonal, Rhythm, and Total) are then converted to Percentile Rank Norms previously developed by Gordon in studies of roughly six thousand students for three groups: College and University Music Majors (Undergraduate and Graduate), College and

University Non-Music Majors (Undergraduate and Graduate), and High School Students.[20] Thirty of the thirty-two banjo players took the music audiation test. Five of the thirty were college graduates. Several had attended community college. All were high school graduates.

Using Gordon's audiation Percentile Rank Norms for High School Students, the results for Total, for Rhythm, and for Tone for the banjo players are as follows: **Total**—Mean 49.4% (median 48.5%, range 14–94%), **Rhythm**—Mean 45.6% (median 45%, range 7–93%), and **Tone**—Mean 53.6% (median 53.5%, range 7–97%).

Using the Two Sample t-test (t-student distribution), the calculated audiation Percentile Rank Norms evaluating the banjo players' scores as College and University **Non-Music Majors** vs. as High School Students for Total, for Rhythm, and for Tone are not statistically significant (Standard p-value >0.05). Consequently, for simplification, the Percentile Rank Norms for High School students will be used for all the banjo players.

However, calculated audiation Percentile Rank Norms evaluating the banjo players' scores as College and University **Music Majors** vs. as High School Students were strikingly lower when compared to Music Majors, and the differences proved to be highly statistically significant. P-values for the banjo players as Music Majors vs. as High School Students for Total, Rhythm, and Tone, were $p=0.00013$, $p=0.00040$, and $p=0.00062$, respectively. Standard p-value in this comparison is ≤ 0.05.

The banjo players' "Total" percentile mean (average) and median were essentially at the 50th percentile for High School students, the "median" meaning that half the banjo players were below the 50th percentile and half were above. Comparing the "Total" percentile scores in the upper and lower half by age, there was no statistical difference. Also, there was no statistical difference between the "Total" percentile scores of the five who had attended college and the twenty-five who had not.

The Music Audiation test is difficult, and the test's "different" tonal or rhythmic changes are, at times, very subtle. In general, the musical exposure of some of the banjo players to different types of music, particularly classical music, is apparently not as extensive as in other parts of the country. The music that most of the banjo players have been primarily exposed to is usually very straightforward rhythmically and is generally not complex or subtle tonally, albeit at times more subtle than rhythmic. It is interesting but not statistically significant that the banjo players' mean Percentile Rank Norm for rhythm is 45.6% and for tone 53.6%. These scores may represent, at least partially, the importance of the cultural nurture of "makin' music" in the musical achievement of the banjo players in this book.[21]

Finally, playing the banjo requires good manual dexterity, and playing rapidly, as the Scruggs style banjo is usually played, requires excellent manual dexterity. This is also true for clawhammer playing as well. Therefore, manual dexterity was not formally evaluated.

NOTES

PREFACE

1. Fiona Ritchie and Doug Orr, *Wayfaring Strangers: The Musical Voyage from Scotland and Ulster to Appalachia* (Chapel Hill: The University of North Carolina Press, 2014), 244.

2. Haywood County. "Demographics. Population," accessed September 14, 2019. https://accessnc.nccommerce.com/DemoGraphiJulycsReports/pdfs/countyProfile/NC/37087.pdf.

3. Haywood County. "Population by Race," accessed September 14, 2019. https://datausa.io/profile/geo/haywood-county-nc.

4. Haywood County. "Population, Incorporated Towns," accessed September 14, 2019. https://www.haywoodcountync.gov/350/About-Haywood-County.

5. Haywood County, "Demographics. Rural/Urban," accessed August 23, 2019. https://accessnc.nccommerce.com/DemoGraphicsReports/pdfs/countyProfile/NC/37087.pdf.

CHAPTER 1: OVERVIEW OF BANJO HISTORY

1. "Slave Voyages, Trans-Atlantic Slave Trade—Estimates," accessed October 17, 2019. https://www.slavevoyages.org/assessment/estimates.

2. Paul Lovejoy, "Table V. Mortality of the Enslaved Population of the Middle Passage," in *The "Middle Passage": The Enforced Migration of Africans across the Atlantic,* accessed October 17, 2019. https://pdfs.semanticscholar.org/10e6/57def8e3ec5de5ec51630afc3eedc43f8127.pdf.

3. "Slave Voyages, Trans-Atlantic Slave Trade—Estimates." www.slavevoyages.org/assessment/estimates.

4. Paul Lovejoy, "Africans in North America," in *The "Middle Passage": The Enforced Migration of Africans across the Atlantic,* accessed October 17, 2019. https://pdfs.semanticscholar.org/10e6/57def8e3ec5de5ec51630afc3eedc43f8127.pdf.

5. Laurent Dubois, *The Banjo: America's African Instrument* (Cambridge, MA and London: The Belknap Press of Harvard University Press, 2016), 139–40.

6. Shlomo Pestcoe, "Banjo Ancestors: West African Plucked Spike Lutes," in *Banjo Roots and Branches,* ed. Robert B. Winans (Urbana, Chicago, and Springfield: University of Illinois Press, 2018), 21–44.

7. Shlomo Pestcoe and Greg Adams, "Banjo Roots Research: Changing Perspectives on the Banjo's African American Origins and West African Heritage," in *Banjo Roots and Branches,* ed. Robert B. Winans (Urbana, Chicago, and Springfield: University of Illinois Press, 2018),

5; Ulf Jagfors, "The African Akonting and the Origin of the Banjo," *The Old-Time Herald* 9, no. 2. (November 2003–January 2004): 26–33.

8. Dena Epstein, *Sinful Tunes and Spirituals: Black Folk Music to the Civil War* (Urbana and Chicago: University of Illinois Press, 2003), 22–38.

9. Pestcoe, "Banjo Ancestors," 35.

10. Epstein, *Sinful Tunes and Spirituals*, 38; William Talmadge, "The Folk Banjo and Clawhammer Performance Practice in the Upper South: A Study of Origins," in *The Appalachian Experience*, ed. Barry M. Buxton (Boone, NC: Appalachian Consortium Press, 1983), 175; Cecilia Conway, "Appalachian Echoes of the African Banjo," in *Appalachians and Race: The Mountain South from Slavery to Segregation*, ed. John Inscoe (Lexington: University Press of Kentucky, 2005), 27–28; George Gibson, "Black Banjo, Fiddle, and Dance in Kentucky," in *Banjo Roots and Branches*, ed. Robert B. Winans (Urbana, Chicago, and Springfield: University of Illinois Press, 2018) 223–55.

11. Pestcoe and Adams, "Banjo Roots Research," 10–11.

12. Dubois, *The Banjo*, 173–204.

13. Bob Carlin, *The Birth of the Banjo: Joel Walker Sweeney and Early Minstrelsy* (Jefferson, NC, and London: McFarland and Company, Inc., 2007), 33; Karen Linn, *That Half-Barbaric Twang: The Banjo in American Popular Culture* (Urbana and Chicago: University of Illinois Press, 1994), 2.

14. Linn, *That Half-Barbaric Twang*, 49–50.

15. Phillip F. Gura and James F. Bollman, *America's Instrument: The Banjo in the Nineteenth Century* (Chapel Hill: The University of North Carolina Press, 1999).

16. Linn, *That Half-Barbaric Twang*, 5–39.

17. Tony Thomas, "Gus Cannon—'The Colored Champion Banjo Pugilist of the World' and the Big World of the Banjo," in *Banjo Roots and Branches*, ed. Robert B. Winans (Urbana, Chicago, and Springfield: University of Illinois Press, 2018), 283.

18. Gura and Bollman, *America's Instrument*, 249.

19. Fiona Ritchie and Doug Orr, *Wayfaring Strangers: The Musical Voyage From Scotland and Ulster to Appalachia* (Chapel Hill: University of North Carolina Press, 2014), 212, 215–26, 260.

20. Linn, *That Half-Barbaric Twang*, 116–18, 121–29.

21. Dubois, *The Banjo*, 275–76.

22. George Gibson, "The Two Phases of the Urban Banjo Revival." Unpublished manuscript, received December 7, 2018.

23. Ritchie and Orr, *Wayfaring Strangers*, 268–69.

24. Bob Carlin, *Banjo: An Illustrated History* (Milwaukee, WI: Backbeat Books, 2016), 210.

25. The Carolina Chocolate Drops. www.carolinachocolatedrops.com, accessed November 6, 2019.

26. MacArthur Fellow, https://www.macfound.org/fellows/class-of-2017/rhiannon-giddens, accessed November 6, 2019.

CHAPTER 2: THE BANJO IN HAYWOOD COUNTY

1. John Preston Arthur, *Western North Carolina: A History (From 1730–1913)* (Asheville, NC: The Edward Buncombe Chapter of the Daughters of the American Revolution, 1914), 268.

2. George Gibson, email message to author, September 29, 2019.

3. John C. Campbell, *The Southern Highlander and His Homeland* (Philadelphia: The Russell Sage Foundation, 1921), 144.

4. George Gibson, email message to author, August 26, 2019.

5. Jeffrey Crow, Paul Escott, and Flora Hatley Wadelington, *A History of African Americans in North Carolina,* 2nd rev. ed. (Raleigh: Office of Archives and History. North Carolina Department of Cultural Resources, 2011), 1–3, 2–4.

6. Ira Berlin, "Foreword," in Paul Heinegg, *Free African Americans of North Carolina, Virginia, and South Carolina: From the Colonial Period to about 1820.* Vols. I and II, 5th ed. (Baltimore, MD: Printed for Clearfield Company by Genealogical Publishing Company, 2005), i–iii.

7. Robert Winans, "Mapping Eighteenth- and Early Nineteenth-Century Citations of Banjo Playing, 1736–1840," in *Banjo Roots and Branches,* ed. Robert Winans (Urbana, Chicago, and Springfield: University of Illinois Press, 2018) 215.

8. Berlin, "Foreword," iii.

9. Crow et al., *A History of African Americans in North Carolina,* 2–4.

10. "Free African American Population in the U. S.: 1790–1860," accessed March 20, 2020. https://www.ncpedia.org/sites/default/files/census_stats_1790-1860.pdf.

11. Crow et al., *A History of African Americans in North Carolina,* 51–52, 56.

12. John Inscoe, "Mountain Masters: Slaveholding in Western North Carolina," *The North Carolina Historical Review,* 61 (April 1984): 168.

13. Darin Waters, "Life Beneath the Veneer. The Black Community in Asheville, North Carolina from 1793 to 1900." Doctoral Dissertation, University of North Carolina at Chapel Hill Department of History. Chapel Hill, 2012.

14. John Inscoe, *Mountain Masters: Slavery and the Sectional Crisis in Western North Carolina* (Knoxville: University of Tennessee Press, 1989), 61–62.

15. Inscoe, 145–46.

16. Michael Beadle, "The Formation of Haywood County, Development of Its Communities and Its Early Leaders" in *Haywood County: Portrait of a Mountain Community. A Bicentennial History,* ed. Curtis W. Wood Jr. (Waynesville, NC: The Historical Society of Haywood County, 2009), 44.

17. Slave Schedule, Haywood County, 1860. www.ncgenweb.us/haywood/censch/1860ss.htm.

18. Inscoe, *Mountain Masters,* 30–33, 61.

19. Kathy Ross and Michael Beadle, "Cherokee and Pioneers in Pre-Haywood County Territory," in *Haywood County: Portrait of a Mountain Community. A Bicentennial History,* ed. Curtis W. Wood Jr. (Waynesville, NC: The Historical Society of Haywood County. 2009), 21–27.

20. Tyler Blethen and Curtis W. Wood Jr., *From Ulster to Carolina: The Migration of the Scotch-Irish to Southwestern North Carolina* (Raleigh: North Carolina Department of Cultural Resources. Office of Archives and History, 2013), 53–54.

21. Ross and Beadle, "Cherokee and Pioneers in Pre-Haywood County Territory," 18–20.

22. Blethen and Wood, *From Ulster to Carolina,* 52–53.

23. Beadle, "The Formation of Haywood County, Development of Its Communities, and Its Early Leaders," 32–33.

24. John Campbell, *The Southern Highlander and His Homeland* (Lexington: University Press of Kentucky, 1969), 41, 49.

25. Blethen and Wood, *From Ulster to Carolina*, 19–20.

26. Campbell, *The Southern Highlander and His Homeland*, 58.

27. Blethen and Wood, *From Ulster to Carolina*, 41–42.

28. Campbell, *The Southern Highlander and His Homeland*, 57–58.

29. Phil Jamison, *Hoedowns, Reels, and Frolics: Roots and Branches of Southern Appalachian Dance* (Urbana, Chicago, and Springfield: University of Illinois Press, 2015),12–13.

30. Blethen and Wood, *From Ulster to Carolina*, 53.

31. Ross and Beadle, "Cherokee and Pioneers in Pre-Haywood County Territory," 24.

32. Blethen and Wood, *From Ulster to Carolina*, 54.

33. Cecilia Conway, *African Banjo Echoes in Appalachia: A Study of Folk Traditions* (Knoxville: The University of Tennessee Press, 1995), 111.

34. *www.hagenbuch.org/scheitholt-early-pennsylvania-german-instrument*. Accessed October 16, 2019.

35. Fiona Ritchie and Doug Orr, *Wayfaring Strangers: The Musical Voyage from Scotland and Ulster to Appalachia* (Chapel Hill: University of North Carolina Press, 2014), 237.

36. Jamison, *Hoedowns Reels and Frolics*, 1–192.

37. Judith Gray, American Folklife Center, Library of Congress, telephone conversation, December 28, 2020, and email message, March 18, 2021.

38. Inscoe, *Mountain Masters*, 53, 54.

39. Personal communication, Phil Hunter, Augusta 16, 2020, and French Kirkpatrick, August 18, 2020.

40. Patrick Willis, "Transportation, Communication, and Utilities," in *Haywood County: Portrait of a Mountain Community. A Bicentennial History*, ed. Curtis W. Wood Jr. (Waynesville, NC: The Historical Society of Haywood County, 2009), 133–38.

41. Inscoe, *Mountain Masters*, 25–52.

42. Gene Wilhelm Jr. "Appalachian Isolation: Fact or Fiction," in *An Appalachian Symposium: Essays Written in Honor of Cratis D. Williams*, ed. J. W. Wilson (Boone, NC: Appalachian State University Press, 1977), 77, 89.

43. Patrick Willis, "Social, Civic, and Community Life," in *Haywood County: Portrait of a Mountain Community. A Bicentennial History*, ed. Curtis W. Wood Jr. (Waynesville, NC: The Historical Society of Haywood County, 2009), 352.

44. Campbell, *The Southern Highlander and His Homeland*, 79, 80–86, 89.

45. Cecil Sharp, "Foreword," in Olive Campbell and Cecil Sharp, *English Folk Songs from the Southern Appalachians* (New York, G. F. Putnam and Sons, 1917), iv–vi.

46. Harry M. Caudill, "Preface," *The Mountain the Miner and the Lord* (Lexington: University Press of Kentucky, 1980), vii–x.

47. Wilhelm Jr., "Appalachian Isolation," 90.

48. George Gibson, email message to author, November 18, 2019.

49. G. Kittredge, "Ballads and Rhymes from Kentucky," *The Journal of American Folklore* 20, no. 79 (Oct.–Dec. 1907): 251–77. https://www.jstor.orgs/stable/i223417.

50. Campbell, *The Southern Highlander and His Homeland*, 146.

51. Elizabeth Williams, ed., *Appalachian Travels: The Diary of Olive Dame Campbell* (Lexington: University Press of Kentucky, 2012), 85–86.

52. Campbell and Sharp, *English Folk Songs from the Southern Appalachians*.

53. David Whisnant. *All That Is Native and Fine: The Politics of Culture in an American Region* (Chapel Hill, The University of North Carolina Press, 2008), 8.

54. Campbell and Sharp, *English Folk Songs from the Southern Appalachians*, viii, iv.

55. Josiah Combs, *Folk Songs of the Southern United States*, ed. and trans. D. K. Wilgus (Austin: Published for the American Folklore Society by the University of Texas Press, 1967), 79.

56. Elizabeth Williams, ed., *Appalachian Travels*, 85.

57. Campbell, *The Southern Highlander and His Homeland*, 143–44.

58. Michael Yates, "Cecil Sharp in America, Collecting in the Appalachians," in *Cecil Sharp in Appalachia: A Brief History*, accessed September 30, 2019. https://cecilsharpinappalachia.org/.

59. George Gibson, email message to author, July 6, 2020.

60. George Gibson, email message to author, November 28, 2019.

61. George Gibson, email message to author, April 15, 2020.

62. Campbell and Sharp, *English Folk Songs from the Southern Appalachians*, xviii.

63. Conway, *African Banjo Echoes in Appalachia: A Study of Folk Traditions*, 304–5.

64. William Attmore, *Journal of a Tour to North Carolina* (Chapel Hill: The University of North Carolina Press. The James Sprunt Historical Publications, Vol. 17, No. 2, 1922, ed. Lida Tunstall Rodman, accessed February 26, 2020, docsouth.unc.edu/nc/attmore/menu.html), 43.

65. Harry McKown, "December: Jonkonnu in North Carolina" in *North Carolina Miscellany*, December 1, 2008. (Chapel Hill, N C, accessed February 26, 2020. https://blogs.lib.unc.edu/ncm/index.php/2008/12/01/this_month_dec_jonkonnu/.

66. *North Carolina Journal*, February 11, 1807, in "The Social Life of the Slave—Recreation" (Chapel Hill: University of North Carolina Library, *Ante-Bellum North Carolina: A Social History: Electronic Edition*. Chapter XVIII, ed. Guion Griffis Johnson), 554.

67. Jean Bradley Anderson, *Durham County. A History of Durham County, North Carolina* (Durham: Duke University Press, 2011), 90.

68. Simon, "For the Register," *Raleigh* (NC) *Register*, August 4, 1858.

69. "Retrospective," *The Roanoke News*, Weldon, NC, August 19, 1915.

70. Conway, *African Banjo Echoes in Appalachia*, 1–83, 120–59.

71. Arthur, *Western North Carolina*, 256, 268.

72. Inscoe, *Mountain Masters*, 47–52.

73. Jamison, *Hoedowns, Reels, and Frolics*, 12.

74. Bruce Whitaker, "The Real Old Drover's Road," *The Fairview* (NC) *Town Crier*, January 2012.

75. Inscoe, *Mountain Masters*, 48.

76. "Registration Scenes." Registration at the South. Scene at Asheville, North Carolina, *Harper's Weekly Magazine*, September 28, 1867, 621.

77. Wilbur Zeigler and Ben Grosscup, *Western North Carolina—The Heart of the Alleghanies* (Raleigh, NC, and Cleveland, OH: A. Williams and Company, 1883), 38.

78. *Historic Webster. A Newsletter of the Webster (NC) Historical Society, Inc.* 4, no. 3 (Summer 1977).

79. Campbell, *The Southern Highlander and His Homeland*, 136.

80. George Reynolds with Wesley Taylor, "Gourd Banjos and Songbows," in *Foxfire 6*, ed. Eliot Wigginton (New York: Anchor Books, 1980), 54–82.

81. Joshua Grant, personal communication, May 1, 2019.

82. Historic Artist, Samantha Bumgarner, Banjo Player, Jackson County, "Blue Ridge National Heritage Area," accessed April 4, 2019. https://www.blueridgeheritage.com/artist/samantha-bumgarner/.

83. Clifford Rorrer. "Charlie Poole, 1892–1931," in *Dictionary of North Carolina Biography*. vol. 5. ed. William S. Powell (Chapel Hill: University of North Carolina Press, 1994), 122.

84. Ray McBride, Don McNeil, and Randy Starnes, "Banjos and Dulcimers," in *Foxfire 3*, ed. Eliot Wigginton (New York: Anchor Books, 1975), 120–185.

85. George Gibson, email message to author, April 4, 2020.

86. George Gibson, "A Brief History of the Folk Banjo." Unpublished manuscript, 5. May 15, 2019.

87. Edward King, "The Great South; Among the Mountains of Western North Carolina," *Scribner's Monthly*, March 1874, 548.

88. Rebecca Harding Davis, "By-paths in the Mountains (II)," *Harper's Magazine*, August 1880, 368.

89. "Letter to the Editor," *The Carolina Mountaineer and Waynesville* (NC) *Courier*, May 5, 1920.

90. Patrick Willis, "Industry and Commerce," in *Haywood County: Portrait of a Mountain Community. A Bicentennial History*, ed. Curtis W. Wood Jr. (Waynesville, NC: The Historical Society of Haywood County, 2009), 236–49.

91. Kathy Ross, "Agriculture and Farm Life," in *Haywood County: Portrait of a Mountain Community. A Bicentennial History*, ed. Curtis W. Wood Jr. (Waynesville: The Historical Society of Haywood County, 2009), 70.

92. Rob Neufeld, "Visiting Our Past: Convict Labor Built the Railroads Here," *Asheville* (NC) *Citizen-Times*, March 3, 2019.

93. Archie Green, in Gene Bluestein, "America's Folk Instrument: Notes on the Five String Banjo," *Western Folklore* 23, no. 4 (October 1964): 243.

94. Ross, "Agriculture and Farm Life," 72.

95. Willis, "Industry and Commerce," 240–43.

96. Cory Vaillancourt, "Good Roots, The African-American Legacy at Sunburst," *Smoky Mountain News* (Waynesville, NC), February 20, 2019.

97. Lewis Oats, telephone conversation with author, May 23, 2020.

98. Canton, North Carolina Mill, Evergreen Packaging. https://evergreenpackaging.com/careers/.

99. Willis, "Industry and Commerce," 240–43.

100. French Kirkpatrick, email message to author, April 15, 2019.

101. Zeigler and Grosscup, *Western North Carolina—The Heart of the Alleghanies*, 155.

102. "Many hotels and inns have served public in this popular mountain resort," *Asheville* (NC) *Citizen-Times*, March 26, 1950.

103. Christina Osborne, "Tourism in Haywood County" in *Haywood County: Portrait of a Mountain Community. A Bicentennial History*, ed. Curtis W. Wood Jr. (Waynesville, NC: The Historical Society of Haywood County, 2009), 149.

104. Henry Foy and Ann Melton, *Waynesville's Early Hotels and Boarding Houses* (Waynesville, NC: Self-published. 2015), 3–241.

105. Osborne, "Tourism in Haywood County," 161–63.

106. Henry Foy and Ann Melton, *Waynesville's Early Hotels and Boarding Houses*, 41.

107. French Kirkpatrick, personal communication, August 18, 2020.

108. Patrick Willis, "Haywood County Enters the 21st Century," in *Haywood County: Portrait of a Mountain Community. A Bicentennial History*, ed. Curtis W. Wood Jr. (Waynesville, NC: The Historical Society of Haywood County, 2009), 416–19.

109. Ritchie and Orr, *Wayfaring Strangers*, 253–267

110. Billy Case, conversation with author, April 5, 2019.

111. Osborne, "Tourism in Haywood County," 170–72.

112. Wayne Erbsen. "Jim Shumate, Bluegrass Fiddler Supreme," *Native Ground Books and Music*, accessed January 20, 2020. https://nativeground.com/jim-shumate-bluegrass-fiddler-supreme.

113. Robert Cantwell, *Bluegrass Breakdown: The Making of the Old Southern Sound* (Urbana and Chicago: University of Illinois Press, 2003), 76.

114. Earl Scruggs, *Earl Scruggs and the 5-String Banjo* (New York: Peer International Corporation, 1968), 147–49, 155.

115. Ralph Rinzler, in C. P. Heaton, "The 5-String Banjo in North Carolina," *Southern Folklore Quarterly* 35, no.1 (1971): 78–79.

116. Barry Willis, "Earl Scruggs, Earl Scruggs and the Foggy Mountain Boys," in *America's Music, Bluegrass: A History of Bluegrass Music in the Words of Its Pioneers* (Franktown, CO: Pine Valley Music, 1997), 178.

117. Willis, 187–89.

118. Willis, 70–76.

119. Willis, 142.

120. Willis, 118, 127, 136.

121. Willis, 131.

CHAPTER 3: THE BANJO PLAYERS

1. Edwin E. Gordon, manual, *Advanced Measures of Music Audiation* (Chicago: GIA Publications, 1989), 5-33.

2. Alessandro Portelli, *They Say in Harlan County: An Oral History* (New York, NY: Oxford University Press, 2011); William Ferris, *Give My Poor Heart Ease: Voices of the Mississippi Blues* (Chapel Hill: The University of North Carolina Press, 2009).

CHAPTER 8: BEGINNING TO LEARN TO PLAY THE BANJO

1. Doug Trantham, personal communication, July 13 and 14, 2021.

CHAPTER 10: WHAT DOES IT FEEL LIKE?

1. Alf Gabrielson, *Strong Experiences with Music: Music is Much More Than Just Music* (New York: Oxford University Press Inc., 2001).

2. Mihalyi Csikszentmihalyi, *Flow: The Psychology of Optimal Experience* (New York: Harper Collins Publishers, 2008), 71.

3. Csikszentmihalyi, 72–74.

CHAPTER 12: THE BANDS, THE PEOPLE, THE PLACES, THE EVENTS

1. "Shape Note Singing," Folkstreams, accessed October 15, 2022. https://www.folkstreams.net/contexts/shape-note-singing.

2. June Smathers-Jolley, email message to author, June 5, 2020.

3. Garret K. Woodward, "Can't Keep a Good Man Down: Banjo Legend Raymond Fairchild on Turning 80, a Life in Music," *Smoky Mountain News*, May 1–7, 2019.

4. French Kirkpatrick, personal communication, March 15, 2020.

5. Tony Trischka, liner notes, "Carroll Best and the White Oak String Band: Old-Time Bluegrass From the Great Smoky Mountains, 1956 & 1959," CD (Gatlinburg, Tennessee: Great Smoky Mountains Association, 2014).

6. Joe Wilson, "Carroll Best, Too Tall to Sleep in the Back of a Car," in *Roots Music in America: Collected Writings of Joe Wilson*, ed. Fred Bartenstein (Knoxville: University of Tennessee Press, 2017), 147.

7. "'Aeonic' by Balsam Range Review: Bluegrass That's Ready to Grow," *Wall Street Journal*, January 9, 2019.

8. "Balsam Range," Balsam Range, accessed June 29, 2019. https://www.balsamrange.com/about.

9. Joe Sam Queen, personal communication, June 15, 2018.

10. "Ole Time Fiddler's and Bluegrass Festival," Library of Congress, accessed October 15, 2022. http://memory.loc.gov/diglib/legacies/loc.afc.afc-legacies.200002909/.

11. Blue Ridge Music Trails, https://www.blueridgemusicnc.com/find-music/event/bascom-lamar-lunsford-minstrel-of-appalachia-festival, accessed June 29, 2019.

12. MerleFest, www.merlefest.org, accessed September 25, 2019.

13. "IBMA and its Raleigh partners announce 3-year extension for the World of Bluegrass event in Raleigh, NC," accessed September 6, 2020. www.ibma.org/press-releases/3993/.

14. "New Free Model A Success for IMBA's Wide Open Bluegrass Festival," accessed October 15, 2022. https://ibma.org/press-releases/new-free-model-a-success-for-ibmas-wide-open-bluegrass-festival/.

CHAPTER 13: THREE JOURNEYS

1. Steve Sorrells, personal communication, August 10, 2019.

2. Western Carolina University, Commencement Ceremony, May 8, 2010.

CHAPTER 14: THE FUTURE

1. "County Estimates," North Carolina Budget and Management, accessed April 20,2020. https://www.osbm.nc.gov/demog/county-estimates.

2. "County Estimates," North Carolina Budget and Management, accessed April 20, 2020. https://www.osbm.nc.gov/demog/county-estimates.

3. "Haywood County North Carolina," accessed August 19, 2019. https://accessnc.nccom merce.com/DemoGraphicsReports/pdfs/countyProfile/NC/37087.pdf.

4. "Net Migration Patterns for US Counties, Net Migration by Age, Haywood County North Carolina," accessed April 11, 2020. www.netmigration.wisc.edu.

5. "County-to-County Migration Flows: 2012–2016. American Community Survey. US Census Bureau," accessed April 20, 2020. https://www.census.gov/data/tables/2016/demo/geographic-mobility/county-to-county-migration-2012-2016.html.

6. "Housing Information," accessed April 15, 2020. https://linc.osbm.nc.gov/pages/home.

7. Ron Breese, REMAX executive, personal communication, April 17, 2019.

8. "Haywood Property Owners by Location of Owners," prepared by Haywood County Economic Development Council, Mark Clasby, executive director (retired), personal communication, August 20, 2019.

9. "Agricultural Statistics, North Carolina," annual publication, North Carolina Department of Agriculture and Consumer Services. United States Department of Agriculture, National Agricultural Statistics Service, Raleigh, North Carolina, NCDA&CS/NASS Print Shop.

10. Vicki Hyatt, "How seven high schools were merged into two," *The Mountaineer*, "50 years strong series," March 1, 2017.

11. Larry Leatherwood, personal communication, September 5, 2019.

12. Bill Teague, personal communication, August 14, 2019.

13. Robert Prince , personal communication, October 26, 2017.

14. Data courtesy of the Southeastern Jurisdiction, United Methodist Church, Lake Junaluska, North Carolina, October 2017.

APPENDIX: ADDITIONAL DEMOGRAPHICS

1. Haywood County, "Income," accessed September 14, 2019. https://datausa.io/profile/geo/haywood-county-nc.

2. "Quick Facts: Haywood, North Carolina," US Census Bureau, accessed October 15, 2022. https://www.census.gov/quickfacts/haywoodcountynorthcarolina.

3. Haywood County, "Education," accessed September 14, 2019. https://datausa.io/profile/geo/haywood-county-nc.

4. Haywood County, "Workers and Employment," accessed September 14, 2019. https://accessnc.nccommerce.com/DemoGraphicsReports/pdfs/countyProfile/NC/37087.pdf.

5. Haywood County Tourism Development Authority, "Reports," accessed September 14, 2019. www.haywoodtda.com.

6. "County Estimates," North Carolina Budget and Management, accessed April 20, 2020. https://www.osbm.nc.gov/demog/county-estimates.

7. "Statistics and Reports," North Carolina Department of Health and Human Services, North Carolina Center for Health Statistics, accessed April 18, 2020. schs.dph.ncdhhs.gov/data/vital.cfm#vitalvol1.

8. "County Estimates," North Carolina Budget and Management, accessed April 20, 2020. https://www.osbm.nc.gov/demog/county-estimates.

9. John Cromartie, Rural Economy Branch, USDA, Economic Research Service, email message to author, August 29, 2019.

10. "Haywood County North Carolina," accessed August 19, 2019. https://accessnc.nccom merce.com/DemoGraphicsReports/pdfs/countyProfile/NC/37087.pdf.

11. Kenneth M. Johnson, Richelle Winkler, Luke T. Rogers, "Age and Lifecycle Patterns Driving U. S. Migration Shifts," Carsey Institute, University of New Hampshire, Issue Brief No. 62, Spring 2013.

12. "Net Migration Patterns for US Counties, Net Migration by Age, Haywood County North Carolina," accessed April 11, 2020. www.netmigration.wisc.edu.

13. "County-to-County Migration Flows: 2012–2016," American Community Survey. US Census Bureau, accessed April 20, 2020. https://www.census.gov/data/tables/2016/demo/ geographic-mobility/county-to-county-migration-2012-2016.html.

14. "Housing Information," accessed April 15, 2020. https://linc.osbm.nc.gov/pages/home.

15. Ron Breese, REMAX executive, personal communication, April 17, 2019.

16. "Haywood Property Owners by Location of Owners," prepared by Haywood County Economic Development Council, Mark Clasby, executive director (retired), personal communication, August 20, 2019.

17. Randy Bolden, personal communication, November 7, 2020.

18. Randy Bolden, personal communication, November 7, 2020.

19. Edwin E. Gordon, Manual, *Advanced Measures of Music Audiation* (Chicago: GIA Publications, 1989), 5.

20. Gordon, 6–33.

21. "Nature vs. Nurture," accessed May 20, 2021. https://www.psychologytoday.com/us/ basics/nature-vs-nurture.

BIBLIOGRAPHY

"Agricultural Statistics. North Carolina." Annual Publication, North Carolina Department of Agriculture and Consumer Services. United States Department of Agriculture, National Agricultural Statistics Service, Raleigh, North Carolina, NCDA&CS/NASS Print Shop.

Anderson, Jean Bradley. *Durham County: A History of Durham County, North Carolina.* Durham: Duke University Press, 2011.

Arthur, John Preston. *Western North Carolina: A History (From 1730–1913).* Raleigh, NC: Edwards and Broughton Printing Company, 1914.

Attmore, William. *Journal of a Tour to North Carolina.* Chapel Hill: The University of North Carolina. *The James Sprunt Historical Publications*, Vol. 17, No. 2, 1922, ed. Lida Tunstall Rodman. Accessed February 26, 2020, 43, docsouth.unc.edu/nc/attmore/menu.html.

Beadle, Michael. "The Formation of Haywood County, Development of Its Communities, and Its Early Leaders." In *Haywood County: Portrait of a Mountain Community. A Bicentennial History*, edited by Curtis W. Wood Jr., 32–54. Waynesville, NC: The Historical Society of Haywood County, 2009.

Berlin, Ira. "Foreword." In Heinegg, Paul, *Free African Americans of North Carolina, Virginia, and South Carolina: From the Colonial Period to about 1820.* Vol. 1, 5th ed., i–iii. Baltimore, MD: Printed for Clearfield Company by Genealogical Publishing Company, 2005.

Blethen, H. Tyler, and Curtis W. Wood Jr. *From Ulster to Carolina: The Migration of the Scotch-Irish to Southwestern North Carolina.* Raleigh: North Carolina Office of Archives and History, 2013.

Blue Ridge National Heritage Area. "Historic Artist, Samantha Bumgarner, Banjo Player, Jackson County." Accessed April 27, 2019. https://www.blueridgeheritage.com/artist/samantha-bumgarner/.

Bluestein, Gene. "America's Folk Instrument: Notes on the Five-String Banjo," *Western Folklore* 23, no. 4 (October 1964): 241–48. https://www.jstor.org/stable/1520666?seq=1.

Campbell, John C. *The Southern Highlander and His Homeland.* Lexington: University Press of Kentucky, 1969.

Campbell, Olive Dame, and Cecil James Sharp. *English Folk Songs from the Southern Appalachians.* New York, NY: Putnam, 1917.

Cantwell, Robert. *Bluegrass Breakdown: The Making of the Old Southern Sound.* Urbana and Chicago: University of Illinois Press, 2003.

Carlin, Bob. *The Birth of the Banjo: Joel Walker Sweeney and Early Minstrelsy.* Jefferson, NC, and London: McFarland and Company, Inc., 2007.

Carlin, Bob. *Banjo, An Illustrated History.* Milwaukee, WI: Backbeat Books, 2016.

Caudill, Harry M. Preface to *The Mountain, the Miner, and the Lord*, vii–x. Lexington: University Press of Kentucky, 1980.

Cecil-Fronsman, Bill. *Common Whites: Class and Culture in Antebellum North Carolina*. Lexington: University Press of Kentucky, 1992.

Combs, Josiah H. *Folk Songs of the Southern United States*. Edited and translated by D. K. Wilgus. Austin: University of Texas Press, 1967. (From Dr. Combs's doctoral dissertation, "Folk Songs du Midi Etats-Unis," University of Paris, 1925.)

Conway, Cecilia. *African Banjo Echoes in Appalachia: A Study of Folk Traditions*. Knoxville: The University of Tennessee Press, 1995.

Conway, Cecilia. "Appalachian Echoes of the African Banjo," in *Appalachians and Race. The Mountain South from Slavery to Segregation*, edited by John Inscoe, Lexington: University Press of Kentucky, 2005.

Crow, Jeffrey J., Paul D. Escott, and Flora J. Hatley Wadelington. *A History of African Americans in North Carolina*. 2nd rev. ed. Raleigh: Office of Archives and History. North Carolina Department of Cultural Resources, 2011.

Csikszentmihalyi, Mihaly. *Flow: The Psychology of Optimal Experience*. New York: Harper Collins Publishers, 2008.

Davis, Rebecca Harding. "By-paths in the Mountains (II)." *Harper's Magazine*, August 1880.

Dubois, Laurent. *The Banjo, America's African Instrument*. Cambridge and London: The Belknap Press of Harvard University Press, 2016.

"1860 Haywood County, NC Slave Schedule," www.ncgenweb.us/haywood/censch/1860ss.htm.

Epstein, Dena J. *Sinful Tunes and Spirituals: Black Folk Music to the Civil War*. Urbana and Chicago: University of Illinois Press, 2003.

Erbsen, Wayne. "Jim Shumate, Bluegrass Fiddler Supreme." Native Ground. Books and Music. https://nativeground.com/jim-shumate-bluegrass-fiddler-supreme.

Ferris, William. *Give My Poor Heart Ease, Voices of the Mississippi Blues*. Chapel Hill: The University of North Carolina Press, 2009.

Foy, Henry and Ann Davis Melton. *Waynesville's Early Hotels and Boarding Houses*. Waynesville, NC: Self-published, 2015.

Gabrielson, Alf. *Strong Experiences with Music: Music Is Much More Than Just Music*. New York: Oxford University Press Inc., 2001.

Gibson, George. "Black Banjo, Fiddle, and Dance in Kentucky and the Amalgamation of African American and Anglo-American Folk Music." In *Banjo Roots and Branches*, edited by Robert B. Winans, 223–55. Urbana, Chicago, and Springfield: University of Illinois Press, 2018.

Gordon, Edwin E. *Manual for the Advanced Measures of Music Audiation*. Chicago: GIA Publications, Inc., 1989.

Green, Archie, in Gene Bluestein. "America's Folk Instrument: Notes on the Five-String Banjo," *Western Folklore* 23, no. 4 (October 1964): 243.

Gura, Phillip F., and James F. Bollman. *America's Instrument: The Banjo in the Nineteenth Century*. Chapel Hill: The University of North Carolina Press, 1999.

Inscoe, John C., "Mountain Masters: Slaveholding in Western North Carolina." *North Carolina Historical Review* 61, no. 2. (April 1984): 143–73. https://www.jstor.org/stable/i23514533.

Inscoe, John C. *Mountain Masters: Slavery and the Sectional Crisis in Western North Carolina*. Knoxville: University of Tennessee Press, 1989.

Jagfors, Ulf, "The African Akonting and the Origin of the Banjo." *The Old-Time Herald* 9, no. 2. (November 2003–January 2004): 26–33.

Jamison, Phil. *Hoedowns, Reels, and Frolics: Roots and Branches of Southern Appalachian Dance*. Urbana, Chicago, and Springfield: University of Illinois Press, 2015.

King, Edward, "The Great South, Among the Mountains of Western North Carolina." *Scribner's Monthly*, March 1874.

Kittredge, G. L., "Ballads and Rhymes from Kentucky." *Journal of American Folklore* 20, no. 79 (Oct.–Dec. 1907): 251–77. https://www.jstor.org/stable/i223417.

Linn, Karen. *That Half-Barbaric Twang: The Banjo in American Popular Culture*. Urbana and Chicago: University of Illinois Press, 1994.

McBride, Ray, Don McNeil, and Randy Starnes. "Banjos and Dulcimers." In *Foxfire 3*, edited by Eliot Wigginton, 120–85. New York: Anchor Books, 1975.

McKown, Harry, "December: Jonkonnu in North Carolina." North Carolina Miscellany, December 1, 2008. Accessed February 26, 2020, https://blogs.lib.unc.edu/ncm/index .php/2008/12/01/this_month_dec_jonkonnu/.

Osborne, Christina Fulcher. "Tourism in Haywood County." In *Haywood County: Portrait of a Mountain Community. A Bicentennial History*, edited by Curtis W. Wood Jr., 147–75. Waynesville, NC: The Historical Society of Haywood County, 2009.

Pestcoe, Shlomo. "Banjo Ancestors, West African Plucked Spike Lutes." In *Banjo Roots and Branches*, edited by Robert B. Winans, 21–44. Urbana, Chicago, and Springfield: University of Illinois Press, 2018.

Pestcoe, Shlomo, and Greg C. Adams. "Banjo Roots Research, Changing Perspectives on the Banjo's African American Origins and West African Heritage." In *Banjo Roots and Branches*, edited by Robert B. Winans, 3–20. Urbana, Chicago, and Springfield: University of Illinois Press, 2018.

Portelli, Alessandro. *They Say in Harlan County, An Oral History*. New York: Oxford University Press, 2011.

Pruett, Marc. *Rascally Mountain Boy*. Waynesville, NC: Self-published, 2019.

Reynolds, George, with Wesley Taylor. "Gourd Banjos and Songbows." In *Foxfire 6*, edited by Eliot Wigginton, 54–82. New York: Anchor Books, 1980.

Rinzler, Ralph. In Heaton, C. P., "The 5-String Banjo in North Carolina." *Southern Folklore Quarterly* 35, no. 1 (1971): 78–79.

Ritchie, Fiona and Doug Orr. *Wayfaring Strangers: The Musical Voyage from Scotland and Ulster to Appalachia*. Chapel Hill: The University of North Carolina Press, 2014.

Rorrer, Clifford Kinney. "Charlie Poole, 1892–1931." In *Dictionary of North Carolina Biography*. Vol. 5. edited by William S. Powell, 122. Chapel Hill: University of North Carolina Press, 1994.

Ross, Kathy. "Agriculture and Farm Life." In *Haywood County: Portrait of a Mountain Community. A Bicentennial History*, edited by Curtis W. Wood Jr., 55–103. Waynesville, NC: The Historical Society of Haywood County, 2009.

Ross, Kathy, and Michael Beadle. In "Cherokee and Pioneers in Pre-Haywood County Territory." In *Haywood County: Portrait of a Mountain Community. A Bicentennial History*, edited by Curtis W. Wood Jr., 14–31. Waynesville, NC: The Historical Society of Haywood County, 2009.

Scruggs, Earl. *Earl Scruggs and the 5-String Banjo*. New York: Peer International Corporation, 1968.

Stueckrath, George H., "The Upper Country of South Carolina, Historical, Reminiscences of Greenville District, South Carolina, Etc." DeBow's Review. *Agricultural, Commercial, Industrial Progress and Resources* 27, no. 6 (December 1859): 688–96.

Talmadge, William. "The Folk Banjo and Clawhammer Performance Practice in the Upper South: A Study of Origins." In *The Appalachian Experience*, edited by Barry M. Buxton, 169–79. Boone, NC: Appalachian Consortium Press, 1983.

Thomas, Tony. "Gus Cannon—'The Colored Champion Banjo Pugilist of the World' and the Big World of the Banjo." In *Banjo Roots and Branches*, edited by Robert B. Winans, 272–89. Urbana, Chicago, and Springfield: University of Illinois Press, 2018.

Vaillancourt, Cory. "Good Roots, The African-American Legacy at Sunburst." *Smoky Mountain* (Waynesville, NC) *News*. February 20, 2019.

Waters, Darin J., "Life Beneath the Veneer, The Black Community in Asheville, North Carolina from 1793 to 1900." Doctoral dissertation, Chapel Hill: University of North Carolina at Chapel Hill, Department of History. 2012.

Whisnant, David E. *All That Is Native and Fine, The Politics of Culture in an American Region*. Chapel Hill: The University of North Carolina Press, 2008.

Wilhelm Jr., Gene. "Appalachian Isolation." In *An Appalachian Symposium: Essays Written in Honor of Cratis D. Williams*, edited by J. W. Williamson, 85–89. Boone, NC: Appalachian State University Press, 1977.

Williams, Elizabeth McCutchen, ed. *Appalachian Travels: The Diary of Olive Dame Campbell*. Lexington: University Press of Kentucky, 2012.

Willis, Barry R. "Earl Scruggs, Earl Scruggs and the Foggy Mountain Boys." In *America's Music: Bluegrass: A History of Bluegrass Music in the Words of Its Pioneers*. 178. Franktown, CO: Pine Valley Music, 1997.

Willis, Patrick. "Haywood County Enters the 21st Century." In *Haywood County: Portrait of a Mountain Community: A Bicentennial History*, edited by Curtis W. Wood Jr., 406–29, Waynesville, NC: The Historical Society of Haywood County, 2009.

Willis, Patrick. "Industry and Commerce." In *Haywood County: Portrait of a Mountain Community. A Bicentennial History*, edited by Curtis W. Wood Jr., 230–59. Waynesville, NC: The Historical Society of Haywood County. 2009.

Willis, Patrick. "Social, Civic, and Community Life." In *Haywood County: Portrait of a Mountain Community. A Bicentennial History*, edited by Curtis W. Wood Jr., 343–69. Waynesville, NC: The Historical Society of Haywood County, 2009.

Willis, Patrick. "Transportation, Communication, and Utilities." In *Haywood County: Portrait of a Mountain Community: A Bicentennial History*, edited by Curtis W. Wood Jr., 122–46. Waynesville, NC: The Historical Society of Haywood County, 2009.

Wilson, Joe. "Carroll Best, Too Tall to Sleep in the Back of a Car." In *Roots Music in America: Collected Writings of Joe Wilson*, edited by Fred Bartenstein, 145–47. Knoxville: University of Tennessee Press, 2017

Wilson, Joe. "The Hicks and Related Families, Carriers of Tradition." In *Roots Music in America. Collected Writings of Joe Wilson*, edited by Fred Bartenstein, 44–46. Charles K. Wolf Music Series, edited by Ted Olson. Knoxville: Tennessee, University of Tennessee Press, 2017.

Winans, Robert B., ed. *Banjo Roots and Branches*. Urbana, Chicago, and Springfield: University of Illinois Press, 2018.

Winans, Robert B. "Mapping Eighteenth- and Early Nineteenth-Century Citations of Banjo
    Playing, 1736–1840." In *Banjo Roots and Branches*, edited by Robert B. Winans, 214–22.
    Urbana, Chicago, and Springfield: University of Illinois Press, 2018.

Wood, Curtis W. Jr., ed. *Haywood County: Portrait of a Mountain Community*. Waynesville,
    NC: The Historical Society of Haywood County, 2009.

Yates, Michael. "Cecil Sharp in America: Collecting in the Appalachians." In *Cecil Sharp in
    Appalachia: A Brief History*, accessed September 30, 2019. https://cecilsharpinappalachia
    .org/.

Zeigler, Wilbur G., and Ben S. Grosscup. *Western North Carolina–The Heart of the Alleghanies*.
    Raleigh, NC, and Cleveland, OH: A. Williams and Company, 1883.

INDEX

ABOUT THE AUTHOR

Photo by Margaret Allsbrook

William C. Allsbrook Jr., MD, is professor emeritus of pathology and surgery (urology) at the Medical College of Georgia, Augusta, Georgia. He and his wife have lived in Waynesville, North Carolina, since 2003. They have three children, eight grandchildren, and one great-grandchild. Several years ago, after beginning banjo lessons, he became aware of the remarkably large number of banjo players in Haywood County and decided to try to understand how this phenomenon occurred. Dr. Allsbrook describes himself as "an enthusiastic and profoundly mediocre" amateur banjo player.

CPSIA information can be obtained
at www.ICGtesting.com
Printed in the USA
BVHW042320210523
664546BV00003BA/6